Oxford Paperback English Texts   General Editor **John Buxton**

James Thomson

The Seasons
and
The Castle of Indolence

James Thomson

The Seasons
and
The Castle of Indolence

Edited by **James Sambrook**

Clarendon Press · Oxford

Oxford University Press, Walton Street, Oxford OX2 6DP

London Glasgow New York Toronto
Delhi Bombay Calcutta Madras Karachi
Kuala Lumpur Singapore Hong Kong Tokyo
Nairobi Dar es Salaam Cape Town
Melbourne Auckland

and associated companies in
Beirut Berlin Ibadan Mexico City Nicosia

Oxford is a trade mark of Oxford University Press

Published in the United States
by Oxford University Press, New York

ISBN 0 19 871070 4

First published 1972
Reprinted with corrections 1984

Printed in Great Britain by
Biddles Ltd., Guildford and Kings Lynn

Acknowledgements

In preparing this edition I have profited from the earlier editorial labours of Robertson and McKillop, and from the very present help of the staff of the Clarendon Press and John Buxton. At Southampton my colleagues have helped with their answers and my undergraduate pupils with their questions; so much so that Thomson's overwrought phrases at *Spring* 1152–3 have at times seemed almost true.

Contents

Introduction

He has joined with great art the most beautiful imagination and the finest reflection together, adorned with a masterly diction and versification, suitable to its other excellencies. And thus he has happily attained the two great ends of poetry, of instructing and delighting the reader. . . . He must be allowed to have the genuine spirit of sublime poetry in him, and bids fair to reach at length the heighth of Milton's character. (*London Journal*, 4 June 1726)[1]

Such a judgement by the first reviewer of *Winter, a Poem* marks the emergence into literary fame of James Thomson who, only a year earlier, had abandoned his studies of divinity in Edinburgh and, like so many Scotsmen of his day, sought his fortune in London. By July 1726 the young poet was hard at work on *Summer* and had published a second edition of *Winter* to which he added a confident preface indicating that he would write poems on the other seasons and outlining his artistic aims:

Nothing can have a better influence towards the revival of poetry than the choosing of great and serious subjects, such as at once amuse the fancy, enlighten the head, and warm the heart. . . . I know no subject more elevating, more amusing, more ready to awake the poetical enthusiasm, the philosophical reflection, and the moral sentiment, than the works of Nature. Where can we meet with such variety, such beauty, such magnificence? All that enlarges and transports the soul![2]

Thomson's intention was to muse (this is the sense of 'amusing') and moralize upon natural description, particularly descriptions of those sublime and beautiful objects that gave especial pleasure to the imagination. The aesthetic underlying this had been expounded fourteen years earlier in Addison's *Spectator* papers on the pleasures of the imagination.[3] Addison drew a distinction between primary and secondary pleasures of the imagination. Poetry could provide only secondary pleasures; the primary pleasures of the imagination came from the observation of Nature itself; the poet's own imagination would be developed by the study of Nature rather than of art.

The growth of Thomson's poem, first to the completed *Seasons* of

---

[1] The whole review is reprinted in A. D. McKillop, *The Background of Thomson's Seasons* (Minneapolis, 1942), pp. 175-7.

[2] The preface was dropped from the complete editions of *The Seasons* published in T.'s lifetime. It is included in the Oxford English Texts edition of T.'s *The Seasons*, ed. James Sambrook (1981), pp. 303-7.

[3] Reprinted in *Critical Essays from The Spectator*, ed. D. F. Bond (Oxford Paperback English Texts, 1970), pp. 175-209.

1730, then to the greatly expanded versions of 1744 and 1746,[1] tended to bring in more natural philosophy (i.e. science) but the work remained essentially a nature-descriptive poem. It was as 'a minute and particular enumeration of circumstances . . . a close and faithful representation of nature' (the phrases are in Joseph Warton's *Essay on the Genius and Writings of Pope*, 1756) that *The Seasons* was most admired in the eighteenth century. Readers were impressed, for instance, by passages describing the mating of birds, building of nests, ruses by which the plover and wild duck distract intruders, and all the other proofs of Thomson's observation. Lessing's *Laokoön* (1766) warned poets not to attempt the detailed factual record of the external world that could be made more effectively in painting, but *The Seasons* was admired through more than a century primarily for its word-paintings—from wide landscapes to tiny vignettes—faithfully depicting all manner of natural scenes.

Johnson, having in mind the essential difference between painting and poetry upon which Lessing had based his treatise, observed 'The great defect of the *Seasons* is want of method; but for this I know not that there was any remedy. Of many appearances subsisting all at once, no rule can be given why one should be mentioned before another' *(Johnson's Lives of the Poets*, ed. J. P. Hardy, p. 325). There is certainly no rule; but, as the constituents of the poem are description and musing or moralizing, its movement—in individual episodes, at least—does reflect the movement of the poet's mind. However, Thomson never seems strongly aware of this truth, and, of course, does not attempt to exalt it into a principle of philosophical or artistic order as Wordsworth was to in *The Prelude*. Thomson is a child of his age in regarding the natural world as wholly external and objective—exciting man's admiration of course, but not answering man's moods. The organizing principle of the poem is the seasonal round as it is observed in the natural world, and though *The Seasons* belongs completely to no one recognized literary *genre* it has most affinities, in both its descriptive and its didactic qualities, with the georgic kind.

Virgil's *Georgics*, described by Addison as 'the most complete, elaborate, and finished piece of all antiquity', provided a model and a challenge for many of the more ambitious poets of the eighteenth century.[2] The first function of the georgic *genre* was to offer matters

---

[1] See the table in Notes on the Text, p. xxiii below.
[2] There are good studies of the English georgic in Dwight L. Durling, *Georgic Tradition in English Poetry* (New York, 1935) and John Chalker, *The English Georgic* (London, 1969).

of fact, descriptions of material objects and accounts of physical processes (with or without their supernatural causes), dressed out with a stylistic artifice which emphasized their dignity and importance without turning them (by metaphor or allegory) into anything else; thus it was the appropriate vehicle for any ambitious Augustan poet who was touched, as Thomson clearly was, by the spirit of scientific inquiry which spread into English culture from the activities of the Royal Society after the 1660s. Moreover, Virgil had woven his detailed and accurate accounts of husbandry into an appealing myth of the innocence, felicity, vigour, and piety of the husbandman's life, and into an inspiring vision of national greatness; Thomson too is idealistic and highly patriotic.

In successive accretions to and revisions of his poem Thomson gradually incorporated more and more material from the great philosophical set-pieces in Virgil's *Georgics*, but his groundwork was still, like Virgil's, agricultural lore, and his framework the annual round of life and labour in the countryside. *The Seasons* took didactic material from other ancient and from many modern sources too, so that the poem in its final form synthesizes instruction in a great range of subjects—husbandry, history and hydrography, meteorology, optics and theology, and enough of science and of art for any man—but in those individual episodes describing the farmer's works and days Thomson is still attempting to synthesize and to find all kinds of harmonies—natural, historical, cultural, social, cosmic. In the description of so commonplace an activity as ploughing (*Spring* 32–77), for instance, he first shows the oxen, faintly humanized, sharing the ploughman's joy in the soft breezes and bird-songs of spring and working in willing partnership with him, the earth too is 'faithful', and man, beast and soil exist in an ideal harmony. Thomson then goes on to elevate the ordinary labours of the field by his reference to Virgil and reminders of the Romans' respect for agriculture. As the poet's view expands the plough turns from a thing into a symbol, and the sharp and concrete particularity of the ploughman bending over and scraping his ploughshare is inflated (or diffused) into generalizations about Autumn's treasures, superior boon and the better blessings of England's export trade. The implication of the whole passage is that the local harmony between the husbandman, his team, and his land is the foundation of the larger harmony of a wide mercantile empire which has cultural links with ancient Rome. A similar point is made in the similarly expansive account of hay-time and sheep-shearing in *Summer*:

A simple scene! yet hence Britannia sees
Her solid grandeur rise.

Critics[1] have pointed to a contradiction between Thomson's fre-
quent idealization of rustic innocence (reaching its idyllic heights in
Autumn 1235–1351) and his no less frequent praise of civic and
mercantile progress (finding its grandest expression in *Autumn*
43–143), and certainly, when, within a few lines of the spring plough-
ing passage I have already referred to, he uses 'pomp' twice with
diametrically opposed implications, he may be accused of a careless
choice of words, but he is not—here or elsewhere in the poem—
opposing pastoral simplicity to urban progress and recommending
one or the other. Rather he is pointing to the plain fact that the
developed civilization of Britain and all the nation's wealth at that
time rested ultimately upon the land and the men who worked it.
This was to be the theme of works as different from one another, yet
as characteristic of their age, as Goldsmith's *The Deserted Village*
and Adam Smith's *The Wealth of Nations*, though the notion
of the fundamental importance of farming is at least as old as
Socrates.

Simple scenes and solid grandeur, though they both provided him
with invigorating patriotic themes, stirred Thomson less than the ad-
vances of man's knowledge. The French imitator of Thomson, Jean
François Saint-Lambert, author of *Les Saisons* (1769), wrote 'les
anciens aimaient et chantaient la campagne, nous admirons et chan-
tons la nature',[2] and Thomson's subject is not merely the country-
side but the secret workings of Nature as these are revealed to the
enlightened eye of the philosopher and scientist. In the preface to the
second edition of *Winter* and in *Autumn* (1353–73) Thomson para-
phrases the passage in the *Georgics* where we are told that the man is
blessed who has been able to win knowledge of the causes of things
('Felix, qui potuit rerum cognoscere causas', II.490), and, like Virgil's
poem, *The Seasons* is strongly influenced throughout by Lucretius'
impassioned expression of scientific speculation concerning the
nature of the universe. The physical law, the hidden mechanism
that, for instance, brought the rainbow into being, arouses Thomson's
admiration, but the poet is equally excited by the human intelligence
that could grasp this law and lay bare this mechanism. Among the
many panegyrics to Newton in the early eighteenth century, parts of

[1] e.g. R. D. Havens, 'Primitivism and the Idea of Progress in Thomson',
Studies in Philology, xxix (1932), 41–52, and A. D. McKillop, *The Background of
Thomson's* Seasons (1942), chap. 3.

[2] *Les Saisons*, ed. le Comte de Boissy-D'Anglos (Paris, 1828), p. xxvii.

The Seasons along with Thomson's *A Poem sacred to the memory of Sir Isaac Newton* (1727) are outstanding.

What Newton meant for Thomson's age is indicated by Addison in *Spectator* 543:

The more extended our reason is, and the more able to grapple with immense objects, the greater still are those discoveries which it makes of wisdom and providence in the work of the Creation. A Sir Isaac Newton, who stands up as the miracle of the present age, can look through a whole planetary system, consider it in its weight, number and measure, and draw from it as many demonstrations of infinite power and wisdom as a more confined understanding is able to deduce from the system of an human body.

Newton's discoveries became the central element in a physico-theological system which demonstrated the existence and the benevolent attributes of God from the evidence of the created universe. It is this system, already outlined in such popular text-books as John Ray's *Wisdom of God manifested in the Works of the Creation* (1691) and William Derham's *Physico-Theology* (1713) and *Astro-Theology* (1715), that provided Thomson with his leading ideas. A friend, recommending *The Seasons* shortly before its first publication in 1730 wrote justly:

Nature and its explainer, and its author are [Thomson's] themes; what indeed could without prophaneness be joined to the praises of the Great Creator, but his works and Newton; his works are his words; he speaks his sublime wisdom and goodness to us in them, and Newton is his interpreter.[1]

In his preface to the second edition of *Winter* Thomson had referred to Virgil's *Georgics* as one of his models but had implied that his own poem had even closer links with a devotional literary tradition which included the Pentateuch, the Book of Job, and *Paradise Lost*. In *The Seasons* Thomson does not allow us to forget the 'informing Author' of the book of Nature. The concluding *Hymn* sketches in little the completed design of the whole poem, according to which the seasons, when viewed by 'reason's eye', are aspects of the 'varied God'; beneath all the appearances of Nature lies the beneficent Art of God. In this world such truth can be seen only dimly—even by the 'sage-instructed' eye—but it will become clearer in the next. However, despite the references to the future life (seen as an evolutionary

---

[1] *James Thomson (1700–1748), Letters and Documents*, ed. A. D. McKillop (Lawrence, Kansas, 1958), p. 62.

extension upwards of the great chain of being) there is no hint of orthodox Christian revelation in the _Hymn_ or the rest of _The Seasons_. Thomson's religious position appears close to deism—believing that the universe sufficiently represents God.

Deist or not, Thomson saw himself as a devotional poet with the highest imaginable artistic and didactic purposes. So, as the appropriate vehicle for his sublime sentiments, he adopted the style of Milton who was already clearly established (largely as a result of Addison's eighteen papers on _Paradise Lost_ in _The Spectator_)[1] as the English master of sublimity. The influence of Milton is omnipresent in the syntax, the handling of the blank verse and, especially, the diction of _The Seasons_. The other sources of Thomson's diction were Virgil (though Thomson tries too extensively to use the elevated style that Virgil kept only for his great set-pieces) and the regular, exact vocabulary of early eighteenth-century scientific writing. Many words that are nowadays used in an extended, abstracted or metaphorical sense (e.g. attraction, austere, bland, benign, concoct, exalt, insipid, involve, refine, spirit, sublime, temperate, tincture) have, in Thomson's poem, an exact scientific significance—often close to an original sense in Latin. Thomson's poetic periphrases are formed on the analogy of scientific classifications; they serve to define precisely particular characteristics or functions of a creature or object, and, if sometimes 'gaudy' they are never 'inane'. John Arthos's remarks on the stock poetic diction of the early eighteenth century apply with especial force to Thomson's:

'nature' was properly the subject of poetry in quite the same sense that it was the subject of science. The function of poetry and science was often the same, and in the tradition of humane learning no hard and fast distinctions were made. The naturalist and the poet borrowed from each other, shared common interests and attitudes, and constructed a common language to fulfill their common functions. In time much of the special vocabulary shared by the two lost its original associations and became identified chiefly as 'poetic diction', partly, probably, through a defect of memory.[2]

If a modern reader loses the scientific precision of much of Thomson's language, so, on the other hand, he may remain unaware of the degree to which Thomson animates his landscapes by a kind of subdued personification. The following description from _Summer_ may appear vague and generalized:

[1] Reprinted in _Critical Essays from The Spectator_, ed. D. F. Bond (Oxford Paperback English Texts, 1970), pp. 62–171.

[2] John Arthos, _The Language of Natural Description in Eighteenth Century Poetry_ (Ann Arbor, Mich., 1949), p. 87.

> O vale of bliss! O softly-swelling hills!
> On which the Power of Cultivation lies,
> And joys to see the wonders of his toil. (1435–7)

But a writer in *The British Magazine*, perhaps Goldsmith, observes:

We cannot conceive a more beautiful image than that of the Genius of Agriculture, distinguished by the implements of his art, imbrowned with labour, glowing with health, crowned with a garland of foliage, flowers, and fruit, lying stretched at his ease on the brow of a gently swelling hill, and contemplating with pleasure the happy effects of his own industry.

On this comment Donald Davie has rightly remarked that the writer 'probably contributes nothing that was not in Thomson's intention. For Thomson could count on finding in his readers a ready allegorical imagination, such as seems lost to us today. The loss is certainly ours.'[1] If an eighteenth-century reader could make so much of a brief reference to the Power of Cultivation, he would have no difficulty in visualizing all those other powers—of Contemplation, of Philosophic Melancholy, the Lubber Power and the rest.

The whole comic hunting and drinking episode in *Autumn* over which the Lubber Power presides serves very strikingly to show the range of Thomson's tone in *The Seasons*, and to remind us that Milton's style was available to Augustan poets not only as a prop for devotional sublimity but as a reference point in mock-epic. The lines of Miltonic imitation in the eighteenth century began with the religious verse of Isaac Watts and the parodies of John Philips, and Thomson, for all his sublimity and gravity, belongs to both lines.

Unlike Miltonic imitation, eighteenth-century imitation of Spenser could in no circumstances be a wholly solemn affair. The first object of it (though not always the final effect) was parody, or, sometimes perhaps, the simple fun of fooling with quaint poetic diction and mock-Gothick allegories. There is no need to assume a more serious original motive for Thomson's *The Castle of Indolence*, a poem which was fourteen or fifteen years in the leisurely making before it was published in May 1748, three months before the author's death. It was begun casually and light-heartedly, as 'little more than a few detached stanzas, in the way of raillery on himself, and on some of his friends, who would reproach him with indolence; while he thought them, at least, as indolent as himself',[2] and, although it grew into a sermon on the Christian duty of work, and an allegory of material

---

[1] Donald Davie, *Purity of Diction in English Verse* (London, 1952), p. 40.
[2] Patrick Murdoch, 'Life' of Thomson in *The Works of James Thomson* (London, 1762), vol. i, p. xiv. Murdoch was one of these friends, and appears in *The Castle of Indolence*, I.lxix.

progress, the whole poem retained the unserious, idyllic-burlesque tone in which it was conceived.

The part of the poem most generally admired is the opening of the first canto where Thomson richly evokes a dreamy, honeyed, languorous drowsiness. In the world's eyes this state of indolence may be selfish, vacuous sloth, but the song (particularly stanzas xvi, xvii) of the enchanter in the Castle contrives to make it indistinguishable from the hedonistic version of that virtuous, philosophic retirement praised by Horace and his innumerable successors.[1] More interestingly, the poet, who is himself one of the indolent dwellers in the allegorical Castle, describes it sometimes (e.g. stanzas v, xiv) in such a way as to suggest that this palace of art and its pastoral setting are representations of the poetic imagination, and that indolence itself is the poet's dream. The first half of Canto I elaborates that allusion to a dream-state in *Spring* 458–66, where, in a state of creative reverie, the poet's mind blends and reshapes images of the external world. Seen in this light the pleasures of indolence seem very like the innocent pleasures of the imagination as they are described by Addison in *The Spectator*. The moral of Thomson's poem, however, requires that we should regard 'indolence', even when it is identified with the state of poetic reverie, as reprehensible if it gives rise to a dream-poetry devoid of moral purpose. Instead of painting landscapes 'Of dreams that wave before the half-shut eye' (I.vi) the poet should perform some 'public' and overtly didactic function (the function that Thomson himself performed with all too depressing results in his heroic political tragedies)—to sing 'of war, and actions fair',

> The sage's calm, the patriot's noble rage,
> Dashing corruption down through every worthless age. (I.xxxii)

Thomson returns briefly to his own role as a poet in the first four stanzas of Canto II, but his larger moral purpose—to condemn indolence and praise progress in its various moral, intellectual and material forms—rules out any possibility that he might explore the nature of the poetic imagination through the dream landscape in which he had placed the half-perceiving, half-creating, dreamer-poet.

For the most part, then, the poem is a simple, objective, moral allegory moving straight towards an unambiguous conclusion. Before the end of the first canto we are shown the dungeon of *ennui*

[1] The Horatian ideal of retirement and its embodiments in English verse to 1760 are fully explored in M.-S. Røstvig, *The Happy Man* (Oslo, vol. i, rev. 1962, vol. ii, 1958).

(I.lxxiii–lxxvii) which lies beneath the Castle of Indolence, and are thus prepared for the destruction of the Castle by the Knight of Arts and Industry in Canto II. The argument of the bard's song (II.xlvii–lxii) justifying the Knight is based upon that Lucretian myth of human progress, outlined in *Autumn* 43–150, where, by the joint activities of mind and body, the race lifted itself from sad, lethargic barbarity into a state of high material civilization and moral and intellectual enlightenment. The bard takes the hedonistic appeal of the enchanter in Canto I further, to show that strenuous physical and moral activity brings true happiness: 'Toil and be glad . . . Who does not act is dead' (II.liv). Man's physical, intellectual and moral activities are not only analogous to God's unceasing work (II.xlvii–xlix) as Thomson had described it in *The Seasons*, but actually serve, in themselves, to bring man to higher states of being in accordance with God's wishes for him (II.lxiii). The underlying notion here is the belief in moral, intellectual and spiritual evolution asserted at several climactic points in *The Seasons*.[1]

Though this idea, that each individual man may rise everlastingly in the scale of being by virtue of his own activities, is fundamental, the emphasis of Canto II is upon public good and the values of society. The allegory, telling how the Knight of Arts and Industry, having brought civilization for a while to Egypt, Greece, and Rome, settles in Britain to develop its trade, manufactures and political institutions (II.xix–xxiv), is a deft rehandling of those Whiggish panegyrics to progress which open *Autumn* and form the whole substance of Thomson's second longest poem, *Liberty*, but the praise of progress here, as in *The Seasons*, borrows from the georgic tradition an idyllic, even nostalgic, note. Thus the art singled out for especial praise is heaven-descended agriculture which combines innocence and profit, delight and use, Nature and Art (II.xix), while the Knight himself, having brought to society the benefits of commerce, retires, like any wealthy Whig city magnate, to a country estate which he improves in the usual enlightened eighteenth-century fashion by enclosing, planting, draining, irrigating, and landscape gardening (II.xxvii–xxviii).

The moral, both as it refers to the advance of society and the spiritual ascent of the individual person, is serious and, in Thomson's eyes, very important, but the Spenserian form, with its continual hints of burlesque, serves to lighten the final effect of the poem and keep it refreshingly free of any of the overstretched or inappropriate sublimity that we occasionally find in *The Seasons*. However,

---

[1] *Spring* 374–9, *Summer* 1796–1805, *Winter* 603–8, *Hymn* 114–18.

Thomson, particularly when he is reflecting upon his own role as poet, is able to divest himself of Spenserian fancy garb—even for whole stanzas at a time—and step, not into the grand Miltonic costume of *The Seasons*, but into a simple dress better cut out for his purpose than either. Quoting Canto II, stanza iii, Professor Dobrée observes:

here is a new note, a different pace, of which one would not have thought Thomson capable; the verse has forgotten sublimity but has a vigour and an ease, almost one would say a lordly Byronic assumption of careless power, not it is true sustained, but never far away.[1]

The last stanza, though, is a broad and vivid Spenserian burlesque (owing a few hints to Pope's *The Alley*) ridiculing miry Brentford, and thus fittingly rounding off a poem whose genesis was light-hearted raillery among the circle of friends at Richmond.

Thomson died on 27 August 1748 and was buried in Richmond church close to the river. In his friendships he was as fortunate after death as in life, for one of his friends William Collins, made him the subject of what is, arguably, the finest short funeral elegy in the language:

ODE OCCASIONED BY THE DEATH OF MR THOMSON

The scene of the following stanzas is supposed to lie on the Thames near Richmond.

> In yonder grave a Druid lies,
>   Where slowly winds the stealing wave!
> The year's best sweets shall duteous rise
>   To deck its poet's sylvan grave!
>
> In yon deep bed of whispering reeds
>   His airy harp shall now be laid,
> That he, whose heart in sorrow bleeds,
>   May love through life the soothing shade.
>
> Then maids and youths shall linger here,
>   And, while its sounds at distance swell,
> Shall sadly seem in Pity's ear
>   To hear the woodland pilgrim's knell.
>
> Remembrance oft shall haunt the shore
>   When Thames in summer wreaths is dressed,
> And oft suspend the dashing oar
>   To bid his gentle spirit rest!

[1] Bonamy Dobrée, *English Literature in the Early Eighteenth Century, 1700–1740* (Oxford, 1959), p. 498.

And oft as Ease and Health retire
    To breezy lawn or forest deep,
The friend shall view yon whitening spire,
    And mid the varied landscape weep.

But thou, who own'st that earthy bed,
    Ah! what will every dirge avail?
Or tears, which Love and Pity shed
    That mourn beneath the gliding sail!

Yet lives there one, whose heedless eye
    Shall scorn thy pale shrine glimmering near?
With him, sweet bard, may Fancy die,
    And Joy desert the blooming year.

But thou, lorn stream, whose sullen tide
    No sedge-crowned Sisters now attend,
Now waft me from the green hill's side,
    Whose cold turf hides the buried friend!

And see, the fairy valleys fade,
    Dun Night has veiled the solemn view!
—Yet once again, dear parted shade,
    Meek Nature's child, again adieu!

The genial meads, assigned to bless
    Thy life, shall mourn thy early doom,
Their hinds and shepherd-girls shall dress
    With simple hands thy rural tomb.

Long, long, thy stone and pointed clay
    Shall melt the musing Briton's eyes:
'O! vales and wild woods', shall he say,
    'In yonder grave your Druid lies!'

Chronological Table

1700   James Thomson born at Ednam or Wideopen in Roxburghshire (baptized 15 Sept.).

1712   T. attends the grammar school in Jedburgh.

1715   T. enters the College of Edinburgh (now Edinburgh University).

1720   T., having finished his Arts course, becomes a student of Divinity with the intention of entering the Presbyterian ministry.

1725   T. leaves Scotland for good, and, in London, writes *Winter*.

1726   *Winter* published (first edn. early April, second edn. with preface July). T. is a tutor in Watts's Academy—a centre for popular study of Newtonian science.

1727   Published *Summer* (Feb.) and *A Poem sacred to the Memory of Sir Isaac Newton* (May).

1728   *Spring* published (May).

1729   *Britannia* published anonymously (Jan.).

1730   *Sophonisba*, a tragedy, acted (Feb.) and printed (Mar.). First collected edn. of *The Seasons*, including 'Autumn' and 'A Hymn' published (June). T. travelling tutor to Charles Talbot; in Paris (Dec.).

1731   T. travels with Talbot extensively in France and Italy; in Rome in Nov.

1732   In Paris (Oct.); returns with Talbot from the Continent at the end of the year or early 1733.

1733   Talbot dies (Sept.); his father (now Lord Chancellor) gives T. the sinecure of Secretary of Briefs in the Court of Chancery.

1735   *Liberty*, Parts I, II, and III published at intervals.

1736   *Liberty*, Parts IV and V published at intervals. T. moves his lodging from London to Richmond.

1737   After the Lord Chancellor's death T. loses his Secretaryship, but receives a pension from Frederick, Prince of Wales.

1738   *Agamemnon*, a tragedy, acted and printed (April).

1739   *Edward and Eleonora*, a tragedy, printed (May), but its performance prohibited for political reasons by the Lord Chamberlain.

1740   *Alfred*, a masque by T. and Mallet, including T.'s ode 'Rule Britannia', performed and printed (Aug.).

1743   T.'s proposal of marriage refused by Elizabeth Young.

1744   Greatly enlarged and much revised edn. of *The Seasons* published (July). George Lyttelton joins the government and gives T. the sinecure of Surveyor-General of the Leeward Islands.

1745   *Tancred and Sigismunda*, a tragedy, acted and printed (Mar.).

1746 Edn. of *The Seasons* including the author's last revisions published.
      T. gives up the Surveyor-Generalship to his deputy, and friend,
      William Paterson.
1747 Writing *Coriolanus*, a tragedy (acted Jan. 1749).
1748 T. loses his pension from the Prince of Wales. *The Castle of Indolence*
      published (May). T. dies at Richmond (27 Aug.).

A Note on the Text

Separate editions of *Winter* (1726, second edition with preface 1726 'fifth edition' 1728), *Summer* (1727), and *Spring* (1728), preceded the first publication of *The Seasons* (1730), and the poem was considerably revised and expanded for later editions. The exact course of these very extensive changes may be followed in James Thomson, *The Seasons*, ed. James Sambrook (Oxford, 1981); the following table, listing the number of verse-lines in each substantially revised edition during Thomson's lifetime, gives some indication of the poem's growth:

		Sp.	*Su.*	*Au.*	*Wi.*	*Hymn*	*Total*
Winter	Mar. 1726				405		
Winter	June 1726				463		
Summer	1727		1146				
Winter	1728				478		
Spring	1728	1082					
The Seasons	1730	1087	1206	1269	781	121	4464
Winter	1730				787		
The Seasons	1744	1173	1796	1375	1069	118	5531
The Seasons	1746	1176	1805	1373	1069	118	5541

The present edition reproduces the text of 1746, modernized in conformity with the principles adopted for the series.

The text of *The Castle of Indolence* is from the second edition (1748), which does not differ substantially from the first edition of the same year. This, too, has been modernized, except for Thomson's deliberately Spenserian-archaic forms.

A Note on the Illustrations

The illustrations to this edition are reproduced from plates designed by William Kent and engraved by Nicolas Tardieu for the quarto edition of *The Seasons* (1730). The upper half of each illustration represents the allegorical regal 'progress' of the personified season as it is described in the opening lines of each book, while the lower half illustrates naturalistically, upon different planes, several episodes or scenes in that book. Such multiple action and such mythological and natural interrelations accord well with Thomson's text. The plate for *Summer* illustrates the Damon and Musidora episode with four bathers, though only three are named in the 1730 text. For the 1744 edition, when Thomson reduced the bathers to one, the plate was redesigned by Kent (engraved by Pierre Fourdrinier) to show only the bather seated on the right.

Abbreviations used in the notes

F.Q.: Spenser's *The Faerie Queene*.

Letters and Documents: *James Thomson (1700–1748), Letters and Documents*, ed. A. D. McKillop (Lawrence, Kansas, 1958).

Lucretius: *De Rerum Natura*.

McKillop: A. D. McKillop, *The Background of Thomson's* Seasons (Minneapolis, 1942).

P. L.: Milton's *Paradise Lost*.

Robertson: *James Thomson, Poetical Works*, ed. J. L. Robertson (London, 1908, reprinted 1965).

Sambrook: James Thomson, *The Seasons*, ed. James Sambrook (Oxford, 1981).

A supralinear 'n' indicates the existence of an end-note, and a supralinear 'e' a gloss in Thomson's 'Explanation of the obsolete words' in *The Castle of Indolence* (pp. 212–13).

Reading List

1. *Editions*

The important early editions are recorded in my Notes on the Text and in the Chronological Table.

ed. J. L. ROBERTSON, *The Seasons and The Castle of Indolence*. Oxford, 1891 (Clarendon Press Editions).

ed. OTTO ZIPPEL, *Thomson's Seasons, Critical Edition*. Berlin: Mayer and Muller, 1908 (*Palaestra*, LXVI).

ed. J. L. ROBERTSON, *Poetical Works*. London, 1908, reprinted 1965 (Oxford Standard Authors).

ed. A. D. McKILLOP, *The Castle of Indolence and Other Poems*. Lawrence: University of Kansas Press, 1961.

ed. JAMES SAMBROOK, *The Seasons*, Oxford 1981 (Oxford English Texts).

2. *Important Books*

ARTHOS, JOHN, *The Language of Natural Description in Eighteenth Century Poetry*. Ann Arbor: University of Michigan Press, 1949.

BARRELL, JOHN, *English Literature in History, 1730–80*. London: Hutchinson, 1983.

CAMPBELL, HILBERT H., *James Thomson (1700–48): An Annotated Bibliography*. New York: Garland, 1976.

—— *James Thomson*. Boston: Twayne, 1979.

COHEN, RALPH, *The Art of Discrimination, Thomson's* The Seasons *and the Language of Criticism*. London: Routledge and Kegan Paul, 1964.

—— *The Unfolding of* The Seasons. London: Routledge and Kegan Paul, 1970.

GRANT, DOUGLAS, *James Thomson, Poet of* The Seasons. London: Cresset Press, 1951.

HAGSTRUM, JEAN, *The Sister Arts: the Tradition of Literary Pictorialism and English Poetry from Dryden to Gray*. Chicago: University of Chicago Press, 1958.

HAVENS, RAYMOND DEXTER, *The Influence of Milton on English Poetry*. Cambridge, Mass.: Harvard University Press, 1922. Chapter VI and Appendix A.

JOHNSON, SAMUEL, 'Life of Thomson'. Many edns. including *Johnson's Lives of the Poets*, ed. J. P. Hardy (Oxford, 1971).

McKILLOP, ALAN DUGALD, *The Background of Thomson's* Seasons. Minneapolis: University of Minnesota Press, 1942.

—— *The Background of Thomson's* Liberty. Houston: Rice Institute Pamphlet XXXVII, No. 2, 1951.

—— (ed.), *James Thomson (1700–1748), Letters and Documents*. Lawrence: University of Kansas Press, 1958.

MOORE, C. A., *Backgrounds of English Literature, 1700–1760*. Minneapolis: University of Minnesota Press, 1953. Chapters I, II, III.

NICOLSON, MARJORIE HOPE, *Newton Demands the Muse, Newton's Opticks and the Eighteenth Century Poets*. Princeton: Princeton University Press, 1946.

SPACKS, PATRICIA MEYER, *The Varied God*. Berkeley and Los Angeles: University of California Press, 1959.

—— *The Poetry of Vision*. Cambridge, Mass.: Harvard University Press, 1967. Chapters I, II, III.

3. *Important Articles*

DRENNON, HERBERT, 'James Thomson's Contact with Newtonianism and his Interest in Natural Philosophy', *PMLA*, xlix (1934), 71–80.

—— 'Scientific Rationalism and James Thomson's Poetic Art', *SP*, xxxi (1934), 453–71.

—— 'James Thomson's Ethical Theory and Scientific Rationalism', *PQ*, xiv (1935), 70–82.

GREENE, DONALD, 'From Accidie to Neurosis: *The Castle of Indolence* revisited', *English Literature in the Age of Disguise*, ed. M. E. Novak. Berkeley: Univ. of California Press (1977).

HAVENS, R. D., 'Primitivism and the Idea of Progress in Thomson', *SP*, xxix (1932), 41–52.

JEFFERSON, D. W., 'The Place of James Thomson', *Proceedings of the British Academy*, lxiv (1978), 233–58.

POTTER, G. R., 'James Thomson and the Evolution of Spirits', *Eng. Studien*, lxi (1926), 57–65.

TODD, WILLIAM B., 'The Text of *The Castle of Indolence*', *English Studies*, xxxiv (1953), 117–21.

TOMPKINS, J. M. S., 'In Yonder Grave a Druid lies', *RES*, xxii (1946), 1–16.

WELLS, J. E., 'Thomson's *Seasons* "Corrected and Amended"', *JEGP*, xlii (1943), 109–14.

The Seasons

A Poem

N. Kent. inv et del.   N. Jardieu Sculp.

Spring

Spring

THE ARGUMENT

The subject proposed. Inscribed to the Countess of Hartford. The Season
is described as it affects the various parts of nature, ascending from the
lower to the higher; and mixed with digressions arising from the subject.
Its influence on inanimate matter, on vegetables, on brute animals, and
last on Man; concluding with a dissuasive from the wild and irregular
passion of Love, opposed to that of a pure and happy kind.

COME, gentle Spring, ethereal mildness, come;
And from the bosom of yon dropping cloud,
While music wakes around, veiled in a shower
Of shadowing roses, on our plains descend.[n]

O Hartford,[n] fitted or to shine in courts   5
With unaffected grace, or walk the plain
With innocence and meditation joined
In soft assemblage, listen to my song,
Which thy own season paints—when Nature all
Is blooming and benevolent, like thee.   10

And see where surly Winter passes off
Far to the north, and calls his ruffian blasts:
His blasts obey, and quit the howling hill,
The shattered forest, and the ravaged vale;
While softer gales succeed, at whose kind touch,   15
Dissolving snows in livid torrents lost,
The mountains lift their green heads to the sky.
    As yet the trembling year is unconfirmed,
And Winter oft at eve resumes the breeze,
Chills the pale morn, and bids his driving sleets   20
Deform the day delightless; so that scarce
The bittern knows his time with bill engulfed
To shake the sounding marsh;[n] or from the shore
The plovers when to scatter o'er the heath,
And sing their wild notes to the listening waste.   25

13 *howling*: dreary, cf. Deut. 32:10.

At last from Aries rolls the bounteous sun,
And the bright Bull receives him. Then no more
The expansive atmosphere is cramped with cold;
But, full of life and vivifying soul,
Lifts the light clouds sublime, and spreads them thin,   30
Fleecy, and white o'er all-surrounding heaven.
    Forth fly the tepid airs; and unconfined,
Unbinding earth, the moving softness strays.
Joyous the impatient husbandman perceives
Relenting Nature, and his lusty steers   35
Drives from their stalls to where the well-used plough
Lies in the furrow loosened from the frost.
There, unrefusing, to the harnessed yoke
They lend their shoulder, and begin their toil,
Cheered by the simple song and soaring lark.   40
Meanwhile incumbent o'er the shining share
The master leans, removes the obstructing clay,
Winds the whole work, and sidelong lays the glebe.
    White through the neighbouring fields the sower stalks
With measured step, and liberal throws the grain   45
Into the faithful bosom of the ground:
The harrow follows harsh, and shuts the scene.
    Be gracious, Heaven, for now laborious man
Has done his part. Ye fostering breezes, blow;
Ye softening dews, ye tender showers, descend;   50
And temper all, thou world-reviving sun,
Into the perfect year. Nor, ye who live
In luxury and ease, in pomp and pride,
Think these lost themes unworthy of your ear:
Such themes as these the rural Maro sung   55
To wide-imperial Rome, in the full height
Of elegance and taste, by Greece refined.
In ancient times the sacred plough employed
The kings and awful fathers of mankind;

---

26 *Aries*: the Ram, the first sign of the zodiac, into which the sun enters at the
   vernal equinox (20 or 21 Mar.). The zodiac is the belt of the heavens through
   which the sun takes its apparent course; it was divided by ancient astronomers in-
   to twelve equal parts—the signs of the zodiac—each named after a constellation.
27 *Bull*: Taurus, the second sign of the zodiac, into which the sun enters about
   21 April; cf. Virgil, *Georgics* I.217–18.
30 *sublime*: high, cf. *P.L.* VII.421.
55 *rural Maro*: Virgil as author of the *Georgics*, cf. *Sp.* 456, *Wi.* 532.

And some, with whom compared your insect-tribes 60
Are but the beings of a summer's day,
Have held the scale of empire, ruled the storm
Of mighty war; then, with victorious hand,
Disdaining little delicacies, seized
The plough, and greatly independent scorned 65
All the vile stores corruption can bestow.
   Ye generous Britons, venerate the plough;
And o'er your hills and long withdrawing vales
Let Autumn spread his treasures to the sun,
Luxuriant and unbounded. As the sea 70
Far through his azure turbulent domain
Your empire owns, and from a thousand shores
Wafts all the pomp of life into your ports;
So with superior boon may your rich soil,
Exuberant, Nature's better blessings pour 75
O'er every land, the naked nations clothe,
And be the exhaustless granary of a world ![n]

   Nor only through the lenient air this change
Delicious breathes: the penetrative Sun,
His force deep-darting to the dark retreat 80
Of vegetation, sets the steaming power
At large, to wander o'er the vernant earth
In various hues; but chiefly thee, gay green!
Thou smiling[n] Nature's universal robe!
United light and shade! where the sight dwells 85
With growing strength and ever-new delight.
   From the moist meadow to the withered hill,
Led by the breeze, the vivid verdure runs,
And swells and deepens to the cherished eye.[n]
The hawthorn whitens; and the juicy groves 90
Put forth their buds, unfolding by degrees,
Till the whole leafy forest stands display'd
In full luxuriance to the sighing gales—
Where the deer rustle through the twining brake,
And the birds sing concealed. At once arrayed 95
In all the colours of the flushing year

60 *some*: e.g. Cincinnatus, Philopoemen, Regulus, and Fabricius, cf. *Su.* 1492,
   Wi. 491, 513, 571.
81 *steaming power*: sap, cf. *Sp.* 79–89 end-note.
82 *vernant*: flourishing in the Spring, cf. *P.L.* X.679.

By Nature's swift and secret-working hand,
The garden glows, and fills the liberal air
With lavish fragrance; while the promised fruit
Lies yet a little embryo, unperceived,   100
Within its crimson folds. Now from the town,
Buried in smoke and sleep and noisome damps,[n]
Oft let me wander o'er the dewy fields
Where freshness breathes, and dash the trembling drops
From the bent bush, as through the verdant maze   105
Of sweet-briar hedges I pursue my walk;
Or taste the smell of dairy;[n] or ascend
Some eminence, Augusta, in thy plains,
And see the country, far-diffused around,
One boundless blush, one white-empurpled shower   110
Of mingled blossoms; where the raptured eye
Hurries from joy to joy, and, hid beneath
The fair profusion, yellow Autumn spies.[n]
If, brushed from Russian wilds, a cutting gale
Rise not, and scatter from his humid wings   115
The clammy mildew; or, dry-blowing, breathe
Untimely frost—before whose baleful blast
The full-blown Spring through all her foliage shrinks,
Joyless and dead, a wide-dejected waste.
For oft, engendered by the hazy north,   120
Myriads on myriads, insect armies waft
Keen in the poisoned breeze, and wasteful eat
Through buds and bark into the blackened core
Their eager way. A feeble race, yet oft
The sacred sons of vengeance, on whose course   125
Corrosive famine waits, and kills the year.
To check this plague, the skilful farmer chaff
And blazing straw before his orchard burns;
Till, all involved in smoke, the latent foe
From every cranny suffocated falls;   130
Or scatters o'er the blooms the pungent dust
Of pepper, fatal to the frosty tribe;[n]
Or, when the envenomed leaf begins to curl,

---

108 *Augusta*: Augusta Trinobantum, a Roman name for London.
110 *white-empurpled*: Lat. *purpureus* referred to any bright colour, cf. *Au.* 674
    (of fruit), Virgil, *Eclogues* V.38 (of narcissus), Horace, *Odes* IV.i.10 (of swans).
121 *waft*: intransitive, cf. *P.L.* II.1042.
132 *frosty tribe*: biting insects. On T.'s periphrases see end-note.

With sprinkled water drowns them in their nest:
Nor, while they pick them up with busy bill,   135
The little trooping birds unwisely scares.[n]
    Be patient, swains; these cruel-seeming winds
Blow not in vain. Far hence they keep repressed
Those deepening clouds on clouds, surcharged with rain,
That o'er the vast Atlantic hither borne   140
In endless train would quench the Summer blaze,
And cheerless drown the crude unripened year.
    The North-east spends his rage, and, now shut up
Within his iron caves,[n] the effusive South
Warms the wide air, and o'er the void of heaven   145
Breathes the big clouds with vernal showers distent.
At first a dusky wreath they seem to rise,
Scarce staining ether; but by fast degrees,
In heaps on heaps the doubling vapour sails
Along the loaded sky, and mingling deep   150
Sits on the horizon round a settled gloom;
Not such as wintry storms on mortals shed,
Oppressing life; but lovely, gentle, kind,
And full of every hope and every joy,
The wish of Nature. Gradual sinks the breeze   155
Into a perfect calm; that not a breath
Is heard to quiver through the closing woods,
Or rustling turn the many-twinkling leaves
Of aspen tall. The uncurling floods, diffused
In glassy breadth, seem through delusive lapse   160
Forgetful of their course. 'Tis silence all,
And pleasing expectation. Herds and flocks
Drop the dry sprig, and mute-imploring eye
The falling verdure. Hushed in short suspense,
The plumy people streak their wings with oil   165
To throw the lucid moisture trickling off,
And wait the approaching sign to strike at once
Into the general choir. Even mountains, vales,

146 *distent*: full, Lat. *distentus*.
148 *ether*: not the 'air' of *Sp.* 145, but the tenuous, fluid medium by which light
    is transmitted. In T. it also refers to the upper sky, since the ether 'is expanded
    through all the heavens' (Newton, *Opticks*, 1704, Query 18). Cf. *Au.* 1213–
    14, *Lucretius* V.498–533.
160 *through delusive lapse*: because their falling cannot be detected, cf. *P.L.* VIII.
    263.
165 *plumy people*: birds. On periphrases see *Sp.* 132 end-note.

And forests seem, impatient, to demand
The promised sweetness. Man superior walks   170
Amid the glad creation, musing praise
And looking lively gratitude. At last
The clouds consign their treasures to the fields,
And, softly shaking on the dimpled pool
Prelusive drops, let all their moisture flow   175
In large effusion o'er the freshened world.
The stealing shower is scarce to patter heard
By such as wander through the forest-walks,
Beneath the umbrageous multitude of leaves.
But who can hold the shade while Heaven descends   180
In universal bounty, shedding herbs
And fruits and flowers on Nature's ample lap ?
Swift fancy fired anticipates their growth;
And, while the milky nutriment distils,
Beholds the kindling country colour round.[n]   185
    Thus all day long the full-distended clouds
Indulge their genial stores, and well-showered earth
Is deep enriched with vegetable life;
Till, in the western sky, the downward Sun
Looks out effulgent from amid the flush   190
Of broken clouds, gay-shifting to his beam.
The rapid radiance instantaneous strikes
The illumined mountain, through the forest streams,
Shakes on the floods, and in a yellow mist,
Far smoking o'er the interminable plain,   195
In twinkling myriads lights the dewy gems.
Moist, bright, and green, the landscape laughs around.
Full swell the woods; their every music wakes,
Mixed in wild concert, with the warbling brooks
Increased, the distant bleatings of the hills,   200
The hollow lows responsive from the vales,
Whence, blending all, the sweetened zephyr springs.
Meantime, refracted from yon eastern cloud,
Bestriding earth, the grand ethereal bow
Shoots up immense; and every hue unfolds,   205
In fair proportion running from the red

184 *milky nutriment*: sap, cf. *Sp.* 79–89 end-note.
196 *gems*: Lat. *gemma* signifies both bud and jewel (cf. Virgil *Georgics* II.335),
    but here the buds do sparkle like gems with sunlight reflected from raindrops;
    T.'s word-painting is etymologically 'witty'.

To where the violet fades into the sky.
Here, awful Newton, the dissolving clouds
Form, fronting on the sun, thy showery prism;
And to the sage-instructed eye unfold   210
The various twine of light, by thee disclosed
From the white mingling maze.[n] Not so the swain;
He wondering views the bright enchantment bend
Delightful o'er the radiant fields, and runs
To catch the falling glory; but amazed   215
Beholds the amusive arch before him fly,
Then vanish quite away. Still night succeeds,
A softened shade, and saturated earth
Awaits the morning beam, to give to light,
Raised through ten thousand different plastic tubes,   220
The balmy treasures of the former day.
    Then spring the living herbs, profusely wild,
O'er all the deep-green earth, beyond the power
Of botanist to number up their tribes:
Whether he steals along the lonely dale   225
In silent search; or through the forest, rank
With what the dull incurious weeds account,
Bursts his blind way; or climbs the mountain-rock,
Fired by the nodding verdure of its brow.
With such a liberal hand has Nature flung   230
Their seeds abroad, blown them about in winds,
Innumerous mixed them with the nursing mould,
The moistening current, and prolific rain.
    But who their virtues can declare ? who pierce
With vision pure into these secret stores   235
Of health and life and joy ? the food of man
While yet he lived in innocence, and told
A length of golden years, unfleshed in blood,
A stranger to the savage arts of life,
Death, rapine, carnage, surfeit, and disease—   240
The lord and not the tyrant of the world.
    The first fresh dawn then waked the gladdened race
Of uncorrupted man, nor blushed to see
The sluggard sleep beneath its sacred beam;
For their light slumbers gently fumed away,   245

220 *plastic tubes*: sap vessels, cf. *Sp*. 79–89 end-note.
227 : with plants which dull and incurious people reckon as weeds.
245 *fumed away*: passed away like smoke.

And up they rose as vigorous as the sun,
Or to the culture of the willing glebe,
Or to the cheerful tendance of the flock.
Meantime the song went round; and dance and sport,
Wisdom and friendly talk successive stole   250
Their hours away; while in the rosy vale
Love breathed his infant sighs, from anguish free,
And full replete with bliss—save the sweet pain
That, inly thrilling, but exalts it more.
Nor yet injurious act nor surly deed   255
Was known among these happy sons of Heaven;
For reason and benevolence were law.
Harmonious Nature too looked smiling on.
Clear shone the skies, cooled with eternal gales,
And balmy spirit all. The youthful Sun   260
Shot his best rays, and still the gracious clouds
Dropped fatness down; as o'er the swelling mead
The herds and flocks commixing played secure.
This when, emergent from the gloomy wood,
The glaring lion saw, his horrid heart   265
Was meekened, and he joined his sullen joy.
For music held the whole in perfect peace:
Soft sighed the flute; the tender voice was heard,
Warbling the varied heart; the woodlands round
Applied their choir; and winds and waters flowed   270
In consonance. Such were those prime of days.

   But now those white unblemished minutes, whence
The fabling poets took their golden age,
Are found no more amid these iron times,[n]
These dregs of life! Now the distempered mind   275
Has lost that concord of harmonious powers
Which forms the soul of happiness; and all
Is off the poise within: the passions all
Have burst their bounds; and Reason, half extinct,
Or impotent, or else approving, sees   280
The foul disorder. Senseless and deformed,
Convulsive Anger storms at large; or, pale
And silent, settles into fell revenge.
Base Envy withers at another's joy,

262 *fatness*: fertility, cf. Ps. 65:12.
266 *sullen joy*: deep-toned roar, cf. *Au.* 416, Milton, *Il Penseroso* 76.

And hates that excellence it cannot reach.   285
Desponding Fear, of feeble fancies full,
Weak and unmanly, loosens every power.
Even Love itself is bitterness of soul,
A pensive anguish pining at the heart;
Or, sunk to sordid interest, feels no more   290
That noble wish, that never-cloyed desire,
Which, selfish joy disdaining, seeks alone
To bless the dearer object of its flame.
Hope sickens with extravagance; and Grief,
Of life impatient, into madness swells,   295
Or in dead silence wastes the weeping hours.
These, and a thousand mixed emotions more,
From ever-changing views of good and ill,
Formed infinitely various, vex the mind
With endless storm: whence, deeply rankling, grows   300
The partial thought, a listless unconcern,
Cold, and averting from our neighbour's good;
Then dark disgust and hatred, winding wiles,
Coward deceit, and ruffian violence.
At last, extinct each social feeling,[n] fell   305
And joyless inhumanity pervades
And petrifies the heart. Nature disturbed
Is deemed, vindictive, to have changed her course.
     Hence, in old dusky time, a deluge came:
When the deep-cleft disparting orb, that arched   310
The central waters round, impetuous rushed
With universal burst into the gulf,
And o'er the high-piled hills of fractured earth
Wide-dashed the waves in undulation vast,
Till, from the centre to the streaming clouds,   315
A shoreless ocean tumbled round the globe.
     The Seasons since have, with severer sway,
Oppressed a broken world: the Winter keen
Shook forth his waste of snows; and Summer shot
His pestilential heats. Great Spring before   320
Greened all the year; and fruits and blossoms blushed
In social sweetness on the self-same bough.[n]
Pure was the temperate air; an even calm
Perpetual reigned, save what the zephyrs bland
Breathed o'er the blue expanse: for then nor storms   325
Were taught to blow, nor hurricanes to rage;

Sound slept the waters; no sulphureous glooms
Swelled in the sky and sent the lightning forth;
While sickly damps and cold autumnal fogs
Hung not relaxing on the springs of life.   330
But now, of turbid elements the sport,
From clear to cloudy tossed, from hot to cold,
And dry to moist, with inward-eating change,
Our drooping days are dwindled down to naught,
Their period finished ere 'tis well begun.   335
   And yet the wholesome herb neglected dies;
Though with the pure exhilarating soul
Of nutriment and health, and vital powers,
Beyond the search of art, 'tis copious blest.
For, with hot ravine fired, ensanguined man   340
Is now become the lion of the plain,
And worse. The wolf, who from the nightly fold
Fierce drags the bleating prey, ne'er drunk her milk,
Nor wore her warming fleece: nor has the steer,
At whose strong chest the deadly tiger hangs,   345
E'er ploughed for him. They too are tempered high,
With hunger stung and wild necessity,
Nor lodges pity in their shaggy breast.
But man, whom Nature formed of milder clay,
With every kind emotion in his heart,   350
And taught alone to weep,—while from her lap
She pours ten thousand delicacies, herbs
And fruits, as numerous as the drops of rain
Or beams that gave them birth,—shall he, fair form!
Who wears sweet smiles, and looks erect on Heaven, 355
E'er stoop to mingle with the prowling herd,
And dip his tongue in gore? The beast of prey,
Blood-stained, deserves to bleed: but you, ye flocks,
What have you done? ye peaceful people, what,
To merit death? you, who have given us milk   360
In luscious streams, and lent us your own coat
Against the Winter's cold? And the plain ox,
That harmless, honest, guileless animal,
In what has he offended? he whose toil,
Patient and ever ready, clothes the land   365
With all the pomp of harvest; shall he bleed,

330 *springs of life*: vital organs, likened to the springs in a machine.
340 *ravine*: rapine.

And struggling groan beneath the cruel hands
Even of the clowns he feeds ? And that, perhaps,
To swell the riot of the autumnal feast,
Won by his labour ? This the feeling heart   370
Would tenderly suggest: but 'tis enough,
In this late age, adventurous to have touched
Light on the numbers of the Samian Sage.
High Heaven forbids the bold presumptuous strain,
Whose wisest will has fixed us in a state   375
That must not yet to pure perfection rise:
Besides, who knows, how, raised to higher life,
From stage to stage, the vital scale ascends ?[n]

   Now, when the first foul torrent of the brooks,
Swelled with the vernal rains, is ebbed away,   380
And whitening down their mossy-tinctured stream
Descends the billowy foam; now is the time,
While yet the dark-brown water aids the guile,
To tempt the trout. The well-dissembled fly,
The rod fine-tapering with elastic spring,   385
Snatched from the hoary steed the floating line,
And all thy slender watery stores prepare.
But let not on thy hook the tortured worm
Convulsive twist in agonizing folds;
Which, by rapacious hunger swallowed deep,   390
Gives, as you tear it from the bleeding breast
Of the weak helpless uncomplaining wretch,
Harsh pain and horror to the tender hand.[n]
   When with his lively ray the potent sun
Has pierced the streams and roused the finny race,   395
Then, issuing cheerful, to thy sport repair;
Chief should the western breezes curling play,
And light o'er ether bear the shadowy clouds.
High to their fount, this day, amid the hills
And woodlands warbling round, trace up the brooks;   400
The next, pursue their rocky-channelled maze,

---

373 *Samian Sage*: Pythagoras, the Greek philosopher and vegetarian born at
   Samos *c.* 580 B.C.
386 *Snatched . . . line*: fishing lines were made of twisted horsehair. Izaak
   Walton recommended 'right, sound, clear, glass-colour hair' (*Compleat Angler*,
   chap. xxi).
393 *horror*: shuddering.
395 *finny race*: fish. On periphrases see *Sp.* 132 end-note.

Down to the river, in whose ample wave
Their little naiads love to sport at large.
Just in the dubious point where with the pool
Is mixed the trembling stream, or where it boils   405
Around the stone, or from the hollowed bank
Reverted plays in undulating flow,
There throw, nice-judging, the delusive fly;
And, as you lead it round in artful curve,
With eye attentive mark the springing game.   410
Straight as above the surface of the flood
They wanton rise, or urged by hunger leap,
Then fix with gentle twitch the barbèd hook—
Some lightly tossing to the grassy bank,
And to the shelving shore slow-dragging some,   415
With various hand proportioned to their force.
If, yet too young and easily deceived,
A worthless prey scarce bends your pliant rod,
Him, piteous of his youth and the short space
He has enjoyed the vital light of heaven,   420
Soft disengage, and back into the stream
The speckled infant throw. But, should you lure
From his dark haunt beneath the tangled roots
Of pendent trees the monarch of the brook,
Behoves you then to ply your finest art.   425
Long time he, following cautious, scans the fly,
And oft attempts to seize it, but as oft
The dimpled water speaks his jealous fear.
At last, while haply o'er the shaded sun
Passes a cloud, he desperate takes the death   430
With sullen plunge. At once he darts along,
Deep-struck, and runs out all the lengthened line;
Then seeks the farthest ooze, the sheltering weed,
The caverned bank, his old secure abode;
And flies aloft, and flounces round the pool,   435
Indignant of the guile. With yielding hand,
That feels him still, yet to his furious course
Give way, you, now retiring, following now
Across the stream, exhaust his idle rage;

403 *naiads*: fish (mock-heroic; lit. water-nymphs).
424 *monarch*: 'the salmon is accounted the king of fresh-water fish' (Walton,
  Compleat Angler, chap. vii), but T.'s description of the haunt suggests that he
  may be referring to the adult trout.

Till floating broad upon his breathless side,   440
And to his fate abandoned, to the shore
You gaily drag your unresisting prize.
   Thus pass the temperate hours: but when the Sun
Shakes from his noon-day throne the scattering clouds,
Even shooting listless languor through the deeps,   445
Then seek the bank where flowering elders crowd,
Where scattered wild the lily of the vale
Its balmy essence breathes, where cowslips hang
The dewy head, where purple violets lurk,
With all the lowly children of the shade;   450
Or lie reclined beneath yon spreading ash
Hung o'er the steep, whence, borne on liquid wing,
The sounding culver shoots, or where the hawk,
High in the beetling cliff, his eyrie builds.
There let the classic page thy fancy lead   455
Through rural scenes, such as the Mantuan swain
Paints in the matchless harmony of song;
Or catch thyself the landscape, gliding swift
Athwart imagination's vivid eye;
Or, by the vocal woods and waters lulled,   460
And lost in lonely musing, in a dream
Confused of careless solitude where mix
Ten thousand wandering images of things,
Soothe every gust of passion into peace—
All but the swellings of the softened heart,   465
That waken, not disturb, the tranquil mind.[n]
   Behold yon breathing prospect bids the Muse
Throw all her beauty forth. But who can paint
Like Nature ? Can imagination boast,
Amid its gay creation, hues like hers ?   470
Or can it mix them with that matchless skill,
And lose them in each other, as appears
In every bud that blows ? If fancy then
Unequal fails beneath the pleasing task,
Ah, what shall language do ? ah, where find words   475
Tinged with so many colours and whose power,
To life approaching, may perfume my lays

---

446 *elders*: not the common elder but the red elder found in Scotland and N.E.
   England which, like the other plants mentioned in *Sp.* 447–9, flowers in Spring.
452 *liquid*: bright, cf. *Lucretius* V.212.
456 *Mantuan swain*: Virgil as author of the *Eclogues*, cf. *Sp.* 55, *Wi.* 532.

With that fine oil, those aromatic gales
That inexhaustive flow continual round?
   Yet, though successless, will the toil delight.   480
Come then, ye virgins and ye youths, whose hearts
Have felt the raptures of refining love;
And thou, Amanda, come, pride of my song!
Formed by the Graces, loveliness itself!
Come with those downcast eyes, sedate and sweet,   485
Those looks demure that deeply pierce the soul,
Where, with the light of thoughtful reason mixed,
Shines lively fancy and the feeling heart:
Oh, come! and, while the rosy-footed May
Steals blushing on, together let us tread   490
The morning dews, and gather in their prime
Fresh-blooming flowers to grace thy braided hair
And thy loved bosom, that improves their sweets.
   See where the winding vale its lavish stores,
well-watered Irriguous, spreads. See how the lily drinks   495
The latent rill, scarce oozing through the grass
Of growth luxuriant, or the humid bank
In fair profusion decks. Long let us walk
Where the breeze blows from yon extended field
Of blossomed beans. Arabia cannot boast   500
A fuller gale of joy than liberal thence
Breathes through the sense, and takes the ravished soul.
Nor is the mead unworthy of thy foot,
Full of fresh verdure and unnumbered flowers,
The negligence of Nature wide and wild,   505
Where, undisguised by mimic art, she spreads
Unbounded beauty to the roving eye.
Here their delicious task the fervent bees
In swarming millions tend. Around, athwart,
Through the soft air, the busy nations fly,   510
Cling to the bud, and with inserted tube
Suck its pure essence, its ethereal soul.
And oft with bolder wing they soaring dare

478 *oil*: the volatile oil that gives scent to plants.
483 *Amanda*: Elizabeth Young who had refused T.'s proposal of marriage in
    1743 (see *Letters and Documents*, pp. 146–61, 164–71, 175–7, 182–4). Lines
    483–8 first appeared in the 1744 edition.
484 *Graces*: see *Wi.* 659 fn.
495 *irriguous*: irrigating, cf. *P.L.* IV.255, Virgil, *Georgics* IV.32.
495 *lily*: lent lily or daffodil.

The purple heath, or where the wild thyme grows,
And yellow load them with the luscious spoil.   515
    At length the finished garden to the view
Its vistas opens and its alleys green.
Snatched through the verdant maze, the hurried eye
Distracted wanders; now the bowery walk
Of covert close, where scarce a speck of day   520
Falls on the lengthened gloom, protracted sweeps;
Now meets the bending sky, the river now
Dimpling along, the breezy ruffled lake,
The forest darkening round, the glittering spire,
The ethereal mountain, and the distant main.   525
But why so far excursive? when at hand,
Along these blushing borders bright with dew,
And in yon mingled wilderness of flowers,
Fair-handed Spring unbosoms every grace—
Throws out the snow-drop and the crocus first,   530
The daisy, primrose, violet darkly blue,
And polyanthus of unnumbered dyes;
The yellow wall-flower, stained with iron brown,
And lavish stock, that scents the garden round:
From the soft wing of vernal breezes shed,   535
Anemones, auriculas, enriched
With shining meal o'er all their velvet leaves;
And full ranunculus of glowing red.
Then comes the tulip-race, where beauty plays
Her idle freaks: from family diffused   540
To family, as flies the father-dust,
The varied colours run; and, while they break
On the charmed eye, the exulting florist marks
With secret pride the wonders of his hand.
No gradual bloom is wanting—from the bud   545
First-born of Spring to Summer's musky tribes;
Nor hyacinths, of purest virgin white,
Low bent and blushing inward; nor jonquils,

518–25 the hurried eye sweeps the bowery walk and meets the bending sky and
    meets the river, etc.
529 *unbosoms*: takes from concealment in the earth.
534 *lavish*: of perfume.
537 *meal*: powder.
541 *father-dust*: pollen.
542 *break*: burst into colour.
546 *musky tribes*: scented flowers. On periphrases see *Sp.* 132 end-note.

Of potent fragrance; nor narcissus fair,
As o'er the fabled fountain hanging still;   550
Nor broad carnations, nor gay-spotted pinks;
Nor, showered from every bush, the damask-rose:
Infinite numbers, delicacies, smells,
With hues on hues expression cannot paint,
The breath of Nature, and her endless bloom.   555
   Hail, Source of Being! Universal Soul
Of heaven and earth! Essential Presence, hail!
To thee I bend the knee; to thee my thoughts
Continual climb, who with a master-hand
Hast the great whole into perfection touched.   560
By thee the various vegetative tribes,
Wrapt in a filmy net and clad with leaves,
Draw the live ether[n] and imbibe the dew.
By thee disposed into congenial soils,
Stands each attractive plant, and sucks, and swells   565
The juicy tide, a twining mass of tubes.
At thy command the vernal sun awakes
The torpid sap, detruded to the root
By wintry winds, that now in fluent dance
And lively fermentation mounting spreads   570
All this innumerous-coloured scene of things.[n]
   As rising from the vegetable world
My theme ascends, with equal wing ascend,
My panting Muse; and hark, how loud the woods
Invite you forth in all your gayest trim.   575
Lend me your song, ye nightingales! oh, pour
The mazy-running soul of melody
Into my varied verse! while I deduce,
From the first note the hollow cuckoo sings,
The symphony of Spring, and touch a theme   580
Unknown to fame—the passion of the groves.

550 *fabled fountain*: Narcissus, in Greek mythology, fell in love with his own
   reflection in a pool, and was turned into a flower; cf. Ovid, *Metamorphoses* III.
   341–510.
557 *Essential Presence*: God, as absolute being, cf. *P.L.* V.841.
562 *filmy net*: system of sap vessels.
565 *attractive*: drawing moisture from the earth.
566 *tubes*: roots.
568 *detruded*: forced down, cf. Virgil, *Aeneid* VII.773.
577 *mazy*: winding, cf. *P.L.* IX.161.
578 *deduce*: trace, cf. Virgil, *Aeneid* X.618.

When first the soul of love is sent abroad
Warm through the vital air, and on the heart
Harmonious seizes, the gay troops begin   *birds!*
In gallant thought to plume the painted wing;   585
And try again the long-forgotten strain,
At first faint-warbled. But no sooner grows
The soft infusion prevalent and wide
Than all alive at once their joy o'erflows
In music unconfined. Up springs the lark,   590
Shrill-voiced and loud, the messenger of morn:
Ere yet the shadows fly, he mounted sings
Amid the dawning clouds, and from their haunts
Calls up the tuneful nations. Every copse
Deep-tangled, tree irregular, and bush   595
Bending with dewy moisture o'er the heads
Of the coy quiristers that lodge within,
Are prodigal of harmony. The thrush
And wood-lark, o'er the kind-contending throng
Superior heard, run through the sweetest length   600
Of notes, when listening Philomela deigns
To let them joy, and purposes, in thought
Elate, to make her night excel their day.
The blackbird whistles from the thorny brake,
The mellow bullfinch answers from the grove;   605
Nor are the linnets, o'er the flowering furze
Poured out profusely, silent. Joined to these
Innumerous songsters, in the freshening shade
Of new-sprung leaves, their modulations mix
Mellifluous. The jay, the rook, the daw,   610
And each harsh pipe, discordant heard alone,
Aid the full concert; while the stock-dove breathes
A melancholy murmur through the whole.
   'Tis love creates their melody, and all

---

584 *gay troops*: birds, cf. 'tuneful nations' (594), 'coy quiristers' (597) where the
   periphrasis emphasizes the attribute under discussion. On periphrases see *Sp.*
   132 end-note.
588 *soft infusion*: what is poured in, i.e. love. Cf. *Sp.* 868, *P.L.* VIII. 474.
599 *kind*: both 'according to their species' and 'affectionately'.
601 *Philomela*: in Greek mythology, the Athenian king's daughter who was
   raped, mutilated, and changed into a nightingale; cf. Ovid, *Metamorphoses*
   VI.438–674.
607 *poured*: the linnets themselves are 'poured' because they fly in large flocks;
   their song, too, is poured.

This waste of music is the voice of love,   615
That even to birds and beasts the tender arts
Of pleasing teaches. Hence the glossy kind
Try every winning way inventive love
Can dictate, and in courtship to their mates
Pour forth their little souls. First, wide around,   620
With distant awe, in airy rings they rove,
Endeavouring by a thousand tricks to catch
The cunning, conscious, half-averted glance
Of their regardless charmer. Should she seem
Softening the least approvance to bestow,   625
Their colours burnish, and, by hope inspired,
They brisk advance; then, on a sudden struck,
Retire disordered; then again approach,
In fond rotation spread the spotted wing,
And shiver every feather with desire.   630
    Connubial leagues agreed, to the deep woods
They haste away, all as their fancy leads,
Pleasure, or food, or secret safety prompts;
That Nature's great command may be obeyed,
Nor all the sweet sensations they perceive   635
Indulged in vain. Some to the holly-hedge
Nestling repair, and to the thicket some;
Some to the rude protection of the thorn
Commit their feeble offspring. The cleft tree
Offers its kind concealment to a few,   640
Their food its insects, and its moss their nests.
Others apart far in the grassy dale,
Or roughening waste, their humble texture weave
But most in woodland solitudes delight,
In unfrequented glooms, or shaggy banks,   645
Steep, and divided by a babbling brook
Whose murmurs soothe them all the live-long day
When by kind duty fixed. Among the roots
Of hazel, pendent o'er the plaintive stream,
They frame the first foundation of their domes—   650
Dry sprigs of trees, in artful fabric laid,

615 *waste*: vast extent.
617 *glossy kind*: birds. T. employs this periphrasis because he is going on to
   show the importance of glossy plumage for mating.
650 *domes*: houses, Lat. *domus* (used of bird's nests in Virgil, *Georgics* II.209); cf.
   Au. 660, 1182.

And bound with clay together. Now 'tis nought
But restless hurry through the busy air,
Beat by unnumbered wings. The swallow sweeps
The slimy pool, to build his hanging house   655
Intent. And often, from the careless back
Of herds and flocks, a thousand tugging bills
Pluck hair and wool; and oft, when unobserved,
Steal from the barn a straw—till soft and warm,
Clean and complete, their habitation grows.   660
   As thus the patient dam assiduous sits,
Not to be tempted from her tender task
Or by sharp hunger or by smooth delight,
Though the whole loosened Spring around her blows,
Her sympathizing lover takes his stand   665
High on the opponent bank, and ceaseless sings
The tedious time away; or else supplies
Her place a moment, while she sudden flits
To pick the scanty meal. The appointed time
With pious toil fulfilled, the callow young,   670
Warmed and expanded into perfect life,
Their brittle bondage break, and come to light,
A helpless family demanding food
With constant clamour. Oh, what passions then,
What melting sentiments of kindly care,   675
On the new parents seize! Away they fly
Affectionate, and undesiring bear
The most delicious morsel to their young;
Which equally distributed, again
The search begins. Even so a gentle pair,   680
By fortune sunk, but formed of generous mould,
And charmed with cares beyond the vulgar breast,
In some lone cot amid the distant woods,
Sustain'd alone by providential Heaven,
Oft, as they weeping eye their infant train,   685
Check their own appetites, and give them all.
   Nor toil alone they scorn: exalting love,
By the great Father of the Spring inspired,
Gives instant courage to the fearful race,
And to the simple art. With stealthy wing,   690

---

682 *charmed with cares*: 'afflicted with anxieties' and, perhaps, 'enchanted by the objects of solicitude (children)'.

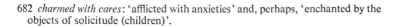

Should some rude foot their woody haunts molest,
Amid a neighbouring bush they silent drop,
And whirring thence, as if alarmed, deceive
The unfeeling schoolboy. Hence, around the head
Of wandering swain, the white-winged plover wheels   695
Her sounding flight, and then directly on
In long excursion skims the level lawn
To tempt him from her nest. The wild-duck, hence,
O'er the rough moss, and o'er the trackless waste
The heath-hen flutters, pious fraud! to lead   700
The hot pursuing spaniel far astray.
   Be not the Muse ashamed here to bemoan
Her brothers[n] of the grove by tyrant man
Inhuman caught, and in the narrow cage
From liberty confined, and boundless air.   705
Dull are the pretty slaves, their plumage dull,
Ragged, and all its brightening lustre lost;
Nor is that sprightly wildness in their notes,
Which, clear and vigorous, warbles from the beech.
Oh then, ye friends of love and love-taught song,   710
Spare the soft tribes, this barbarous art forbear!
If on your bosom innocence can win,
Music engage, or piety persuade.
   But let not chief the nightingale lament
Her ruined care, too delicately framed   715
To brook the harsh confinement of the cage.
Oft when, returning with her loaded bill,
The astonished mother finds a vacant nest,
By the hard hand of unrelenting clowns
Robbed, to the ground the vain provision falls;   720
Her pinions ruffle, and, low-drooping, scarce
Can bear the mourner to the poplar shade;
Where, all abandoned to despair, she sings
Her sorrows through the night, and, on the bough
Sole-sitting, still at every dying fall   725
Takes up again her lamentable strain
Of winding woe, till wide around the woods

---

696 *sounding*: diving (the lapwing's flight is highly erratic when it is trying to
  decoy predators away from its nest).
697 *excursion*: running out, cf. Virgil, *Georgics* IV.194.
700 *heath-hen*: black grouse.
715 *ruined care*: lost offspring.

      Sigh to her song and with her wail resound.[n]
      But now the feathered youth their former bounds,
    Ardent, disdain; and, weighing oft their wings,   730
    Demand the free possession of the sky.
    This one glad office more, and then dissolves
    Parental love at once, now needless grown:
    Unlavish Wisdom never works in vain.
    'Tis on some evening, sunny, grateful, mild,   735
    When nought but balm is breathing through the woods
    With yellow lustre bright, that the new tribes
    Visit the spacious heavens, and look abroad
    On Nature's common, far as they can see
    Or wing, their range and pasture. O'er the boughs   740
    Dancing about, still at the giddy verge
    Their resolution fails; their pinions still,
    In loose libration stretched, to trust the void
    Trembling refuse—till down before them fly
    The parent-guides, and chide, exhort, command,   745
    Or push them off. The surging air receives
    The plumy burden; and their self-taught wings
    Winnow the waving element. On ground
    Alighted, bolder up again they lead,
    Farther and farther on, the lengthening flight;   750
    Till, vanished every fear, and every power
    Roused into life and action, light in air
    The acquitted parents see their soaring race,
    And, once rejoicing, never know them more.
      High from the summit of a craggy cliff,   755
    Hung o'er the deep, such as amazing frowns
    On utmost Kilda's shore, whose lonely race
    Resign the setting sun to Indian worlds,
    The royal eagle draws his vigorous young,
    Strong-pounced, and ardent with paternal fire,   760
    Now fit to raise a kingdom of their own,
    He drives them from his fort, the towering seat
    For ages of his empire—which in peace

729 *feathered youth*: fledglings.
730 *weighing oft their wings*: balancing themselves.
757 *Kilda*: St. Kilda, the most westerly and remote of the Outer Hebrides, known in the eighteenth century by the famous description in Martin Martin, *A Late Voyage to St. Kilda* (1698).
761–5 To obtain enough food a single pair of golden eagles needs to prey over a large area.

Unstained he holds, while many a league to sea
He wings his course, and preys in distant isles.   765
   Should I my steps turn to the rural seat
Whose lofty elms and venerable oaks
Invite the rook, who high amid the boughs
In early Spring his airy city builds,
And ceaseless caws amusive; there, well-pleased,   770
I might the various polity survey
Of the mixed household-kind. The careful hen
Calls all her chirping family around,
Fed and defended by the fearless cock,
Whose breast with ardour flames, as on he walks   775
Graceful, and crows defiance. In the pond
The finely-chequered duck before her train
Rows garrulous. The stately-sailing swan
Gives out his snowy plumage to the gale,
And, arching proud his neck, with oary feet   780
Bears forward fierce, and guards his osier-isle,[n]
Protective of his young. The turkey nigh,
Loud-threatening, reddens; while the peacock spreads
His every-coloured glory to the sun,
And swims in radiant majesty along.   785
O'er the whole homely scene the cooing dove
Flies thick in amorous chase, and wanton rolls
The glancing eye, and turns the changeful neck.
   While thus the gentle tenants of the shade
Indulge their purer loves, the rougher world   790
Of brutes below rush furious into flame
And fierce desire. Through all his lusty veins
The bull, deep-scorched, the raging passion feels.
Of pasture sick, and negligent of food,
Scarce seen he wades among the yellow broom,   795
While o'er his ample sides the rambling sprays
Luxuriant shoot; or through the mazy wood
Dejected wanders, nor the enticing bud
Crops, though it presses on his careless sense.
And oft, in jealous maddening fancy wrapt,   800
He seeks the fight; and idly-butting, feigns
His rival gored in every knotty trunk.
Him should he meet, the bellowing war begins:

769 *airy city*: rookery.

Their eyes flash fury; to the hollowed earth,
Whence the sand flies, they mutter bloody deeds, 805
And, groaning deep, the impetuous battle mix:
While the fair heifer, balmy-breathing near,
Stands kindling up their rage. The trembling steed,
With this hot impulse seized in every nerve,
Nor heeds the rein, nor hears the sounding thong; 810
Blows are not felt; but, tossing high his head,
And by the well-known joy to distant plains
Attracted strong, all wild he bursts away;
O'er rocks, and woods, and craggy mountains flies;
And, neighing, on the aerial summit takes 815
The exciting gale; then, steep-descending, cleaves
The headlong torrents foaming down the hills,
Even where the madness of the straitened stream
Turns in black eddies round: such is the force
With which his frantic heart and sinews swell. 820
    Nor undelighted by the boundless Spring
Are the broad monsters of the foaming deep:
From the deep ooze and gelid cavern roused,
They flounce and tumble in unwieldy joy.
Dire were the strain and dissonant to sing 825
The cruel raptures of the savage kind:
How, by this flame their native wrath sublimed,
They roam, amid the fury of their heart,
The far-resounding waste in fiercer bands,
And growl their horrid loves.[n] But this the theme 830
I sing enraptured to the British fair
Forbids, and leads me to the mountain-brow
Where sits the shepherd on the grassy turf,
Inhaling healthful the descending sun.
Around him feeds his many-bleating flock, 835
Of various cadence; and his sportive lambs,
This way and that convolved in friskful glee,
Their frolics play. And now the sprightly race
Invites them forth; when swift, the signal given,
They start away, and sweep the massy mound 840
That runs around the hill—the rampart once

---

826 *kind*: species (but its conjunction with 'savage' gives the effect of oxymoron).
830–2 T.'s theme—gentle love—forbids him to sing any longer this dire and dissonant song of sexual violence. There is perhaps, a hint of self-parody in T.'s genteel self-censorship.

Of iron war, in ancient barbarous times,
When disunited Britain ever bled,
Lost in eternal broil, ere yet she grew
To this deep-laid indissoluble state   845
Where wealth and commerce lift the golden head,
And o'er our labours liberty and law
Impartial watch, the wonder of a world![n]
    What is this mighty breath, ye curious, say,
That in a powerful language, felt, not heard,   850
Instructs the fowls of heaven, and through their breast
These arts of love diffuses ? What, but God ?
Inspiring God ! who, boundless spirit all
And unremitting energy, pervades,
Adjusts, sustains, and agitates the whole.   855
He ceaseless works alone, and yet alone
Seems not to work; with such perfection framed
Is this complex, stupendous scheme of things.
But, though concealed, to every purer eye
The informing Author in his works appears: 860
Chief, lovely Spring, in thee and thy soft scenes
The smiling God[n] is seen—while water, earth,
And air attest his bounty, which exalts
The brute-creation to this finer thought,
And annual melts their undesigning hearts   865
Profusely thus in tenderness and joy.
    Still let my song a nobler note assume,
And sing the infusive force of Spring on man;
When heaven and earth, as if contending, vie
To raise his being and serene his soul.   870
Can he forbear to join the general smile
Of Nature ? Can fierce passions vex his breast,
While every gale is peace, and every grove
Is melody ? Hence ! from the bounteous walks
Of flowing Spring ye sordid sons of earth,   875
Hard, and unfeeling of another's woe,
Or only lavish to yourselves—away !
But come, ye generous minds, in whose wide thought,
Of all his works, Creative Bounty burns

860 *informing*: giving life to, cf. *Su.* 104, 1754.   864 *finer thought*: love.
865 *undesigning*: actuated by instinct.
870 *serene*: make calm.
875 *sons of earth*: oppressors who have no thought of Heaven, cf. Ps. 10:18.

With warmest beam, and on your open front   880
And liberal eye sits, from his dark retreat
Inviting modest Want. Nor till invoked
Can restless Goodness wait; your active search
Leaves no cold wintry corner unexplored;
Like silent-working Heaven, surprising oft   885
The lonely heart with unexpected good.
For you the roving spirit of the wind
Blows Spring abroad; for you the teeming clouds
Descend in gladsome plenty o'er the world;
And the Sun sheds his kindest rays for you,   890
Ye flower of human race ! In these green days,
Reviving Sickness lifts her languid head;
Life flows afresh; and young-eyed Health exalts
The whole creation round. Contentment walks
The sunny glade, and feels an inward bliss   895
Spring o'er his mind, beyond the power of kings
To purchase. Pure Serenity apace
Induces thought, and contemplation still.
By swift degrees the love of Nature works,
And warms the bosom; till at last, sublimed   900
To rapture and enthusiastic heat,
We feel the present Deity, and taste
The joy of God to see a happy world ![n]
    These are the sacred feelings of thy heart,
Thy heart informed by reason's purer ray,   905
O Lyttelton,[n] the friend ! Thy passions thus
And meditations vary, as at large,
Courting the muse, through Hagley Park[n] you stray—
Thy British Tempe ! There along the dale
With woods o'erhung, and shagged with mossy rocks   910
Whence on each hand the gushing waters play,
And down the rough cascade white-dashing fall
Or gleam in lengthened vista through the trees,
You silent steal; or sit beneath the shade
Of solemn oaks, that tuft the swelling mounts   915
Thrown graceful round by Nature's careless hand,
And pensive listen to the various voice
Of rural peace—the herds, the flocks, the birds,

---

891 *green*: verdurous.
909 *Tempe*: the beautiful vale in Thessaly, celebrated by classical poets.
910 *shagged*: made rough, cf. *Comus*, 428, *Wi.* 281, 918.

The hollow-whispering breeze, the plaint of rills,
That, purling down amid the twisted roots   920
Which creep around, their dewy murmurs shake
On the soothed ear. From these abstracted oft,
You wander through the philosophic world;
Where in bright train continual wonders rise
Or to the curious or the pious eye.   925
And oft, conducted by historic truth,
You tread the long extent of backward time,
Planning with warm benevolence of mind
And honest zeal, unwarped by party-rage,
Britannia's weal,—how from the venal gulf   930
To raise her virtue and her arts revive.
Or, turning thence thy view, these graver thoughts
The Muses charm—while, with sure taste refined,
You draw the inspiring breath of ancient song,
Till nobly rises emulous thy own.   935
Perhaps thy loved Lucinda shares thy walk,
With soul to thine attuned. Then Nature all
Wears to the lover's eye a look of love;
And all the tumult of a guilty world,
Tossed by ungenerous passions, sinks away.   940
The tender heart is animated peace;
And, as it pours its copious treasures forth
In varied converse, softening every theme,
You, frequent pausing turn, and from her eyes,
Where meekened sense and amiable grace   945
And lively sweetness dwell, enraptured drink
That nameless spirit of ethereal joy,
Inimitable happiness! which love
Alone bestows, and on a favoured few.
Meantime you gain the height, from whose fair brow   950
The bursting prospect spreads immense around;
And, snatched o'er hill and dale, and wood and lawn,
And verdant field, and darkening heath between,
And villages embosomed soft in trees,
And spiry towns by surging columns marked   955
Of household smoke, your eye excursive roams—
Wide-stretching from the Hall in whose kind haunt

---

936 *Lucinda*: Lucy Fortescue, married to Lyttelton 1742, died 1747, prompting
  Lyttelton's celebrated *Monody*.

The hospitable Genius lingers still,
To where the broken landscape, by degrees
Ascending, roughens into rigid hills   960
O'er which the Cambrian mountains, like far clouds
That skirt the blue horizon, dusky rise.
    Flushed by the spirit of the genial year,
Now from the virgin's cheek a fresher bloom
Shoots less and less the live carnation round;   965
Her lips blush deeper sweets; she breathes of youth;
The shining moisture swells into her eyes
In brighter flow; her wishing bosom heaves
With palpitations wild; kind tumults seize
Her veins, and all her yielding soul is love.   970
From the keen gaze her lover turns away,
Full of the dear ecstatic power, and sick
With sighing languishment. Ah then, ye fair!
Be greatly cautious of your sliding hearts:
Dare not the infectious sigh; the pleading look,   975
Downcast and low, in meek submission dressed,
But full of guile. Let not the fervent tongue,
Prompt to deceive with adulation smooth,
Gain on your purposed will. Nor in the bower
Where woodbines flaunt and roses shed a couch,   980
While evening draws her crimson curtains round,
Trust your soft minutes with betraying man.
    And let the aspiring youth beware of love,
Of the smooth glance beware; for 'tis too late,
When on his heart the torrent-softness pours.   985
Then wisdom prostrate lies, and fading fame
Dissolves in air away; while the fond soul,
Wrapt in gay visions of unreal bliss,
Still paints the illusive form, the kindling grace,
The enticing smile, the modest-seeming eye,   990
Beneath whose beauteous beams, belying Heaven,
Lurk searchless cunning, cruelty, and death:
And still, false-warbling in his cheated ear,
Her siren voice enchanting draws him on

965 *live carnation*: pinkness.
992 *searchless*: resisting investigation.
994 *siren*: the Sirens in Greek mythology were beautiful women (or half-woman
    monsters) who lured men to destruction by their enchanting song; cf. Homer,
    Odyssey, XII, 39–200.

To guileful shores and meads of fatal joy.   995
   Even present, in the very lap of love
Inglorious laid—while music flows around,
Perfumes, and oils, and wine, and wanton hours—
Amid the roses fierce repentance rears
Her snaky crest: a quick-returning pang   1000
Shoots through the conscious heart, where honour still
And great design, against the oppressive load
Of luxury, by fits, impatient heave.[n]
   But absent, what fantastic woes, aroused,
Rage in each thought, by restless musing fed,   1005
Chill the warm cheek, and blast the bloom of life!
Neglected fortune flies; and, sliding swift,
Prone into ruin fall his scorned affairs.
'Tis nought but gloom around: the darkened sun
Loses his light. The rosy-bosomed Spring   1010
To weeping fancy pines; and yon bright arch,
Contracted, bends into a dusky vault.
All Nature fades extinct; and she alone
Heard, felt, and seen, possesses every thought,
Fills every sense, and pants in every vein.   1015
Books are but formal dulness, tedious friends;
And sad amid the social band he sits,
Lonely and unattentive. From the tongue
The unfinished period falls: while, borne away
On swelling thought, his wafted spirit flies   1020
To the vain bosom of his distant fair;
And leaves the semblance of a lover, fixed
In melancholy site, with head declined,
And love-dejected eyes. Sudden he starts,
Shook from his tender trance, and restless runs   1025
To glimmering shades and sympathetic glooms,
Where the dun umbrage o'er the falling stream
Romantic hangs; there through the pensive dusk
Strays, in heart-thrilling meditation lost,
Indulging all to love—or on the bank   1030
Thrown, amid drooping lilies, swells the breeze
With sighs unceasing, and the brook with tears.

1002 *great design*: noble purpose.
1011 *arch*: the sky.
1021 *vain*: empty.
1023 *site*: attitude.

Thus in soft anguish he consumes the day,
Nor quits his deep retirement till the Moon
Peeps through the chambers of the fleecy east,   1035
Enlightened by degrees, and in her train
Leads on the gentle hours; then forth he walks,
Beneath the trembling languish of her beam,
With softened soul, and woos the bird of eve
To mingle woes with his; or, while the world   1040
And all the sons of care lie hushed in sleep,
Associates with the midnight shadows drear,
And, sighing to the lonely taper, pours
His idly-tortured heart into the page
Meant for the moving messenger of love,   1045
Where rapture burns on rapture, every line
With rising frenzy fired. But if on bed
Delirious flung, sleep from his pillow flies.
All night he tosses, nor the balmy power
In any posture finds; till the grey morn   1050
Lifts her pale lustre on the paler wretch,
Exanimate by love—and then perhaps
Exhausted nature sinks a while to rest,
Still interrupted by distracted dreams
That o'er the sick imagination rise   1055
And in black colours paint the mimic scene.
Oft with the enchantress of his soul he talks;
Sometimes in crowds distressed; or, if retired
To secret-winding flower-enwoven bowers,
Far from the dull impertinence of man,   1060
Just as he, credulous, his endless cares
Begins to lose in blind oblivious love,
Snatched from her yielded hand, he knows not how,
Through forests huge, and long untravelled heaths
With desolation brown, he wanders waste,   1065
In night and tempest wrapt; or shrinks aghast
Back from the bending precipice; or wades
The turbid stream below, and strives to reach
The farther shore where, succourless and sad,

1035: shines through clouds in the eastern sky; cf. *Wi.* 15.
1038 *languish*: tender glance, cf. Pope, *Iliad* XVIII.50.
1039 *bird of eve*: nightingale; on the reason for the nightingale's woes cf. *Sp.* 601
    fn.
1060 *impertinence*: intrusion.
1065 *waste*: to no purpose.

She with extended arms his aid implores,   1070
But strives in vain: borne by the outrageous flood
To distance down, he rides the ridgy wave,
Or whelmed beneath the boiling eddy sinks.[n]
   These are the charming agonies of love,
Whose misery delights. But through the heart   1075
Should jealousy its venom once diffuse,
'Tis then delightful misery no more,
But agony unmixed, incessant gall,
Corroding every thought, and blasting all
Love's Paradise. Ye fairy prospects, then,   1080
Ye bed of roses and ye bowers of joy,
Farewell! Ye gleamings of departed peace,
Shine out your last! The yellow-tinging plague
Internal vision taints, and in a night
Of livid gloom imagination wraps.   1085
Ah then! instead of love-enlivened cheeks,
Of sunny features, and of ardent eyes
With flowing rapture bright, dark looks succeed,
Suffused, and glaring with untender fire,
A clouded aspect, and a burning cheek   1090
Where the whole poisoned soul malignant sits,
And frightens love away. Ten thousand fears
Invented wild, ten thousand frantic views
Of horrid rivals hanging on the charms
For which he melts in fondness, eat him up   1095
With fervent anguish and consuming rage.
In vain reproaches lend their idle aid,
Deceitful pride, and resolution frail,
Giving false peace a moment. Fancy pours
Afresh her beauties on his busy thought,   1100
Her first endearments twining round the soul
With all the witchcraft of ensnaring love.
Straight the fierce storm involves his mind anew,
Flames through the nerves, and boils along the veins;
While anxious doubt distracts the tortured heart: 1105
For even the sad assurance of his fears
Were peace to what he feels. Thus the warm youth,
Whom love deludes into his thorny wilds
Through flowery-tempting paths, or leads a life

1071 *outrageous*: violent, cf. *P.L.* VII.212.
1083 *yellow-tinging plague*: jealousy.

Of fevered rapture or of cruel care— 1110
His brightest aims extinguished all, and all
His lively moments running down to waste.
    But happy they ! the happiest of their kind !
Whom gentler stars unite, and in one fate
Their hearts, their fortunes, and their beings blend. 1115
'Tis not the coarser tie of human laws,
Unnatural oft, and foreign to the mind,
That binds their peace, but harmony itself,
Attuning all their passions into love;
Where friendship full-exerts her softest power, 1120
Perfect esteem enlivened by desire
Ineffable and sympathy of soul,
Thought meeting thought, and will preventing will,
With boundless confidence: for nought but love
Can answer love, and render bliss secure. 1125
Let him, ungenerous, who, alone intent
To bless himself, from sordid parents buys
The loathing virgin, in eternal care
Well-merited consume his nights and days;
Let barbarous nations, whose inhuman love 1130
Is wild desire, fierce as the suns they feel;
Let eastern tyrants from the light of heaven
Seclude their bosom-slaves, meanly possessed
Of a mere lifeless, violated form:
While those whom love cements in holy faith 1135
And equal transport free as nature live,
Disdaining fear. What is the world to them,
Its pomp, its pleasure, and its nonsense all,
Who in each other clasp whatever fair
High fancy forms, and lavish hearts can wish ? 1140
Something than beauty dearer, should they look
Or on the mind or mind-illumined face;
Truth, goodness, honour, harmony, and love,
The richest bounty of indulgent Heaven !
Meantime a smiling offspring rises round, 1145
And mingles both their graces. By degrees
The human blossom blows; and every day,
Soft as it rolls along, shows some new charm,
The father's lustre and the mother's bloom.

1123 *preventing*: anticipating.
1139 *fair*: beauty, cf. *P.L.* IX. 608.

Then infant reason grows apace, and calls   1150
For the kind hand of an assiduous care.
Delightful task! to rear the tender thought,
To teach the young idea how to shoot,
To pour the fresh instruction o'er the mind,
To breathe the enlivening spirit, and to fix   1155
The generous purpose in the glowing breast.
Oh, speak the joy! ye, whom the sudden tear
Surprises often, while you look around,
And nothing strikes your eye but sights of bliss,
All various Nature pressing on the heart—   1160
An elegant sufficiency, content,
Retirement, rural quiet, friendship, books,
Ease and alternate labour, useful life,
Progressive virtue, and approving Heaven!
These are the matchless joys of virtuous love;   1165
And thus their moments fly. The Seasons thus,
As ceaseless round a jarring world they roll,
Still find them happy; and consenting Spring
Sheds her own rosy garland on their heads:
Till evening comes at last, serene and mild;   1170
When after the long vernal day of life,
Enamoured more, as more remembrance swells
With many a proof of recollected love,
Together down they sink in social sleep;
Together freed, their gentle spirits fly   1175
To scenes where love and bliss immortal reign.

W. Kent inv. et del.   N. Tardieu Sculp.

Summer

Summer

FROM brightening fields of ether fair-disclosed,
Child of the Sun, refulgent Summer comes
In pride of youth, and felt through Nature's depth:
He comes attended by the sultry Hours
And ever-fanning breezes on his way;   5
While from his ardent look the turning Spring
Averts her blushful face, and earth and skies
All-smiling to his hot dominion leaves.[n]
   Hence let me haste into the mid-wood shade,
Where scarce a sunbeam wanders through the gloom,   10
And on the dark-green grass, beside the brink
Of haunted stream that by the roots of oak
Rolls o'er the rocky channel, lie at large
And sing the glories of the circling year.
   Come, Inspiration! from thy hermit-seat,   15
By mortal seldom found: may fancy dare,
From thy fixed serious eye and raptured glance
Shot on surrounding Heaven, to steal one look

1 *ether*: see *Sp.* 148 fn.
4 *Hours*: in Greek mythology the goddesses of weather who were supposed to
  preside over the changes of the seasons.
12 *haunted*: i.e. by the Muses, cf. Milton, *L'Allegro* 129–30, *P.L.* III.26–8.
15 *hermit*: lonely (Gk. *eremia*, desert).

Creative of the poet, every power
Exalting to an ecstasy of soul.[n]   20
    And thou, my youthful Muse's early friend,
In whom the human graces all unite—
Pure light of mind and tenderness of heart,
Genius and wisdom, the gay social sense
By decency chastised, goodness and wit   25
In seldom-meeting harmony combined,
Unblemished honour, and an active zeal
For Britain's glory, liberty, and man:
O Dodington![n] attend my rural song,
Stoop to my theme, inspirit every line,   30
And teach me to deserve thy just applause.

    With what an awful world-revolving power
Were first the unwieldy planets launched along
The illimitable void!—thus to remain,
Amid the flux of many thousand years   35
That oft has swept the toiling race of men,
And all their laboured monuments away,
Firm, unremitting, matchless in their course;
To the kind-tempered change of night and day,
And of the seasons ever stealing round,   40
Minutely faithful: such the all-perfect Hand
That poised, impels, and rules the steady whole![n]
    When now no more the alternate Twins are fired,
And Cancer reddens with the solar blaze,
Short is the doubtful empire of the night;   45
And soon, observant of approaching day,
The meek-eyed Morn appears, mother of dews,
At first faint-gleaming in the dappled east;
Till far o'er ether spreads the widening glow,
And, from before the lustre of her face,   50
White break the clouds away. With quickened step,
Brown Night retires. Young Day pours in apace,
And opens all the lawny prospect wide.
The dripping rock, the mountain's misty top
Swell on the sight and brighten with the dawn.   55

43 *Twins*: Gemini, the third sign of the zodiac into which the sun enters about
    21 May.
44 *Cancer*: the Crab, the fourth sign of the zodiac into which the sun enters at
    the summer solstice (21 or 22 June).
49 *ether*: see *Sp.* 148 fn.
55 *Swell on the sight*: are revealed more distinctly.

Blue through the dusk the smoking currents shine;
And from the bladed field the fearful hare
Limps awkward; while along the forest glade
The wild deer trip, and often turning gaze
At early passenger. Music awakes,   60
The native voice of undissembled joy;
And thick around the woodland hymns arise.
Roused by the cock, the soon-clad shepherd leaves
His mossy cottage, where with peace he dwells,
And from the crowded fold in order drives   65
His flock to taste the verdure of the morn.
   Falsely luxurious, will not man awake,
And, springing from the bed of sloth, enjoy
The cool, the fragrant, and the silent hour,
To meditation due and sacred song?   70
For is there aught in sleep can charm the wise?
To lie in dead oblivion, losing half
The fleeting moments of too short a life—
Total extinction of the enlightened soul!
Or else, to feverish vanity alive,   75
Wildered, and tossing through distempered dreams!
Who would in such a gloomy state remain
Longer than nature craves; when every muse
And every blooming pleasure wait without
To bless the wildly-devious morning walk?   80
   But yonder comes the powerful king of day[n]
Rejoicing in the east. The lessening cloud,
The kindling azure, and the mountain's brow
Illumed with fluid gold,[n] his near approach
Betoken glad. Lo! now, apparent all,   85
Aslant the dew-bright earth and coloured air,
He looks in boundless majesty abroad,
And sheds the shining day, that burnished plays
On rocks, and hills, and towers, and wandering streams
High-gleaming from afar. Prime cheerer, Light!   90
Of all material beings first and best!
Efflux divine! Nature's resplendent robe,
Without whose vesting beauty all were wrapt
In unessential gloom; and thou, O Sun!

56 *smoking currents*: rising mists.   60 *passenger*: traveller on foot.
80 *wildly devious*: circuitous.
94 *unessential*: without substance or being, cf. *Sp.* 557, *P.L.* II.439, III.1–6.

Soul of surrounding worlds! in whom best seen   95
Shines out thy Maker! may I sing of thee?
  'Tis by thy secret, strong, attractive force,
As with a chain indissoluble bound,
Thy system rolls entire[n]—from the far bourne
Of utmost Saturn, wheeling wide his round   100
Of thirty years, to Mercury, whose disc
Can scarce be caught by philosophic eye,
Lost in the near effulgence of thy blaze.
  Informer of the planetary train!
Without whose quickening glance their cumbrous orbs   105
Were brute unlovely mass, inert and dead,
And not, as now, the green abodes of life![n]
How many forms of being wait on thee,
Inhaling spirit, from the unfettered mind,
By thee sublimed, down to the daily race,   110
The mixing myriads of thy setting beam!
  The vegetable world is also thine,
Parent of Seasons! who the pomp precede
That waits thy throne, as through thy vast domain,
Annual, along the bright ecliptic road   115
In world-rejoicing state it moves sublime.
Meantime the expecting nations, circled gay
With all the various tribes of foodful earth,
Implore thy bounty, or send grateful up
A common hymn: while, round thy beaming car,   120
High-seen, the Seasons lead, in sprightly dance
Harmonious knit, the rosy-fingered Hours,
The zephyrs floating loose, the timely rains,
Of bloom ethereal the light-footed dews,
And, softened into joy, the surly storms.   125
These, in successive turn, with lavish hand

---

100 *utmost*: Saturn was thought to be the outermost member of the solar
    system.
102 *Can scarce be caught*: because it is never above the horizon longer than two
    hours after sunset or before sunrise. *philosophic*: of the scientist.
104 *Informer*: the sun, as 'best image' (cf. *Hymn* 66) of God (cf. *Sp.* 860).
108 *wait*: are dependent.
109 *unfettered mind*: disembodied spirit (of angelic beings).
110 *daily race*: insects that live for a single day. On periphrases see *Sp.* 132 end-
    note.
117 *nations*: of men.
118 *tribes*: of animals and vegetables.
122 *Hours*: see *Su.* 4 fn.; 'rosy-fingered' is Homer's epithet for morning.

Shower every beauty, every fragrance shower,
Herbs, flowers, and fruits; till, kindling at thy touch,
From land to land is flushed the vernal year.
    Nor to the surface of enlivened earth,   130
Graceful with hills and dales, and leafy woods,
Her liberal tresses, is thy force confined;
But, to the bowelled cavern darting deep,
The mineral kinds confess thy mighty power.
Effulgent hence the veiny marble shines;   135
Hence labour draws his tools; hence burnished war
Gleams on the day; the nobler works of peace
Hence bless mankind; and generous commerce binds
The round of nations in a golden chain.
    The unfruitful rock itself, impregned by thee,   140
In dark retirement forms the lucid stone.[n]
The lively diamond drinks thy purest rays,
Collected light compact; that, polished bright,
And all its native lustre let abroad,
Dares, as it sparkles on the fair one's breast,   145
With vain ambition emulate her eyes.
At thee the ruby lights its deepening glow,
And with a waving radiance inward flames.
From thee the sapphire, solid ether, takes
Its hue cerulean; and, of evening tinct,   150
The purple-streaming amethyst is thine.
With thy own smile the yellow topaz burns;
Nor deeper verdure dyes the robe of Spring,
When first she gives it to the southern gale,
Than the green emerald shows. But, all combined,[n]   155
Thick through the whitening opal play thy beams;
Or, flying several from its surface, form
A trembling variance of revolving hues
As the site varies in the gazer's hand.
    The very dead creation from thy touch   160
Assumes a mimic life. By thee refined,
In brighter mazes the relucent stream
Plays o'er the mead. The precipice abrupt,

---

134 *kinds*: indicating that minerals grow and live like other objects of creation.
136–9: referring to metallic ores.
140 *impregned*: made fruitful, cf. *P.L.* IV.500.
150 *tinct*: dyed, Lat. *tinctus*.
159 *site*: position, cf. *Sp.* 1023.

Projecting horror on the blackened flood,
Softens at thy return. The desert joys   165
Wildly through all his melancholy bounds.
Rude ruins glitter; and the briny deep,
Seen from some pointed promontory's top
Far to the blue horizon's utmost verge,
Restless reflects a floating gleam.[n] But this,   170
And all the much-transported Muse can sing,
Are to thy beauty, dignity, and use
Unequal far, great delegated Source
Of light and life and grace and joy below!
    How shall I then attempt to sing of Him   175
Who, Light Himself, in uncreated light
Invested deep, dwells awfully retired
From mortal eye or angel's purer ken;
Whose single smile has, from the first of time,
Filled overflowing all those lamps of heaven   180
That beam for ever through the boundless sky:[n]
But, should He hide his face, the astonished sun
And all the extinguished stars would, loosening, reel
Wide from their spheres, and chaos come again.
    And yet, was every faltering tongue of man,   185
Almightly Father! silent in thy praise,
Thy works themselves would raise a general voice;
Even in the depth of solitary woods,
By human foot untrod, proclaim thy power;
And to the choir celestial Thee resound,   190
The eternal cause, support, and end of all!
    To me be Nature's volume broad displayed;
And to peruse its all-instructing page,
Or, haply catching inspiration thence,
Some easy passage, raptured, to translate,   195
My sole delight,[n] as through the falling glooms
Pensive I stray, or with the rising dawn
On fancy's eagle-wing excursive soar.

    Now, flaming up the heavens, the potent sun
Melts into limpid air the high-raised clouds   200
And morning fogs that hovered round the hills

---

164 *Projecting horror*: casting a rough, bristling shadow; cf. Milton, *Comus* 38.
Lat. *horrere*, to bristle.
184 *spheres*: orbits.

In parti-coloured bands; till wide unveiled
The face of nature shines from where earth seems,
Far-stretched around, to meet the bending sphere.

    Half in a blush of clustering roses lost,   205
Dew-dropping Coolness to the shade retires;
There, on the verdant turf or flowery bed,
By gelid founts and careless rills to muse;
While tyrant Heat, dispreading through the sky
With rapid sway, his burning influence darts   210
On man and beast and herb and tepid stream.

    Who can unpitying see the flowery race,
Shed by the morn, their new-flushed bloom resign
Before the parching beam? So fade the fair,
When fevers revel through their azure veins.   215
But one, the lofty follower of the sun,
Sad when he sets, shuts up her yellow leaves,
Drooping all night; and, when he warm returns,
Points her enamoured bosom to his ray.[n]

    Home from his morning task the swain retreats,   220
His flock before him stepping to the fold;
While the full-uddered mother lows around
The cheerful cottage then expecting food,
The food of innocence and health! The daw,
The rook, and magpie, to the grey-grown oaks   225
(That the calm village in their verdant arms,
Sheltering, embrace) direct their lazy flight;
Where on the mingling boughs they sit embowered
All the hot noon, till cooler hours arise.
Faint underneath the household fowls convene;   230
And, in a corner of the buzzing shade,
The house-dog with the vacant greyhound lies
Out-stretched and sleepy. In his slumbers one
Attacks the nightly thief, and one exults
O'er hill and dale; till, wakened by the wasp,   235
They starting snap. Nor shall the muse disdain
To let the little noisy summer-race
Live in her lay and flutter through her song:
Not mean though simple—to the sun allied,
From him they draw their animating fire.   240

---

209 *dispreading*: extending.   213 *shed by the morn*: cf. *Su.* 120–9.
223 *food*: milk (expected by the cottage household).   232 *vacant*: listless.
237 *summer-race*: short-lived insects. On periphrases see *Sp.* 132 end-note.

Waked by his warmer ray, the reptile young
Come winged abroad, by the light air upborne,
Lighter, and full of soul. From every chink
And secret corner, where they slept away
The wintry storms, or rising from their tombs   245
To higher life, by myriads forth at once
Swarming they pour, of all the varied hues
Their beauty-beaming parent can disclose.
Ten thousand forms, ten thousand different tribes
People the blaze. To sunny waters some   250
By fatal instinct fly; where on the pool
They sportive wheel, or, sailing down the stream,
Are snatched immediate by the quick-eyed trout
Or darting salmon. Through the green-wood glade
Some love to stray; there lodged, amused, and fed   255
In the fresh leaf. Luxurious, others make
The meads their choice, and visit every flower
And every latent herb: for the sweet task
To propagate their kinds, and where to wrap
In what soft beds their young, yet undisclosed,   260
Employs their tender care. Some to the house,
The fold, and dairy hungry bend their flight;
Sip round the pail, or taste the curdling cheese:
Oft, inadvertent, from the milky stream
They meet their fate; or, weltering in the bowl,   265
With powerless wings around them wrapt, expire.
    But chief to heedless flies the window proves
A constant death; where, gloomily retired,
The villain spider lives, cunning and fierce,
Mixture abhorred! Amid a mangled heap   270
Of carcases in eager watch he sits,
O'erlooking all his waving snares around.
Near the dire cell the dreadless wanderer oft
Passes; as oft the ruffian shows his front.
The prey at last ensnared, he dreadful darts   275
With rapid glide along the leaning line;
And, fixing in the wretch his cruel fangs,
Strikes backward grimly pleased: the fluttering wing
And shriller sound declare extreme distress,
And ask the helping hospitable hand.[n]   280

---

241 *reptile*: crawling.   **245** *tombs*: chrysalises.   **248** *parent*: the sun.

Resounds the living surface of the ground:
Nor undelightful is the ceaseless hum
To him who muses through the woods at noon,
Or drowsy shepherd as he lies reclined,
With half-shut eyes, beneath the floating shade   285
Of willows grey, close-crowding o'er the brook.
  Gradual from these what numerous kinds descend,
Evading even the microscopic eye!
Full Nature swarms with life; one wondrous mass
Of animals, or atoms organized   290
Waiting the vital breath when Parent-Heaven
Shall bid his spirit blow. The hoary fen
In putrid streams emits the living cloud
Of pestilence. Through subterranean cells,
Where searching sunbeams scarce can find a way,   295
Earth animated heaves. The flowery leaf
Wants not its soft inhabitants. Secure
Within its winding citadel the stone
Holds multitudes. But chief the forest boughs,
That dance unnumbered to the playful breeze,   300
The downy orchard, and the melting pulp
Of mellow fruit the nameless nations feed
Of evanescent insects. Where the pool
Stands mantled o'er with green, invisible
Amid the floating verdure millions stray.   305
Each liquid too, whether it pierces, soothes,
Inflames, refreshes, or exalts the taste,
With various forms abounds. Nor is the stream
Of purest crystal, nor the lucid air,
Though one transparent vacancy it seems,   310
Void of their unseen people. These, concealed
By the kind art of forming Heaven, escape
The grosser eye of man: for, if the worlds
In worlds inclosed should on his senses burst,
From cates ambrosial and the nectared bowl   315
He would abhorrent turn; and in dead night,
When Silence sleeps o'er all, be stunned with noise.[n]
  Let no presuming impious railer tax
Creative Wisdom, as if aught was formed
In vain, or not for admirable ends.   320
Shall little haughty Ignorance pronounce
His works unwise, of which the smallest part

Exceeds the narrow vision of her mind?
As if upon a full-proportioned dome,
On swelling columns heaved, the pride of art!   325
A critic fly, whose feeble ray scarce spreads
An inch around, with blind presumption bold
Should dare to tax the structure of the whole.[n]
And lives the man whose universal eye
Has swept at once the unbounded scheme of things,   330
Marked their dependence so and firm accord,
As with unfaltering accent to conclude
That this availeth nought? Has any seen
The mighty chain of beings,[n] lessening down
From infinite perfection to the brink   335
Of dreary nothing, desolate abyss!
From which astonished thought recoiling turns?
Till then, alone let zealous praise ascend
And hymns of holy wonder to that Power
Whose wisdom shines as lovely on our minds   340
As on our smiling eyes his servant-sun.

　　Thick in yon stream of light, a thousand ways,
Upward and downward, thwarting and çonvolved,
The quivering nations sport; till, tempest-winged,
Fierce Winter sweeps them from the face of day.   345
Even so luxurious men, unheeding, pass
An idle summer life in fortune's shine,
A season's glitter! Thus they flutter on
From toy to toy, from vanity to vice;
Till, blown away by death, oblivion comes   350
Behind and strikes them from the book of life.[n]

　　Now swarms the village o'er the jovial mead—
The rustic youth, brown with meridian toil,
Healthful and strong; full as the summer rose
Blown by prevailing suns, the ruddy maid,   355
Half naked, swelling on the sight, and all
Her kindled graces burning o'er her cheek.
Even stooping age is here; and infant hands
Trail the long rake, or, with the fragrant load

---

344 *quivering nations*: dancing insects. On periphrases see *Sp.* 132 end-note.
355 *blown*: caused to blossom.
356 *swelling on the sight*: i.e. she is dressed in stays and skirt, and her breasts are
　　half-revealed. A sly echo of *Su.* 55.

O'ercharged, amid the kind oppression roll.   360
Wide flies the tedded grain; all in a row
Advancing broad, or wheeling round the field,
They spread their breathing harvest to the sun,
That throws refreshful round a rural smell;
Or, as they rake the green-appearing ground,   365
And drive the dusky wave along the mead,
The russet hay-cock rises thick behind
In order gay: while heard from dale to dale,
Waking the breeze, resounds the blended voice
Of happy labour, love, and social glee.   370
    Or, rushing thence, in one diffusive band
They drive the troubled flocks, by many a dog
Compelled, to where the mazy-running brook
Forms a deep pool, this bank abrupt and high,
And that fair-spreading in a pebbled shore.   375
Urged to the giddy brink, much is the toil,
The clamour much of men and boys and dogs
Ere the soft, fearful people to the flood
Commit their woolly sides. And oft the swain,
On some impatient seizing, hurls them in: 380
Emboldened then, nor hesitating more,
Fast, fast they plunge amid the flashing wave,
And, panting, labour to the farther shore.
Repeated this, till deep the well-washed fleece
Has drunk the flood, and from his lively haunt   385
The trout is banished by the sordid stream.
Heavy and dripping, to the breezy brow
Slow move the harmless race; where, as they spread
Their swelling treasures to the sunny ray,
Inly disturbed, and wondering what this wild   390
Outrageous tumult means, their loud complaints
The country fill; and, tossed from rock to rock,
Incessant bleatings run around the hills.
At last, of snowy white the gathered flocks

---

360 *kind oppression*: i.e. the children are loaded with an uninjurious weight.
361 *grain*: seeded grass.   363 *breathing*: fragrant.
367 *thick*: numerous.
373 *mazy*: winding, cf. *Sp.* 577.
378 *soft fearful people*: sheep; cf. *Su.* 388, 417. On periphrases see *Sp.* 132 end-note.
389 *treasures*: fleeces (anticipating the wool harvest; cf. *Sp.* 112–13 on the corn harvest).

Are in the wattled pen innumerous pressed,   395
Head above head; and, ranged in lusty rows,
The shepherds sit, and whet the sounding shears.
The housewife waits to roll her fleecy stores,
With all her gay-drest maids attending round.
One, chief, in gracious dignity enthroned,   400
Shines o'er the rest, the pastoral queen, and rays
Her smiles sweet-beaming on her shepherd-king;
While the glad circle round them yield their souls
To festive mirth, and wit that knows no gall.
Meantime, their joyous task goes on apace: 405
Some mingling stir the melted tar, and some,
Deep on the new-shorn vagrant's heaving side
To stamp his master's cipher ready stand;
Others the unwilling wether drag along;
And, glorying in his might, the sturdy boy   410
Holds by the twisted horns the indignant ram.
Behold where bound, and of its robe bereft
By needy man, that all-depending lord,
How meek, how patient, the mild creature lies!
What softness in its melancholy face,   415
What dumb complaining innocence appears!
Fear not, ye gentle tribes! 'tis not the knife
Of horrid slaughter that is o'er you waved;
No, 'tis the tender swain's well-guided shears,
Who having now, to pay his annual care,   420
Borrowed your fleece, to you a cumbrous load,
Will send you bounding to your hills again.
    A simple scene! yet hence Britannia sees
Her solid grandeur rise: hence she commands
The exalted stores of every brighter clime,   425
The treasures of the sun without his rage:
Hence, fervent all with culture, toil, and arts,
Wide glows her land: her dreadful thunder hence
Rides o'er the waves sublime, and now, even now,
Impending hangs o'er Gallia's humbled coast;   430

407 *vagrant*: because shearing has temporarily removed the owner's mark from
  its side.
420 *annual care*: rent; an ironic adaptation of *cura* in Virgil's *Georgics*—a
  constant word for the tasks of the shepherd and farmer.
425 *stores*: imports from the tropics.
430 *Gallia*: France. Though Britain did not declare war until March 1744 her
  ships before then were blockading Brest and Toulon.

Hence rules the circling deep, and awes the world.[n]

   'Tis raging noon; and, vertical, the Sun
Darts on the head direct his forceful rays.
O'er heaven and earth, far as the ranging eye
Can sweep, a dazzling deluge reigns; and all   435
From pole to pole is undistinguished blaze.
In vain the sight dejected to the ground
Stoops for relief; thence hot ascending steams
And keen reflection pain. Deep to the root
Of vegetation parched, the cleaving fields   440
And slippery lawn an arid hue disclose,
Blast fancy's blooms, and wither even the soul.
Echo no more returns the cheerful sound
Of sharpening scythe: the mower, sinking, heaps
O'er him the humid hay, with flowers perfumed;   445
And scarce a chirping grasshopper is heard
Through the dumb mead. Distressful nature pants.
The very streams look languid from afar,
Or, through the unsheltered glade, impatient seem
To hurl into the covert of the grove.   450
   All-conquering heat, oh, intermit thy wrath!
And on my throbbing temples potent thus
Beam not so fierce! Incessant still you flow,
And still another fervent flood succeeds,
Poured on the head profuse.[n] In vain I sigh,   455
And restless turn, and look around for night:
Night is far off; and hotter hours approach.
Thrice happy he, who on the sunless side
Of a romantic mountain, forest-crowned,
Beneath the whole collected shade reclines;   460
Or in the gelid caverns, woodbine-wrought
And fresh bedewed with ever-spouting streams,
Sits coolly calm;[n] while all the world without,
Unsatisfied and sick, tosses in noon.
Emblem instructive of the virtuous man,   465
Who keeps his tempered mind serene and pure,

---

437 *dejected*: cast down, cf. *Su*. 974, 1066.
440 *cleaving*: with surface cracked by heat.
459 *romantic*: redolent of romance. The word was very widely used in the
   eighteenth century to describe wild landscapes; cf. *Au*. 880 and end-note. See
   Logan Pearsall Smith, 'Four Romantic Words' in *Words and Idioms* (1925).
461 *wrought*; decorated with.

And every passion aptly harmonized
Amid a jarring world with vice inflamed.
　　Welcome, ye shades! ye bowery thickets, hail!
Ye lofty pines! ye venerable oaks!   470
Ye ashes wild, resounding o'er the steep!
Delicious is your shelter to the soul
As to the hunted hart the sallying spring
Or stream full-flowing, that his swelling sides
Laves as he floats along the herbaged brink.   475
Cool through the nerves your pleasing comfort glides;
The heart beats glad; the fresh-expanded eye
And ear resume their watch; the sinews knit;
And life shoots swift through all the lightened limbs.
　　Around the adjoining brook, that purls along   480
The vocal grove, now fretting o'er a rock,
Now scarcely moving through a reedy pool,
Now starting to a sudden stream, and now
Gently diffused into a limpid plain,
A various group the herds and flocks compose,   485
Rural confusion! On the grassy bank
Some ruminating lie, while others stand
Half in the flood and, often bending, sip
The circling surface. In the middle droops
The strong laborious ox, of honest front,   490
Which incomposed he shakes; and from his sides
The troublous insects lashes with his tail,
Returning still. Amid his subjects safe
Slumbers the monarch-swain, his careless arm
Thrown round his head on downy moss sustained;   495
Here laid his scrip with wholesome viands filled,
There, listening every noise, his watchful dog.[n]
　　Light fly his slumbers, if perchance a flight
Of angry gad-flies fasten on the herd,
That startling scatters from the shallow brook   500
In search of lavish stream. Tossing the foam,
They scorn the keeper's voice, and scour the plain
Through all the bright severity of noon;
While from their labouring breasts a hollow moan
Proceeding runs low-bellowing round the hills.[n]   505
　　Oft in this season too, the horse, provoked,

490 *front*: forehead, cf. *Au.* 521,
491 *incomposed*: discomposed, cf. *P.L.* II. 989.

While his big sinews full of spirits swell,
Trembling with vigour, in the heat of blood
Springs the high fence, and, o'er the field effused,
Darts on the gloomy flood with steadfast eye   510
And heart estranged to fear: his nervous chest,
Luxuriant and erect, the seat of strength,
Bears down the opposing stream; quenchless his thirst,
He takes the river at redoubled draughts,
And with wide nostrils, snorting, skims the wave.[n]   515
  Still let me pierce into the midnight depth
Of yonder grove, of wildest largest growth,
That, forming high in air a woodland choir,
Nods o'er the mount beneath. At every step,
Solemn and slow the shadows blacker fall,   520
And all is awful listening gloom around.
  These are the haunts of meditation, these
The scenes where ancient bards the inspiring breath
Ecstatic felt, and, from this world retired,
Conversed with angels and immortal forms,   525
On gracious errands bent—to save the fall
Of virtue struggling on the brink of vice;
In waking whispers and repeated dreams
To hint pure thought, and warn the favoured soul,
For future trials fated, to prepare;   530
To prompt the poet, who devoted gives
His muse to better themes; to soothe the pangs
Of dying worth, and from the patriot's breast
(Backward to mingle in detested war,
But foremost when engaged) to turn the death;   535
And numberless such offices of love,
Daily and nightly, zealous to perform.
  Shook sudden from the bosom of the sky,
A thousand shapes or glide athwart the dusk
Or stalk majestic on, Deep-roused, I feel   540
A sacred terror, a severe delight,
Creep through my mortal frame; and thus, methinks,
A voice, than human more, the abstracted ear
Of fancy strikes—'Be not of us afraid,
Poor kindred man! thy fellow-creatures, we   545

518 *choir*: chancel, cf. Shakespeare, *Sonnet* lxxiii.4.

From the same Parent-Power our beings drew,
The same our Lord and laws and great pursuit.
Once some of us, like thee, through stormy life
Toiled tempest-beaten ere we could attain
This holy calm, this harmony of mind,   550
Where purity and peace immingle charms.
Then fear not us; but with responsive song,
Amid these dim recesses, undisturbed
By noisy folly and discordant vice,
Of Nature sing with us, and Nature's God.   555
Here frequent, at the visionary hour,
When musing midnight reigns or silent noon,
Angelic harps are in full concert heard,
And voices chaunting from the wood-crown'd hill,
The deepening dale, or inmost sylvan glade: 560
A privilege bestow'd by us alone
On contemplation, or the hallow'd ear
Of poet swelling to seraphic strain.'[n]
      And art thou, Stanley, of that sacred band?
Alas! for us too soon! Though raised above   565
The reach of human pain, above the flight
Of human joy, yet with a mingled ray
Of sadly pleased remembrance, must thou feel
A mother's love, a mother's tender woe—
Who seeks thee still in many a former scene,   570
Seeks thy fair form, thy lovely beaming eyes,
Thy pleasing converse, by gay lively sense
Inspired, where moral wisdom mildly shone
Without the toil of art, and virtue glowed
In all her smiles without forbidding pride.   575
But, O thou best of parents! wipe thy tears;
Or rather to parental Nature pay
The tears of grateful joy, who for a while
Lent thee this younger self, this opening bloom
Of thy enlightened mind and gentle worth.   580
Believe the Muse—the wintry blast of death

546 *Parent-Power*: perhaps Nature, rather than God; cf. *Su.* 577.
556 *visionary hour*: supernatural beings are most likely to be encountered at noon
  or midnight; cf. Homer, *Odyssey* IV.400, 450, *P.L.* IV.682.
564 *Stanley*: Miss Elizabeth Stanley who died in 1738, aged 18. T. wrote the
  epitaph on her in Holyrood Church, Southampton. Her mother (569) was
  daughter of Sir Hans Sloane, an early friend of T.'s. Lines 564–84 were first
  added in the 1744 edition.

Kills not the buds of virtue; no, they spread
Beneath the heavenly beam of brighter suns
Through endless ages into higher powers.
    Thus up the mount, in airy vision rapt, 585
I stray, regardless whither; till the sound
Of a near fall of water every sense
Wakes from the charm of thought: swift-shrinking back,
I check my steps and view the broken scene.
    Smooth to the shelving brink a copious flood 590
Rolls fair and placid; where, collected all
In one impetuous torrent, down the steep
It thundering shoots, and shakes the country round.
At first, an azure sheet, it rushes broad;
Then, whitening by degrees as prone it falls, 595
And from the loud-resounding rocks below
Dashed in a cloud of foam, it sends aloft
A hoary mist and forms a ceaseless shower.
Nor can the tortured wave here find repose;
But, raging still amid the shaggy rocks, 600
Now flashes o'er the scattered fragments, now
Aslant the hollow channel rapid darts;
And, falling fast from gradual slope to slope,
With wild infracted course and lessened roar
It gains a safer bed, and steals at last 605
Along the mazes of the quiet vale.[n]
    Invited from the cliff, to whose dark brow
He clings, the steep-ascending eagle soars
With upward pinions through the flood of day,
And, giving full his bosom to the blaze, 610
Gains on the Sun; while all the tuneful race,
Smit by afflictive noon, disordered droop
Deep in the thicket, or, from bower to bower
Responsive, force an interrupted strain.
The stock-dove only through the forest coos, 615
Mournfully hoarse; oft ceasing from his plaint,
Short interval of weary woe! again
The sad idea of his murdered mate,
Struck from his side by savage fowler's guile,
Across his fancy comes; and then resounds 620

595 *prone*: headless.   604 *infracted*: broken.
611 *tuneful race*: singing birds. On periphrases see *Sp.* 132 end-note.
614 *responsive*: answering one another.

A louder song of sorrow through the grove.
  Beside the dewy border let me sit,
All in the freshness of the humid air,
There on that hollowed rock, grotesque and wild,
An ample chair moss-lined, and over head   625
By flowering umbrage shaded; where the bee
Strays diligent, and with the extracted balm
Of fragrant woodbine loads his little thigh.[n]
  Now, while I taste the sweetness of the shade,
While Nature lies around deep-lulled in noon,   630
Now come, bold fancy, spread a daring flight
And view the wonders of the torrid zone:
Climes unrelenting! with whose rage compared,
Yon blaze is feeble and yon skies are cool.
  See how at once the bright effulgent Sun,   635
Rising direct, swift chases from the sky
The short-lived twilight, and with ardent blaze
Looks gaily fierce o'er all the dazzling air!
He mounts his throne; but kind before him sends,
Issuing from out the portals of the morn,   640
The general breeze[n] to mitigate his fire
And breathe refreshment on a fainting world.
Great are the scenes, with dreadful beauty crowned
And barbarous wealth, that see, each circling year,
Returning suns and double seasons pass;   645
Rocks rich in gems,[n] and mountains big with mines,
That on the high equator ridgy rise,
Whence many a bursting stream auriferous plays;
Majestic woods of every vigorous green,
Stage above stage high waving o'er the hills,   650
Or to the far horizon wide-diffused,
A boundless deep immensity of shade.
Here lofty trees, to ancient song unknown,
The noble sons of potent heat and floods
Prone-rushing from the clouds, rear high to heaven   655
Their thorny stems, and broad around them throw
Meridian gloom. Here, in eternal prime,
Unnumbered fruits of keen delicious taste

---

645 *Returning . . . seasons*: 'In all places between the tropics the sun, as he passes and repasses in his annual motion, is twice a year perpendicular, which produces this effect.' (T.)

And vital spirit drink, amid the cliffs
And burning sands that bank the shrubby vales,   660
Redoubled day, yet in their rugged coats
A friendly juice to cool its rage contain.[n]
   Bear me, Pomona! to thy citron groves;
To where the lemon and the piercing lime,
With the deep orange glowing through the green,   665
Their lighter glories blend. Lay me reclined
Beneath the spreading tamarind, that shakes,
Fanned by the breeze, its fever-cooling fruit.
Deep in the night the massy locust sheds
Quench my hot limbs; or lead me through the maze,   670
Embowering endless, of the Indian fig;
Or, thrown at gayer ease on some fair brow,
Let me behold, by breezy murmurs cooled,
Broad o'er my head the verdant cedar wave,
And high palmettos lift their graceful shade.   675
Oh, stretched amid these orchards of the sun,
Give me to drain the coco's milky bowl,
And from the palm to draw its freshening wine!
More bounteous far than all the frantic juice
Which Bacchus pours. Nor, on its slender twigs   680
Low-bending, be the full pomegranate scorned;
Nor, creeping through the woods, the gelid race
Of berries. Oft in humble station dwells
Unboastful worth, above fastidious pomp.
Witness, thou best anana, thou the pride   685
Of vegetable life, beyond whate'er
The poets imaged in the golden age:
Quick let me strip thee of thy tufty coat,
Spread thy ambrosial stores, and feast with Jove!

659 *of . . . vital spirit*: yielding life-sustaining fluids; cf. *P.L.* V.484.
663 *Pomona*: Roman goddess of fruit-trees.
669 *locust*: the very large courbaril tree of Guiana and the West Indies.
671 *Indian fig*: the huge banyan tree whose extensive branches drop shoots which root and grow into trunks, so that one tree assumes the appearance of a dense and dark grove; cf. Pliny, *Natural History* XII.xi.22–3, *P.L.* IX.1101–10.
674 *verdant cedar*: the cedar of Lebanon—an exotic, not to be planted in quantity in England before about 1760.
675 *palmettos*: palm trees in general—not as now, 'dwarf palms'.
677 *coco*: coconut.   678 *wine*: coconut milk.
679 *frantic*: intoxicating.   680 *Bacchus*: Roman god of wine.
682 *gelid*: refreshing.
683 *in humble station*: growing close to the ground.
685 *anana*: pineapple (first cultivated in the later 17c., and highly prized).

From these the prospect varies. Plains immense   690
Lie stretched below, interminable meads
And vast savannas, where the wandering eye,
Unfixed, is in a verdant ocean lost.
Another Flora there, of bolder hues
And richer sweets beyond our garden's pride,   695
Plays o'er the fields, and showers with sudden hand
Exuberant spring—for oft these valleys shift
Their green-embroidered robe to fiery brown,
And swift to green again, as scorching suns
Or streaming dews and torrent rains prevail.   700
Along these lonely regions, where, retired
From little scenes of art, great Nature dwells
In awful solitude, and naught is seen
But the wild herds that own no master's stall,
Prodigious rivers roll their fattening seas;   705
On whose luxuriant herbage, half-concealed,
Like a fallen cedar, far diffused his train,
Cased in green scales, the crocodile extends.
The flood disparts: behold! in plaited mail
Behemoth rears his head. Glanced from his side,   710
The darted steel in idle shivers flies:
He fearless walks the plain, or seeks the hills,
Where, as he crops his varied fare, the herds,
In widening circle round, forget their food
And at the harmless stranger wondering gaze.   715
   Peaceful beneath primeval trees that cast
Their ample shade o'er Niger's yellow stream,
And where the Ganges rolls his sacred wave,
Or mid the central depth of blackening woods,
High-raised in solemn theatre around,   720
Leans the huge elephant—wisest of brutes!
Oh, truly wise! with gentle might endowed,
Though powerful not destructive! Here he sees
Revolving ages sweep the changeful earth,
And empires rise and fall; regardless he   725

694 *Flora*: ancient Italian goddess of flowers and fertility.
703 *solitude*: without man.
705 *fattening*: making fertile by irrigation.
707 *diffused his train*: his tail stretched out; cf. Milton, *Samson Agonistes* 118.
710 *Behemoth*: 'the hippopotamus, or river-horse'. (T.) Cf. Job 40:15-24.
720 *theatre*: natural amphitheatre; cf. *P.L.* IV.141-2, Dryden, *Aeneid* V.377-8.

Of what the never-resting race of men
Project: thrice happy, could he 'scape their guile
Who mine, from cruel avarice, his steps,
Or with his towery grandeur swell their state,
The pride of kings! or else his strength pervert,   730
And bid him rage amid the mortal fray,
Astonished at the madness of mankind.
    Wide o'er the winding umbrage of the floods,
Like vivid blossoms glowing from afar,
Thick-swarm the brighter birds. For Nature's hand,   735
That with a sportive vanity has decked
The plumy nations, there her gayest hues
Profusely pours. But, if she bids them shine
Arrayed in all the beauteous beams of day,
Yet, frugal still, she humbles them in song.   740
Nor envy we the gaudy robes they lent
Proud Montezuma's realm, whose legions cast
A boundless radiance waving on the sun,
While Philomel is ours, while in our shades,
Through the soft silence of the listening night,[n]   745
The sober-suited songstress trills her lay.
    But come, my Muse, the desert-barrier burst,
A wild expanse of lifeless sand and sky;
And, swifter than the toiling caravan,
Shoot o'er the vale of Sennar; ardent climb   750
The Nubian mountains, and the secret bounds
Of jealous Abyssinia boldly pierce.
Thou art no ruffian, who beneath the mask
Of social commerce com'st to rob their wealth;
No holy fury thou, blaspheming Heaven,   755
With consecrated steel to stab their peace,

728 *mine . . . his steps*: trap by means of a camouflaged pit.
733 *winding umbrage*: forests on the river banks.
738 *But . . . shine*: 'In all the regions of the torrid zone the birds, though more
    beautiful in their plumage, are observed to be less melodious than ours.' (T.)
    This is not altogether true; cf. *McKillop*, p. 150.
739 : because as Newton had shown, sunlight is the source of colour.
742 *Montezuma*: (1466–1520), the last Aztec ruler of Mexico before it was con-
    quered by Spain. The Aztecs wove feathers into a costly kind of cloth, and their
    soldiers ornamented headdresses and shields with feathers.
744 *Philomel*: see *Sp*. 601 fn.
750 *Sennar*: a kingdom and city in the upper Blue Nile valley, now part of the
    Sudan close to the Abyssinian border.
751 *Nubian*: Nubia was the ancient name for the upper Nile regions.
752 *jealous*: inhospitable to explorers.

And through the land, yet red from civil wounds,
To spread the purple tyranny of Rome.
Thou, like the harmless bee, mayst freely range
From mead to mead bright with exalted flowers,   760
From jasmine grove to grove; mayst wander gay
Through palmy shades and aromatic woods
That grace the plains, invest the peopled hills,
And up the more than Alpine mountains wave.
There on the breezy summit, spreading fair   765
For many a league, or on stupendous rocks,
That from the sun-redoubling valley lift,
Cool to the middle air, their lawny tops,
Where palaces and fanes and villas rise,
And gardens smile around and cultured fields,   770
And fountains gush, and careless herds and flocks
Securely stray—a world within itself,
Disdaining all assault: there let me draw
Ethereal soul, there drink reviving gales
Profusely breathing from the spicy groves   775
And vales of fragrance, there at distance hear
The roaring floods and cataracts that sweep
From disembowelled earth the virgin gold,
And o'er the varied landscape restless rove,
Fervent with life of every fairer kind.   780
A land of wonders! which the sun still eyes
With ray direct, as of the lovely realm
Enamoured, and delighting there to dwell.[n]
   How changed the scene! In blazing height of noon,
The sun, oppressed, is plunged in thickest gloom.   785
Still horror reigns, a dreary twilight round,
Of struggling night and day malignant mixed.
For to the hot equator crowding fast,
Where, highly rarefied, the yielding air
Admits their stream, incessant vapours roll,   790

---

758 *purple tyranny*: in the sixteenth and early seventeenth centuries Jesuit
    missionaries sought to convert the Coptic Christians of Abyssinia to Rome; their
    success in converting the Emperor provoked a bloody civil war.
767 *sun-redoubling valley*: one that by reflecting the sun's rays from its side in-
    creases their heat.
768 *middle air*: a cold vaporous region—the second of the three layers into which
    medieval philosophers divided the atmosphere; cf. *P.L.* I.516, *Au.* 707–10 end-
    note.
773 *Disdaining all assault*: because ringed by mountains.

Amazing clouds on clouds continual heaped;
Or whirled tempestuous by the gusty wind,
Or silent borne along, heavy and slow,
With the big stores of steaming oceans charged.
Meantime, amid these upper seas, condensed   795
Around the cold aerial mountain's brow,
And by conflicting winds together dashed,
The Thunder holds his black tremendous throne;
From cloud to cloud the rending Lightnings rage;
Till, in the furious elemental war   800
Dissolved, the whole precipitated mass
Unbroken floods and solid torrents pours.[n]
   The treasures these, hid from the bounded search
Of ancient knowledge, whence with annual pomp,
Rich king of floods! o'erflows the swelling Nile.[n]   805
From his two springs in Gojam's sunny realm
Pure-welling out, he through the lucid lake
Of fair Dambea rolls his infant stream.
There, by the Naiads nursed, he sports away
His playful youth amid the fragrant isles   810
That with unfading verdure smile around.
Ambitious thence the manly river breaks,
And, gathering many a flood, and copious fed
With all the mellowed treasures of the sky,
Winds in progressive majesty along: 815
Through splendid kingdoms now devolves his maze,
Now wanders wild o'er solitary tracts
Of life-deserted sand; till, glad to quit
The joyless desert, down the Nubian rocks
From thundering steep to steep he pours his urn,   820
And Egypt joys beneath the spreading wave.
   His brother Niger too, and all the floods
In which the full-formed maids of Afric lave
Their jetty limbs, and all that from the tract
Of woody mountains stretched thro' gorgeous Ind   825
Fall on Cormandel's coast or Malabar;

806 *Gojam*: a region of N.W. Abyssinia.
808 *Dambea*: Lake Tana in Abyssinia.
809 *Naiads*: water-nymphs, cf. *Sp.* 403.
819 *Nubian rocks*: the Cataracts, cf. *Su.* 751.
820 *pours his urn*: the image is of a statue or other representation of the river-god;
   the reference is to the annual flooding of Lower Egypt.
826 Coromandel is the east, and Malabar the west coast of India.

From Menam's orient stream[n] that nightly shines
With insect-lamps, to where Aurora sheds
On Indus' smiling banks the rosy shower—
All, at this bounteous season, ope their urns   830
And pour untoiling harvest o'er the land.
     Nor less thy world, Columbus, drinks refreshed
The lavish moisture of the melting year.
Wide o'er his isles the branching Oronoque
Rolls a brown deluge, and the native drives   835
To dwell aloft on life-sufficing trees—[n]
At once his dome, his robe, his food, and arms.
Swelled by a thousand streams, impetuous hurled
From all the roaring Andes, huge descends
The mighty Orellana. Scarce the muse   840
Dares stretch her wing o'er this enormous mass
Of rushing water; scarce she dares attempt
The sea-like Plata, to whose dread expanse,
Continuous depth, and wondrous length of course
Our floods are rills. With unabated force   845
In silent dignity they sweep along,
And traverse realms unknown, and blooming wilds,
And fruitful deserts—worlds of solitude
Where the sun smiles and seasons teem in vain,
Unseen and unenjoyed. Forsaking these,   850
O'er peopled plains they fair-diffusive flow
And many a nation feed, and circle safe
In their soft bosom many a happy isle,
The seat of blameless Pan, yet undisturbed
By Christian crimes and Europe's cruel sons.   855
Thus pouring on they proudly seek the deep,
Whose vanquish'd tide, recoiling from the shock,
Yields to this liquid weight of half the globe;
And Ocean trembles for his green domain.[n]
     But what avails this wondrous waste of wealth,   860

828 *Aurora*: in Roman mythology the goddess of dawn.
830–1 the monsoon floods making alluvial deposits on the land.
834 *Oronoque*: Orinoco.
840 *Orellana*: 'The river of the Amazons' (T.); named after its first navigator
    Francisco de Orellana, a follower of Pizarro.
854 *Pan*: the Greek god of flocks, shepherds, and pastoral song. In Christian
    legend (based on a story in Plutarch) a mysterious cry 'The great god Pan is
    dead' was heard about the time that Christ was born.
855 *cruel sons*: Spanish and Portuguese.

This gay profusion of luxurious bliss,
This pomp of Nature? what their balmy meads,
Their powerful herbs, and Ceres void of pain?
By vagrant birds dispersed and wafting winds,
What their unplanted fruits? what the cool draughts,   865
The ambrosial food, rich gums, and spicy health
Their forests yield? their toiling insects what,
Their silky pride and vegetable robes?
Ah! what avail their fatal treasures, hid
Deep in the bowels of the pitying earth,   870
Golconda's gems, and sad Potosi's mines
Where dwelt the gentlest children of the Sun?
What all that Afric's golden rivers roll,
Her odorous woods, and shining ivory stores?
Ill-fated race! the softening arts of peace,   875
Whate'er the humanizing Muses teach,
The godlike wisdom of the tempered breast,
Progressive truth, the patient force of thought,
Investigation calm whose silent powers
Command the world, the light that leads to Heaven,   880
Kind equal rule, the government of laws,
And all-protecting freedom which alone
Sustains the name and dignity of man—
These are not theirs. The parent Sun himself
Seems o'er this world of slaves to tyrannize,   885
And, with oppressive ray the roseate bloom
Of beauty blasting, gives the gloomy hue
And feature gross—or, worse, to ruthless deeds.
Mad jealousy, blind rage, and fell revenge
Their fervid spirit fires. Love dwells not there,   890
The soft regards, the tenderness of life,
The heart-shed tear, the ineffable delight
Of sweet humanity: these court the beam
Of milder climes—in selfish fierce desire
And the wild fury of voluptuous sense   895

863 *Ceres*: Roman goddess of agriculture; here signifying harvest ('void of pain',
    i.e. without labour).
871 *Golconda*: the town near Hyderabad in India where diamonds were brought
    to be cut and polished.
871 *Potosi*: the extremely rich silver-mining area in what is now Bolivia; 'sad'
    because the Spaniards treated their native labourers cruelly.
872 *children of the sun*: the Inca of ancient Peru worshipped the sun, of which
    their emperor was held to be a descendant.

There lost. The very brute creation there
This rage partakes, and burns with horrid fire.[n]
　　Lo! the green serpent, from his dark abode,
Which even imagination fears to tread,
At noon forth-issuing, gathers up his train　　　　　　900
In orbs immense, then, darting out anew,
Seeks the refreshing fount, by which diffused
He throws his folds; and while, with threatening tongue
And deathful jaws erect, the monster curls
His flaming crest, all other thirst appalled　　　　　　905
Or shivering flies, or checked at distance stands,
Nor dares approach.[n] But still more direful he,
The small close-lurking minister of fate,
Whose high-concocted venom through the veins
A rapid lightning darts, arresting swift　　　　　　910
The vital current. Formed to humble man,
This child of vengeful Nature! There, sublimed
To fearless lust of blood, the savage race
Roam, licensed by the shading hour of guilt
And foul misdeed, when the pure day has shut　　　　　915
His sacred eye. The tiger, darting fierce
Impetuous on the prey his glance has doomed;
The lively-shining leopard, speckled o'er
With many a spot, the beauty of the waste;
And, scorning all the taming arts of man,　　　　　　920
The keen hyena, fellest of the fell—
These, rushing from the inhospitable woods
Of Mauritania, or the tufted isles
That verdant rise amid the Libyan wild,
Innumerous glare around their shaggy king　　　　　　925
Majestic stalking o'er the printed sand;
And with imperious and repeated roars
Demand their fated food. The fearful flocks
Crowd near the guardian swain; the nobler herds,
Where round their lordly bull in rural ease　　　　　930
They ruminating lie, with horror hear
The coming rage. The awakened village starts;

905 *thirst*: thirsty creatures.　　　　　908 *minister of fate*: asp.
909 *high-concocted*: brought to perfection by heat. According to myth the asp
　　was formed by the sun's heat on a clot of Medusa's blood; cf. Lucan, *Pharsalia*
　　IX.700–5.
923 *Mauritania*: the Mediterranean costal regions of what are now Morocco and
　　western Algeria.　　　　　923 *tufted isles*: oases.　　　　　925 *king*: the lion.

And to her fluttering breast the mother strains
Her thoughtless infant. From the pirate's den,
Or stern Morocco's tyrant fang escaped,   935
The wretch half wishes for his bonds again;
While, uproar all, the wilderness resounds
From Atlas eastward to the frighted Nile.
Unhappy he! who, from the first of joys,
Society, cut off, is left alone   940
Amid this world of death! Day after day,
Sad on the jutting eminence he sits,
And views the main that ever toils below;
Still fondly forming in the farthest verge,
Where the round ether mixes with the wave,   945
Ships, dim-discovered, dropping from the clouds;[n]
At evening, to the setting sun he turns
A mournful eye, and down his dying heart
Sinks helpless; while the wonted roar is up,
And hiss continual through the tedious night.   950
Yet here, even here, into these black abodes
Of monsters, unappalled, from stooping Rome
And guilty Caesar, Liberty retired,
Her Cato[n] following through Numidian wilds—
Disdainful of Campania's gentle plains   955
And all the green delights Ausonia pours,
When for them she must bend the servile knee,
And, fawning, take the splendid robber's boon.
   Nor stop the terrors of these regions here.
Commissioned demons[n] oft, angels of wrath,   960
Let loose the raging elements. Breathed hot
From all the boundless furnace of the sky,
And the wide glittering waste of burning sand,
A suffocating wind the pilgrim smites
With instant death. Patient of thirst and toil,   965
Son of the desert! even the camel feels,
Shot through his withered heart, the fiery blast.
Or from the black-red ether, bursting broad,
Sallies the sudden whirlwind. Straight the sands,
Commoved around, in gathering eddies play;   970

934 *thoughtless*: free from care.   938 *Atlas*: see *Au.* 798 fn.
952 *stooping*: declining.   954 *Numidia*: what is now eastern Algeria.
955 *Campania*: the fertile region around Naples.
956 *Ausonia*: Italy.   958 *splendid robber*: Julius Caesar.

Nearer and nearer still they darkening come;
Till, with the general all-involving storm
Swept up, the whole continuous wilds arise;
And by their noon-day fount dejected thrown,
Or sunk at night in sad disastrous sleep, 975
Beneath descending hills the caravan
Is buried deep.[n] In Cairo's crowded streets
The impatient merchant, wondering, waits in vain,
And Mecca saddens at the long delay.
But chief at sea, whose every flexile wave 980
Obeys the blast, the aerial tumult swells.
In the dread ocean, undulating wide,
Beneath the radiant line that girts the globe,
The circling typhon, whirled from point to point,
Exhausting all the rage of all the sky, 985
And dire ecnephia[n] reign. Amid the heavens,
Falsely serene, deep in a cloudy speck
Compressed, the mighty tempest brooding dwells.
Of no regard, save to the skilful eye,
Fiery and foul, the small prognostic hangs 990
Aloft, or on the promontory's brow
Musters its force. A faint deceitful calm,
A fluttering gale, the demon sends before
To tempt the spreading sail. Then down at once
Precipitant descends a mingled mass 995
Of roaring winds and flame and rushing floods.
In wild amazement fixed the sailor stands.
Art is too slow. By rapid fate oppressed,
His broad-winged vessel drinks the whelming tide,
Hid in the bosom of the black abyss. 1000
With such mad seas the daring Gama fought,
For many a day and many a dreadful night
Incessant labouring round the stormy Cape,—
By bold ambition led, and bolder thirst
Of gold. For then from ancient gloom emerged 1005

974 *dejected*: down.   983 *radiant line*: Equator.
987 *a cloudy speck*: 'called by the sailors the ox-eye, being in appearance at first no bigger' (T.).
989 *of no regard*: unnoticeable.
993 *gale*: gentle breeze, cf. *Sp.* 873; not the 'gale' of *Su.* 1018.
998 *art*: seamanship (in furling the sails).
1001 *Gama*: 'Vasco da Gama, the first that sailed round Africa, by the Cape of Good Hope, to the East Indies' (T.). He made his first voyage to India in 1497–9.

The rising world of trade: the genius then
Of navigation, that in hopeless sloth
Had slumbered on the vast Atlantic deep
For idle ages, starting, heard at last
The Lusitanian Prince, who, heaven-inspired,   1010
To love of useful glory roused mankind,
And in unbounded commerce mixed the world.
    Increasing still the terrors of these storms,
His jaws horrific armed with threefold fate,
Here dwells the direful shark. Lured by the scent   1015
Of steaming crowds, of rank disease, and death,
Behold! he rushing cuts the briny flood,
Swift as the gale can bear the ship along;
And from the partners of that cruel trade
Which spoils unhappy Guinea of her sons   1020
Demands his share of prey—demands themselves.
The stormy fates descend: one death involves
Tyrants and slaves; when straight, their mangled limbs
Crashing at once, he dyes the purple seas
With gore, and riots in the vengeful meal.[n]   1025
    When o'er this world, by equinoctial rains
Flooded immense, looks out the joyless sun,
And draws the copious steam from swampy fens,
Where putrefaction into life ferments
And breathes destructive myriads, or from woods,   1030
Impenetrable shades, recesses foul,
In vapours rank and blue corruption wrapt,
Whose gloomy horrors yet no desperate foot
Has ever dared to pierce; then wasteful forth
Walks the dire power of pestilent disease.[n]   1035
A thousand hideous fiends her course attend,
Sick nature blasting, and to heartless woe
And feeble desolation, casting down
The towering hopes and all the pride of man:
Such as of late at Carthagena quenched   1040
The British fire. You, gallant Vernon,[n] saw
The miserable scene; you, pitying, saw

1010 *Lusitanian Prince*: 'Don Henry, third son to John the First, King of Portugal.
  His strong genius to the discovery of new countries was the source of all the
  modern improvements in navigation' (T.). He is generally known as Henry the
  Navigator; Lusitania was the ancient name for Portugal.
1014 *threefold fate*: the shark has three rows of teeth.

To infant-weakness sunk the warrior's arm;
Saw the deep-racking pang, the ghastly form,
The lip pale-quivering, and the beamless eye   1045
No more with ardour bright; you heard the groans
Of agonizing ships from shore to shore,
Heard, nightly plunged amid the sullen waves,
The frequent corse, while, on each other fixed
In sad presage, the blank assistants seemed   1050
Silent to ask whom fate would next demand.

What need I mention those inclement skies
Where frequent o'er the sickening city, plague,
The fiercest child of Nemesis divine,
Descends? From Ethiopia's poisoned woods,[n]   1055
From stifled Cairo's filth, and fetid fields
With locust armies putrefying heaped,
This great destroyer sprung. Her awful rage
The brutes escape: Man is her destined prey,
Intemperate man! and o'er his guilty domes   1060
She draws a close incumbent cloud of death;
Uninterrupted by the living winds,
Forbid to blow a wholesome breeze; and stained
With many a mixture by the Sun suffused
Of angry aspect. Princely wisdom then   1065
Dejects his watchful eye; and from the hand
Of feeble justice ineffectual drop
The sword and balance; mute the voice of joy,
And hushed the clamour of the busy world.
Empty the streets, with uncouth verdure clad;[n]   1070
Into the worst of deserts sudden turned
The cheerful haunt of men—unless, escaped
From the doomed house, where matchless horror reigns,
Shut up by barbarous fear, the smitten wretch
With frenzy wild breaks loose, and, loud to Heaven   1075
Screaming, the dreadful policy arraigns,

1045 *beamless*: unshining, or, perhaps, blind (referring to the Pythagorean theory
of vision—that sight emanated from the eye).
1050 *blank*: pale, cf. *Wi*. 124, *P.L.* X.656.
1054 *Nemesis*: in Greek and Roman mythology the goddess of retribution, who
punished insolence towards the gods. I have found no ancient reference to her
being the mother of plague; usually she is represented as a virgin.
1065 *angry aspect*: a position in the heavens that, according to astrologers, fore-
told disaster.
1066 *dejects*: throws down, cf. *Su*. 437, 974.

Inhuman and unwise. The sullen door,
Yet uninfected, on its cautious hinge
Fearing to turn, abhors society:
Dependents, friends, relations, Love himself,   1080
Savaged by woe, forget the tender tie,
The sweet engagement of the feeling heart.
But vain their selfish care: the circling sky,
The wide enlivening air is full of fate;
And, struck by turns, in solitary pangs   1085
They fall, unblessed, untended, and unmourned.
Thus o'er the prostrate city black Despair
Extends her raven wing; while, to complete
The scene of desolation stretched around,
The grim guards stand, denying all retreat,   1090
And give the flying wretch a better death.
     Much yet remains unsung: the rage intense
Of brazen-vaulted skies, of iron fields,
Where drought and famine starve the blasted year;
Fired by the torch of noon to tenfold rage,   1095
The infuriate hill that shoots the pillared flame;
And, roused within the subterranean world,
The expanding earthquake, that resistless shakes
Aspiring cities from their solid base,
And buries mountains in the flaming gulf.   1100
But 'tis enough; return, my vagrant muse;
A nearer scene of horror calls thee home.
     Behold, slow-settling o'er the lurid grove
Unusual darkness broods, and, growing, gains
The full possession of the sky, surcharged   1105
With wrathful vapour, from the secret beds
Where sleep the mineral generations drawn.
Thence nitre, sulphur and the fiery spume
Of fat bitumen, steaming on the day,
With various-tinctured trains of latent flame,   1110
Pollute the sky, and in yon baleful cloud,
A reddening gloom, a magazine of fate,
Ferment; till, by the touch ethereal roused,
The dash of clouds, or irritating war

1090 *grim guards*: the *cordon sanitaire*.
1099 *Aspiring*: towering, cf. Spenser, *Ruines of Time* 408.
1109 *fat*: richly resinous.
1113 *touch ethereal*: contact with the upper air.

Of fighting winds, while all is calm below,   1115
They furious spring.[n] A boding silence reigns
Dread through the dun expanse—save the dull sound
That from the mountain, previous to the storm,
Rolls o'er the muttering earth, disturbs the flood,
And shakes the forest-leaf without a breath.   1120
Prone to the lowest vale the aerial tribes
Descend: the tempest-loving raven scarce
Dares wing the dubious dusk. In rueful gaze
The cattle stand, and on the scowling heavens
Cast a deploring eye—by man forsook,   1125
Who to the crowded cottage hies him fast,
Or seeks the shelter of the downward cave.
   'Tis listening fear and dumb amazement all:[n]
When to the startled eye the sudden glance
Appears far south, eruptive through the cloud,   1130
And, following slower, in explosion vast
The thunder raises his tremendous voice.
At first, heard solemn o'er the verge of heaven,
The tempest growls; but as it nearer comes,
And rolls its awful burden on the wind,   1135
The lightnings flash a larger curve, and more
The noise astounds, till overhead a sheet
Of livid flame discloses wide, then shuts
And opens wider, shuts and opens still
Expansive, wrapping ether in a blaze.   1140
Follows the loosened aggravated roar,
Enlarging, deepening, mingling, peal on peal
Crushed horrible, convulsing heaven and earth.
   Down comes a deluge of sonorous hail,
Or prone-descending rain. Wide-rent, the clouds   1145
Pour a whole flood; and yet, its flame unquenched,
The unconquerable lightning struggles through,
Ragged and fierce, or in red whirling balls,
And fires the mountains with redoubled rage.
Black from the stroke, above, the smouldering pine   1150
Stands a sad shattered trunk; and, stretched below,
A lifeless group the blasted cattle lie:
Here the soft flocks, with that same harmless look
They wore alive, and ruminating still

1121 *aerial tribes*: birds. On periphrases see *Sp.* 132 end-note.
1138 *discloses*: (intrans.), i.e. opens.

In fancy's eye, and there the frowning bull   1155
And ox half-raised. Struck on the castled cliff,
The venerable tower and spiry fane
Resign their aged pride. The gloomy woods
Start at the flash, and from their deep recess
Wide-flaming out, their trembling inmates shake.   1160
Amid Caernarvon's mountains rages loud
The repercussive roar: with mighty crush,
Into the flashing deep, from the rude rocks
Of Penmaen-Mawr heaped hideous to the sky,
Tumble the smitten cliffs; and Snowdon's peak,   1165
Dissolving, instant yields his wintry load.
Far seen, the heights of heathy Cheviot blaze,
And Thule bellows through her utmost isles.
     Guilt hears appalled, with deeply troubled thought;
And yet not always on the guilty head   1170
Descends the fated flash. Young Celadon
And his Amelia were a matchless pair,
With equal virtue formed and equal grace
The same, distinguished by their sex alone:
Hers the mild lustre of the blooming morn,   1175
And his the radiance of the risen day.
     They loved: but such their guileless passion was
As in the dawn of time informed the heart
Of innocence and undissembling truth.
'Twas friendship heightened by the mutual wish,   1180
The enchanting hope and sympathetic glow
Beamed from the mutual eye. Devoting all
To love, each was to each a dearer self,
Supremely happy in the awakened power
Of giving joy. Alone amid the shades,   1185
Still in harmonious intercourse they lived
The rural day, and talked the flowing heart,
Or sighed and looked unutterable things.
So passed their life, a clear united stream,
By care unruffled; till, in evil hour,   1190
The tempest caught them on the tender walk,
Heedless how far and where its mazes strayed,

1164 *Penmaen-Mawr*: the hill in north Wales, overlooking Conway Bay.
1168 *Thule*: the name given by ancient geographers to an island north of Britain;
perhaps the Shetlands here.

While with each other blest, creative Love
Still bade eternal Eden smile around.
Heavy with instant fate, her bosom heaved   1195
Unwonted sighs, and, stealing oft a look
Of the big gloom, on Celadon her eye
Fell tearful, wetting her disordered cheek.
In vain assuring love and confidence
In Heaven repressed her fear; it grew, and shook   1200
Her frame near dissolution. He perceived
The unequal conflict, and, as angels look
On dying saints, his eyes compassion shed,
With love illumined high. 'Fear not,' he said,
'Sweet innocence! thou stranger to offence   1205
And inward storm! he, who yon skies involves
In frowns of darkness, ever smiles on thee
With kind regard. O'er thee the secret shaft
That wastes at midnight, or the undreaded hour
Of noon, flies harmless: and that very voice,   1210
Which thunders terror through the guilty heart,
With tongues of seraphs whispers peace to thine.
'Tis safety to be near thee sure, and thus
To clasp perfection!' From his void embrace,
Mysterious Heaven! that moment to the ground,   1215
A blackened corse, was struck the beauteous maid.
But who can paint the lover, as he stood
Pierced by severe amazement, hating life,
Speechless, and fixed in all the death of woe?
So, faint resemblance! on the marble tomb   1220
The well-dissembled mourner stooping stands,
For ever silent and for ever sad.[n]
     As from the face of Heaven the shattered clouds
Tumultuous rove, the interminable sky
Sublimer swells, and o'er the world expands   1225
A purer azure. Nature from the storm
Shines out afresh; and through the lightened air
A higher lustre and a clearer calm
Diffusive tremble; while, as if in sign
Of danger past, a glittering robe of joy,   1230
Set off abundant by the yellow ray,

1195 *instant*: imminent.
1221 *dissembled*: simulated, cf. Dryden, *Aeneid* VIII.880.
1225 *sublimer*: higher.

Invests the fields, yet dropping from distress.
'Tis beauty all, and grateful song around,[n]
Joined to the low of kine, and numerous bleat
Of flocks thick-nibbling through the clovered vale.   1235
And shall the hymn be marred by thankless man,
Most-favoured, who with voice articulate
Should lead the chorus of this lower world ?
Shall he, so soon forgetful of the hand
That hushed the thunder, and serenes the sky,   1240
Extinguished feel that spark the tempest waked,
That sense of powers exceeding far his own,
Ere yet his feeble heart has lost its fears ?
    Cheered by the milder beam, the sprightly youth
Speeds to the well-known pool, whose crystal depth   1245
A sandy bottom shows. Awhile he stands
Gazing the inverted landscape, half afraid
To meditate the blue profound below;
Then plunges headlong down the circling flood.
His ebon tresses and his rosy cheek   1250
Instant emerge; and through the obedient wave,
At each short breathing by his lip repelled,
With arms and legs according well, he makes,
As humour leads, an easy-winding path;
While from his polished sides a dewy light   1255
Effuses on the pleased spectators round.
    This is the purest exercise of health,
The kind refresher of the summer heats;
Nor, when cold winter keens the brightening flood,
Would I weak-shivering linger on the brink.   1260
Thus life redoubles, and is oft preserved
By the bold swimmer, in the swift illapse
Of accident disastrous. Hence the limbs
Knit into force; and the same Roman arm
That rose victorious o'er the conquered earth   1265
First learned, while tender, to subdue the wave.
Even from the body's purity the mind
Receives a secret sympathetic aid.[n]

1240 *serenes*: makes calm, cf. *Sp.* 870.
1247 *gazing*: (trans.) staring at, cf. *P.L.* VIII.258.
1248 *meditate*: (trans.) fix the attention upon; cf. *Au.* 670, Pope, *Windsor Forest* 102.
1248 *profound*: depth, cf. *P.L.* II.980.
1259 *keens*: sharpens, cf. *Cas. Ind.* II.l.4.   1262 *illapse*: falling.

Close in the covert of an hazel copse,
Where, winded into pleasing solitudes,   1270
Runs out the rambling dale, young Damon sat
Pensive, and pierced with love's delightful pangs.
There to the stream that down the distant rocks
Hoarse-murmuring fell, and plaintive breeze that played
Among the bending willows, falsely he   1275
Of Musidora's cruelty complained.
She felt his flame; but deep within her breast,
In bashful coyness or in maiden pride,
The soft return concealed; save when it stole
In side-long glances from her downcast eye,   1280
Or from her swelling soul in stifled sighs.
Touched by the scene, no stranger to his vows,
He framed a melting lay to try her heart;
And, if an infant passion struggled there,
To call that passion forth. Thrice happy swain!   1285
A lucky chance, that oft decides the fate
Of mighty monarchs, then decided thine!
For, lo! conducted by the laughing Loves,
This cool retreat his Musidora sought:
Warm in her cheek the sultry season glowed;   1290
And, robed in loose array, she came to bathe
Her fervent limbs in the refreshing stream.
What shall he do? In sweet confusion lost,
And dubious flutterings, he a while remained.
A pure ingenuous elegance of soul,   1295
A delicate refinement, known to few,
Perplexed his breast and urged him to retire:
But love forbade. Ye prudes in virtue, say,
Say, ye severest, what would you have done?
Meantime, this fairer nymph than ever blest   1300
Arcadian stream, with timid eye around
The banks surveying, stripped her beauteous limbs
To taste the lucid coolness of the flood.
Ah! then, not Paris on the piny top
Of Ida panted stronger, when aside   1305
The rival goddesses the veil divine

1288 *Loves*: Cupids, or frolicsome boy-gods of love: cf. Spenser, *Amoretti* xvi.6.
1301 *Arcadia*: the mountain district of central Greece where, in ancient times,
    Pan was worshipped. After it was mentioned in Virgil's *Eclogues* it came to
    be regarded as an ideal region of rural joy.

Cast unconfined, and gave him all their charms,[n]
Than, Damon, thou; as from the snowy leg
And slender foot the inverted silk she drew;
As the soft touch dissolved the virgin zone;   1310
And, through the parting robe, the alternate breast,
With youth wild-throbbing, on thy lawless gaze
In full luxuriance rose. But, desperate youth,
How durst thou risk the soul-distracting view
As from her naked limbs of glowing white,   1315
Harmonious swelled by nature's finest hand,
In folds loose-floating fell the fainter lawn,
And fair exposed she stood, shrunk from herself,
With fancy blushing, at the doubtful breeze
Alarmed, and starting like the fearful fawn?[n]   1320
Then to the flood she rushed: the parted flood
Its lovely guest with closing waves received;
And every beauty softening, every grace
Flushing anew, a mellow lustre shed—
As shines the lily through the crystal mild,   1325
Or as the rose amid the morning dew,
Fresh from Aurora's hand, more sweetly glows.
While thus she wantoned, now beneath the wave
But ill-concealed, and now with streaming locks,
That half-embraced her in a humid veil,   1330
Rising again, the latent Damon drew
Such maddening draughts of beauty to the soul
As for a while o'erwhelmed his raptured thought
With luxury too daring. Checked, at last,
By love's respectful modesty, he deemed   1335
The theft profane, if aught profane to love
Can e'er be deemed, and, struggling from the shade,
With headlong hurry fled: but first these lines,
Traced by his ready pencil, on the bank
With trembling hand he threw—'Bathe on, my fair,   1340
Yet unbeheld save by the sacred eye
Of faithful love: I go to guard thy haunt;
To keep from thy recess each vagrant foot
And each licentious eye.' With wild surprise,
As if to marble struck, devoid of sense,   1345

1319 *doubtful*: causing apprehension.
1325 *crystal*: clear water, cf. Denham, *Cooper's Hill* 322.
1327 *Aurora*: see *Su.* 828 fn.

A stupid moment motionless she stood:
So stands the statue that enchants the world;
So, bending, tries to veil the matchless boast,
The mingled beauties, of exulting Greece.
Recovering, swift she flew to find those robes   1350
Which blissful Eden knew not; and, arrayed
In careless haste, the alarming paper snatched.
But, when her Damon's well-known hand she saw,
Her terrors vanished, and a softer train
Of mixed emotions, hard to be described,   1355
Her sudden bosom seized: shame void of guilt,
The charming blush of innocence, esteem
And admiration of her lover's flame,
By modesty exalted, even a sense
Of self-approving beauty stole across   1360
Her busy thought. At length, a tender calm
Hushed by degrees the tumult of her soul;
And on the spreading beech, that o'er the stream
Incumbent hung, she with the sylvan pen
Of rural lovers this confession carved,   1365
Which soon her Damon kissed with weeping joy:
'Dear youth! sole judge of what these verses mean,
By fortune too much favoured, but by love,
Alas! not favoured less, be still as now
Discreet: the time may come you need not fly.'   1370
      The Sun has lost his rage: his downward orb[n]
Shoots nothing now but animating warmth
And vital lustre; that with various ray,
Lights up the clouds, those beauteous robes of heaven,
Incessant rolled into romantic shapes,   1375
The dream of waking fancy! Broad below,
Covered with ripening fruits, and swelling fast
Into the perfect year, the pregnant earth
And all her tribes rejoice. Now the soft hour
Of walking comes for him who lonely loves   1380
To seek the distant hills, and there converse

1347 *statue . . . world*: 'The Venus of Medici.' (T.) Often copied, it was regarded
  as 'the standard of all female beauty' (Joseph Spence, *Polymetis* (1747), p. 66).
  T. describes it in *Liberty* IV (1736), 175–84.
1356 *sudden*: impetuous, cf. *P.L.* II.738.
1364 *sylvan pen*: knife. (The implausibility of Musidora's feat of carving suggests
  that T. may have regarded this whole episode as agreeable nonsense.)

With nature, there to harmonize his heart,
And in pathetic song to breathe around
The harmony to others. Social friends,
Attuned to happy unison of soul—   1385
To whose exalting eye a fairer world,
Of which the vulgar never had a glimpse,
Displays its charms; whose minds are richly fraught
With philosophic stores, superior light;
And in whose breast enthusiastic burns   1390
Virtue, the sons of interest deem romance—
Now called abroad, enjoy the falling day:
Now to the verdant Portico of woods,
To nature's vast Lyceum, forth they walk;
By that kind school where no proud master reigns,   1395
The full free converse of the friendly heart,
Improving and improved. Now from the world,
Sacred to sweet retirement, lovers steal,
And pour their souls in transport, which the sire
Of love approving hears, and calls it good.   1400
Which way, Amanda, shall we bend our course?
The choice perplexes. Wherefore should we choose?
All is the same with thee. Say, shall we wind
Along the streams? or walk the smiling mead?
Or court the forest glades? or wander wild   1405
Among the waving harvests? or ascend,
While radiant Summer opens all its pride,
Thy hill, delightful Shene? Here let us sweep
The boundless landscape; now the raptured eye,
Exulting swift, to huge Augusta send,   1410
Now to the sister hills that skirt her plain,
To lofty Harrow now, and now to where
Majestic Windsor lifts his princely brow.

1383 *pathetic*: sympathetic.
1391 *sons of interest*: self-interested people; cf. 'sons of party', *Cas. Ind.* I.liv.1.
1393 *Portico*: the Painted Porch in ancient Athens where Zeno taught his philo-
    sophy.
1394 *Lyceum*: the garden with covered walks at Athens where Aristotle taught
    his philosophy.
1401 *Amanda*: see *Sp.* 483 fn.
1408 *Shene*: 'The old name of Richmond, signifying in Saxon shining or splen-
    dour.' (T.) Richmond Hill commanded one of the eighteenth century's most
    praised views; after 1736 it was T.'s home.
1410 *Augusta*: see *Sp.* 108 fn.
1411 *the sister hills*: 'Highgate and Hampstead' (T.).

In lovely contrast to this glorious view,
Calmly magnificent, then will we turn   1415
To where the silver Thames first rural grows.
There let the feasted eye unwearied stray;
Luxurious, there, rove through the pendent woods
That nodding hang o'er Harrington's retreat;
And, stooping thence to Ham's embowering walks,   1420
Beneath whose shades, in spotless peace retired,
With her the pleasing partner of his heart,
The worthy Queensberry yet laments his Gay,
And polished Cornbury woos the willing muse,[n]
Slow let us trace the matchless vale of Thames;   1425
Fair-winding up to where the muses haunt
In Twit'nam's bowers, and for their Pope implore
The healing god; to royal Hampton's pile,
To Clermont's terraced height, and Esher's groves,
Where in the sweetest solitude, embraced   1430
By the soft windings of the silent Mole,
From courts and senates Pelham finds repose.[n]
Enchanting vale! beyond whate'er the muse
Has of Achaia or Hesperia sung!
O vale of bliss! O softly-swelling hills!   1435
On which the Power of Cultivation lies,
And joys to see the wonders of his toil.[n]
        Heavens! what a goodly prospect spreads around,
Of hills, and dales, and woods, and lawns, and spires,
And glittering towns, and gilded streams, till all   1440
The stretching landscape into smoke decays!
Happy Britannia![n] where the Queen of Arts,
Inspiring vigour, Liberty, abroad
Walks unconfined even to thy farthest cots,
And scatters plenty with unsparing hand.[n]   1445
        Rich is thy soil, and merciful thy clime;
Thy streams unfailing in the Summer's drought;

1414 *contrast*: juxtaposition of forms, colours, etc., as in painting.
1427 *Twit'nam's*: Alexander Pope had laid out a famous garden at his house at
    Twickenham. He fell fatally ill early in 1744, shortly before T. wrote these lines,
    and died 30 May. Cf. *Wi.* 550–4.
1434 *Achaia*: the Roman province of southern Greece.
1434 *Hesperia*: 'western land'; the Greek name for Italy and the Roman name
    for Spain. T. means Italy.
1441 *smoke*: blue haze (as in a Claude Lorrain landscape painting, cf. *Cas. Ind.*
    I.xxxviii.8).

Unmatched thy guardian-oaks; thy valleys float
With golden waves; and on thy mountains flocks
Bleat numberless; while, roving round their sides,   1450
Bellow the blackening herds in lusty droves.
Beneath, thy meadows glow, and rise unquelled
Against the mower's scythe. On every hand
Thy villas shine. Thy country teems with wealth;
And Property assures it to the swain,   1455
Pleased and unwearied in his guarded toil.
    Full are thy cities with the sons of art;
And trade and joy, in every busy street,
Mingling are heard: even Drudgery himself,
As at the car he sweats, or, dusty, hews   1460
The palace stone, looks gay. Thy crowded ports,
Where rising masts an endless prospect yield,
With labour burn, and echo to the shouts
Of hurried sailor, as he hearty waves
His last adieu, and, loosening every sheet,   1465
Resigns the spreading vessel to the wind.
    Bold, firm, and graceful, are thy generous youth,
By hardship sinewed, and by danger fired,
Scattering the nations where they go; and first
Or in the listed plain or stormy seas.   1470
Mild are thy glories too, as o'er the plans
Of thriving peace thy thoughtful sires preside—
In genius and substantial learning, high;
For every virtue, every worth, renowned;
Sincere, plain-hearted, hospitable, kind,   1475
Yet like the mustering thunder when provoked,
The dread of tyrants, and the sole resource
Of those that under grim oppression groan.
    Thy sons of glory many! Alfred thine,
In whom the splendour of heroic war,   1480
And more heroic peace, when governed well,
Combine; whose hallowed name the Virtues saint,
And his own Muses love; the best of kings!
With him thy Edwards and thy Henrys shine,
Names dear to fame; the first who deep impressed   1485

1465 *sheet*: sail (not what a sailor would call a sheet, cf. *Au.* 125).
1470 *listed plain*: ground enclosed for tilting, cf. Milton, *Samson Agonistes* 1087.
1472 *thoughtful sires*: Pelham's cabinet—which in 1744 favoured peace (though
  the war against France was not ended until 1748).

On haughty Gaul the terror of thy arms,
That awes her genius still. In statesmen thou,
And patriots, fertile. Thine a steady More,[n]
Who, with a generous though mistaken zeal,
Withstood a brutal tyrant's useful rage;   1490
Like Cato[n] firm, like Aristides[n] just,
Like rigid Cincinnatus[n] nobly poor—
A dauntless soul erect, who smiled on death.
Frugal and wise, a Walsingham is thine;
A Drake, who made thee mistress of the deep,   1495
And bore thy name in thunder round the world.
Then flamed thy spirit high. But who can speak
The numerous worthies of the maiden reign?
In Raleigh mark their every glory mixed—
Raleigh, the scourge of Spain! whose breast with all   1500
The sage, the patriot, and the hero burned.
Nor sunk his vigour when a coward reign
The warrior fettered, and at last resigned,
To glut the vengeance of a vanquished foe.
Then, active still and unrestrained, his mind   1505
Explored the vast extent of ages past,
And with his prison-hours enriched the world;
Yet found no times, in all the long research,
So glorious, or so base, as those he proved,
In which he conquered, and in which he bled.[n]   1510
Nor can the muse the gallant Sidney pass,
The plume of war! with early laurels crowned,
The lover's myrtle and the poet's bay.
A Hampden too is thine, illustrious land!
Wise, strenuous, firm, of unsubmitting soul,   1515
Who stemmed the torrent of a downward age
To slavery prone, and bade thee rise again,
In all thy native pomp of freedom bold.[n]

1488 *More*: Sir Thomas More (1478–1535); and see end-note.
1491 *Cato*: perhaps Cato the Censor; but see end-note.
1494 *Walsingham*: Sir Francis Walsingham (1536–90), diplomat and statesman.
1496 During his circumnavigation of the world, 1577–80, Sir Francis Drake
   captured or destroyed many Spanish ships.
1498 *maiden reign*: of Elizabeth I.
1502 *coward reign*: of James I.
1509 *proved*: experienced.
1511 *Sidney*: Sir Philip Sidney (1554–86), courtier, soldier, statesman, poet, and
   novelist.
1514 *Hampden*: John Hampden (1594–1643), Parliamentarian.

Bright at his call thy age of men effulged;
Of men on whom late time a kindling eye   1520
Shall turn, and tyrants tremble while they read.
Bring every sweetest flower, and let me strew
The grave where Russell lies, whose tempered blood,
With calmest cheerfulness for thee resigned,
Stained the sad annals of a giddy reign   1525
Aiming at lawless power, though meanly sunk
In loose inglorious luxury. With him
His friend, the British Cassius,[n] fearless bled;
Of high determined spirit, roughly brave,
By ancient learning to the enlightened love   1530
Of ancient freedom warmed. Fair thy renown
In awful sages and in noble bards;
Soon as the light of dawning Science spread
Her orient ray, and waked the Muses' song.
Thine is a Bacon,[n] hapless in his choice,   1535
Unfit to stand the civil storm of state,
And, through the smooth barbarity of courts,
With firm but pliant virtue forward still
To urge his course: him for the studious shade
Kind Nature formed, deep, comprehensive, clear,   1540
Exact, and elegant; in one rich soul,
Plato, the Stagyrite, and Tully joined.
The great deliverer he, who, from the gloom
Of cloistered monks and jargon-teaching schools,
Led forth the true Philosophy, there long   1545
Held in the magic chain of words and forms
And definitions void: he led her forth,
Daughter of Heaven! that, slow-ascending still,
Investigating sure the chain of things,
With radiant finger points to Heaven again.[n]   1550
The generous Ashley[n] thine, the friend of man,

1519 *effulged*: shone, cf. 'effulgence', *P.L.* III.388.
1520 *late time*: the distant future.
1523 *Russell*: William, Lord Russell (1639–83), executed for complicity in the
  Rye House Plot; greatly admired in life and death by the Whigs.
1525 *giddy reign*: of Charles II.
1528 *British Cassius*: 'Algernon Sidney' (T.); and see end-note.
1542 *the Stagyrite*: Aristotle, native of the ancient Macedonian city of Stagira.
1542 *Tully*: Cicero, cf. *Wi.* 521.
1551 *Ashley*: 'Anthony Ashley Cooper, Earl of Shaftesbury' (T.), and see end-
  note.

Who scanned his nature with a brother's eye,
His weakness prompt to shade, to raise his aim,
To touch the finer movements of the mind,
And with the moral beauty charm the heart.   1555
Why need I name thy Boyle, whose pious search,
Amid the dark recesses of his works,
The great Creator sought ? And why thy Locke,
Who made the whole internal world his own ?
Let Newton, pure intelligence, whom God   1560
To mortals lent to trace his boundless works
From laws sublimely simple, speak thy fame
In all philosophy.[n] For lofty sense,
Creative fancy, and inspection keen
Through the deep windings of the human heart,   1565
Is not wild Shakespeare[n] thine and Nature's boast ?
Is not each great, each amiable muse
Of classic ages in thy Milton met ?[n]
A genius universal as his theme,
Astonishing as chaos, as the bloom   1570
Of blowing Eden fair, as heaven sublime !
Nor shall my verse that elder bard forget,
The gentle Spenser, fancy's pleasing son;
Who, like a copious river, poured his song
O'er all the mazes of enchanted ground:[n]   1575
Nor thee, his ancient master, laughing sage,
Chaucer, whose native manners-painting verse,
Well moralized, shines through the Gothic cloud
Of time and language o'er thy genius thrown.
      May my song soften as thy daughters I,   1580
Britannia, hail ! for beauty is their own,
The feeling heart, simplicity of life,
And elegance, and taste; the faultless form,
Shaped by the hand of harmony; the cheek,
Where the live crimson, through the native white   1585
Soft-shooting, o'er the face diffuses bloom
And every nameless grace; the parted lip,
Like the red rosebud moist with morning dew,
Breathing delight; and, under flowing jet,

1556 *Boyle*: Hon. Robert Boyle (1627–91), chemist, physicist, and theologian,
   and a founder of the Royal Society.
1559 refers to Locke's *Essay concerning Human Understanding* (1690); cf. *Su.*
   1788–1805 end-notes.

Or sunny ringlets, or of circling brown,   1590
The neck slight-shaded and the swelling breast;
The look resistless, piercing to the soul,
And by the soul informed, when, dressed in love,
She sits high-smiling in the conscious eye.
    Island of bliss! amid the subject seas   1595
That thunder round thy rocky coasts, set up,
At once the wonder, terror, and delight,
Of distant nations, whose remotest shore
Can soon be shaken by thy naval arm;
Not to be shook thyself, but all assaults   1600
Baffling, like thy hoar cliffs the loud sea-wave.
    O Thou, by whose almighty nod the scale
Of empire rises, or alternate falls,
Send forth the saving Virtues round the land
In bright patrol—white Peace, and social Love;   1605
The tender-looking Charity, intent
On gentle deeds, and shedding tears through smiles;
Undaunted Truth, and Dignity of mind;
Courage, composed and keen; sound Temperance,
Healthful in heart and look; clear Chastity,   1610
With blushes reddening as she moves along,
Disordered at the deep regard she draws;
Rough Industry; Activity untired,
With copious life informed, and all awake:
While in the radiant front superior shines   1615
That first paternal virtue, Public Zeal,
Who throws o'er all an equal, wide survey,
And, ever musing on the common weal,
Still labours glorious with some great design.[n]
    Low walks the Sun, and broadens by degrees,   1620
Just o'er the verge of day. The shifting clouds
Assembled gay, a richly-gorgeous train,
In all their pomp attend his setting throne.
Air, earth, and ocean smile immense. And now,
As if his weary chariot sought the bowers   1625
Of Amphitritè and her tending nymphs,

1594 *She*: the soul.   1602 *Thou*: God.
1620 *broadens*: because its light, passing at a low angle through a broad belt of
atmosphere, is refracted. The personification is not very happily allied to the
science.
1626 *Amphitritè*: wife of Poseidon the sea-god; her bower is the sea and her
tending nymphs the Oceanids.

(So Grecian fable sung) he dips his orb;
Now half-immersed; and now, a golden curve,
Gives one bright glance, then total disappears.
    For ever running an enchanted round,   1630
Passes the day, deceitful, vain, and void;
As fleets the vision o'er the formful brain,
This moment hurrying wild the impassioned soul,
The next in nothing lost. 'Tis so to him,
The dreamer of this earth, an idle blank—   1635
A sight of horror to the cruel wretch,
Who, all day long in sordid pleasure rolled,
Himself an useless load, has squandered vile
Upon his scoundrel train what might have cheered
A drooping family of modest worth.   1640
But to the generous, still-improving mind
That gives the hopeless heart to sing for joy,
Diffusing kind beneficence around
Boastless as now descends the silent dew—
To him the long review of ordered life   1645
Is inward rapture only to be felt.[n]
    Confessed from yonder slow-extinguished clouds,
All ether softening, sober Evening takes
Her wonted station in the middle air,
A thousand shadows at her beck. First this   1650
She sends on earth; then that of deeper dye
Steals soft behind; and then a deeper still,
In circle following circle, gathers round
To close the face of things. A fresher gale
Begins to wave the wood and stir the stream,   1655
Sweeping with shadowy gust the fields of corn,
While the quail clamours for his running mate.
Wide o'er the thistly lawn, as swells the breeze,
A whitening shower of vegetable down
Amusive floats. The kind impartial care   1660
Of Nature naught disdains: thoughtful to feed
Her lowest sons, and clothe the coming year,
From field to field the feathered seeds she wings.
    His folded flock secure, the shepherd home
Hies, merry-hearted; and by turns relieves   1665

1647 *confessed*: disclosed.
1649 *middle air*: see *Su.* 768 fn.

The ruddy milk-maid of her brimming pail—
The beauty whom perhaps his witless heart,
Unknowing what the joy-mixed anguish means,
Sincerely loves, by that best language shown
Of cordial glances and obliging deeds.   1670
Onward they pass, o'er many a panting height
And valley sunk and unfrequented; where
At fall of eve the fairy people throng,
In various game and revelry to pass
The summer night, as village stories tell.   1675
But far about they wander from the grave
Of him whom his ungentle fortune urged
Against his own sad breast to lift the hand
Of impious violence. The lonely tower
It also shunned; whose mournful chambers hold,   1680
So night-struck fancy dreams, the yelling ghost.[n]
     Among the crooked lanes, on every hedge,
The glow-worm lights his gem; and, through the dark,
A moving radiance twinkles. Evening yields
The world to Night; not in her winter robe   1685
Of massy Stygian woof, but loose arrayed
In mantle dun. A faint erroneous ray,
Glanced from the imperfect surfaces of things,
Flings half an image on the straining eye;
While wavering woods, and villages, and streams,   1690
And rocks, and mountain-tops that long retained
The ascending gleam are all one swimming scene,
Uncertain if beheld. Sudden to heaven
Thence weary vision turns; where, leading soft
The silent hours of love, with purest ray   1695
Sweet Venus shines; and, from her genial rise,
When daylight sickens, till it springs afresh,
Unrivalled reigns, the fairest lamp of night.
As thus the effulgence tremulous I drink,
With cherished gaze, the lambent lightnings shoot   1700
Across the sky, or horizontal dart[n]
In wondrous shapes—by fearful murmuring crowds

1686 *Stygian*: black as the River Styx in Hades (the infernal regions of classical
     mythology).
1687 *erroneous*: wandering. 'This circle, by being placed here, stopped much of
     the erroneous light' (Newton, *Opticks* (1721), p. 91); cf. *P.L.* VII.20.
1700 *lambent lightnings*: comets.

Portentous deemed. Amid the radiant orbs
That more than deck, that animate the sky,
The life-infusing suns of other worlds,   1705
Lo! from the dread immensity of space
Returning with accelerated course,
The rushing comet to the sun descends;
And, as he sinks below the shading earth,
With awful train projected o'er the heavens,   1710
The guilty nations tremble. But, above
Those superstitious horrors that enslave
The fond sequacious herd, to mystic faith
And blind amazement prone, the enlightened few,
Whose godlike minds philosophy exalts,   1715
The glorious stranger hail. They feel a joy
Divinely great; they in their powers exult,
That wondrous force of thought, which mounting spurns
This dusky spot, and measures all the sky;
While, from his far excursion through the wilds   1720
Of barren ether, faithful to his time,
They see the blazing wonder rise anew,
In seeming terror clad, but kindly bent,
To work the will of all-sustaining love—
From his huge vapoury train perhaps to shake   1725
Reviving moisture on the numerous orbs
Through which his long ellipsis winds, perhaps
To lend new fuel to declining suns,
To light up worlds, and feed the eternal fire.[n]
    With thee, serene Philosophy, with thee,   1730
And thy bright garland, let me crown my song!
Effusive source of evidence and truth!
A lustre shedding o'er the ennobled mind,
Stronger than summer-noon, and pure as that
Whose mild vibrations soothe the parted soul,[n]   1735
New to the dawning of celestial day.
Hence through her nourished powers, enlarged by thee,
She springs aloft, with elevated pride,
Above the tangling mass of low desires,
That bind the fluttering crowd; and, angel-winged,   1740

1705 *worlds*: the planets of distant stars (referring to the theory of the plurality of
    worlds, cf. *Su.* 107 end-note).
1730 *Philosophy*: natural philosophy, i.e. science, which should tutor poetry, cf.
    Su. 1753.

The heights of science and of virtue gains,
Where all is calm and clear; with Nature round,
Or in the starry regions or the abyss,
To reason's and to fancy's eye displayed—
The first up-tracing, from the dreary void,   1745
The chain of causes and effects to Him,
The world-producing Essence, who alone
Possesses being; while the last receives
The whole magnificence of heaven and earth,
And every beauty, delicate or bold,   1750
Obvious or more remote, with livelier sense,
Diffusive painted on the rapid mind.[n]
   Tutored by thee, hence Poetry exalts
Her voice to ages; and informs the page
With music, image, sentiment, and thought,   1755
Never to die;[n] the treasure of mankind,
Their highest honour, and their truest joy!
   Without thee what were unenlightened man?
A savage, roaming through the woods and wilds
In quest of prey; and with the unfashioned fur   1760
Rough-clad; devoid of every finer art
And elegance of life. Nor happiness
Domestic, mixed of tenderness and care,
Nor moral excellence, nor social bliss,
Nor guardian law were his; nor various skill   1765
To turn the furrow, or to guide the tool
Mechanic; nor the heaven-conducted prow
Of Navigation bold, that fearless braves
The burning line or dares the wintry pole,
Mother severe of infinite delights!   1770
Nothing, save rapine, indolence, and guile,
And woes on woes, a still-revolving train!
Whose horrid circle had made human life
Than non-existence worse: but, taught by thee,
Ours are the plans of policy and peace;   1775
To live like brothers, and, conjunctive all,
Embellish life. While thus laborious crowds
Ply the tough oar, Philosophy directs
The ruling helm; or, like the liberal breath
Of potent heaven, invisible, the sail   1780

1747 *Essence*: God, cf. *Sp*. 557.   1754 *informs*: gives life to, cf. *Sp*. 860.

Swells out, and bears the inferior world along.[n]
  Nor to this evanescent speck of earth
Poorly confined; the radiant tracts on high
Are her exalted range; intent to gaze
Creation through; and, from that full complex   1785
Of never-ending wonders, to conceive
Of the Sole Being right, who spoke the word,
And Nature moved complete. With inward view,
Thence on the ideal kingdom swift she turns
Her eye; and instant, at her powerful glance,   1790
The obedient phantoms vanish or appear;
Compound, divide, and into order shift,
Each to his rank, from plain perception up
To the fair forms of fancy's fleeting train;
To reason then, deducing truth from truth,   1795
And notion quite abstract; where first begins
The world of spirits, action all, and life
Unfettered and unmixed. But here the cloud,
So wills Eternal Providence, sits deep.[n]
Enough for us to know that this dark state,   1800
In wayward passions lost and vain pursuits,
This infancy of being, cannot prove
The final issue of the works of God,
By boundless love and perfect wisdom formed,
And ever rising with the rising mind.[n]   1805

1789 *ideal kingdom*: the mind, with its ideas, i.e. objects of understanding; cf.
Locke, *Essay concerning Human Understanding* I.i.8.

W. Kent . inv et del .   N. Parr . Sculp .

Autumn

Autumn

THE ARGUMENT

The subject proposed. Addressed to Mr. Onslow. A prospect of the fields ready for harvest. Reflections in praise of industry raised by that view. Reaping. A tale relative to it. A harvest storm. Shooting and hunting; their barbarity. A ludicrous account of foxhunting. A view of an orchard. Wall fruit. A vineyard. A description of fogs, frequent in the latter part of Autumn; whence a digression, inquiring into the rise of fountains and rivers. Birds of season considered, that now shift their habitation. The prodigious number of them that cover the northern and western isles of Scotland. Hence a view of the country. A prospect of the discoloured, fading woods. After a gentle dusky day, moonlight. Autumnal meteors. Morning; to which succeeds a calm, pure sunshiny day, such as usually shuts up the season. The harvest being gathered in, the country dissolved in joy. The whole concludes with a panegyric on a philosophical country life.

CROWNED with the sickle and the wheaten sheaf
While Autumn nodding o'er the yellow plain
Comes jovial on,[n] the Doric reed[n] once more
Well-pleased I tune. Whate'er the Wintry frost
Nitrous prepared,[n] the various-blossomed Spring   5
Put in white promise forth, and Summer-suns
Concocted strong, rush boundless now to view,
Full, perfect all, and swell my glorious theme.
  Onslow! the Muse, ambitious of thy name
To grace, inspire, and dignify her song,   10
Would from the Public Voice thy gentle ear
A while engage. Thy noble cares she knows,
The patriot-virtues that distend thy thought,
Spread on thy front, and in thy bosom glow;
While listening senates hang upon thy tongue,   15
Devolving through the maze of eloquence
A roll of periods, sweeter than her song.

3 *Doric reed*: rustic pipe; and see end-note.
7 *concocted*: ripened, cf. *Su.* 909.
9 *Onslow*: Arthur Onslow (1691–1768), Speaker of the House of Commons, 1727–61.
12 *Public Voice*: Parliament.

But she too pants for public virtue; she,
Though weak of power, yet strong in ardent will,
Whene'er her country rushes on her heart,   20
Assumes a bolder note, and fondly tries
To mix the patriot's with the poet's flame.

When the bright Virgin gives the beauteous days,
And Libra weighs in equal scales the year,
From heaven's high cope the fierce effulgence shook   25
Of parting Summer, a serener blue,
With golden light enlivened, wide invests
The happy world. Attempered suns arise
Sweet-beamed, and shedding oft through lucid clouds
A pleasing calm; while broad and brown, below,   30
Extensive harvests hang the heavy head.
Rich, silent, deep they stand; for not a gale
Rolls its light billows o'er the bending plain;
A calm of plenty! till the ruffled air
Falls from its poise, and gives the breeze to blow.   35
Rent is the fleecy mantle of the sky;
The clouds fly different; and the sudden sun
By fits effulgent gilds the illumined field,
And black by fits the shadows sweep along—
A gaily chequered, heart-expanding view,   40
Far as the circling eye can shoot around,
Unbounded tossing in a flood of corn.
    These are thy blessings, Industry, rough power!
Whom labour still attends, and sweat, and pain;
Yet the kind source of every gentle art   45
And all the soft civility of life:
Raiser of human kind! by Nature cast
Naked and helpless out amid the woods
And wilds to rude inclement elements;
With various seeds of art[n] deep in the mind   50
Implanted, and profusely poured around
Materials infinite; but idle all,
Still unexerted, in the unconscious breast

18 *pants for public virtue*: desires to serve the state.
23 *Virgin*: Virgo, the sixth sign of the zodiac, into which the sun enters towards
the end of August.
24 *Libra*: the Scales, the seventh sign of the zodiac, into which the sun enters at
the autumnal equinox (22 or 23 Sept.)—hence 'equal scales', cf. Virgil, *Georgics*
I.208.

Slept the lethargic powers; Corruption still
Voracious swallowed what the liberal hand   55
Of Bounty scattered o'er the savage year.
And still the sad barbarian roving mixed
With beasts of prey; or for his acorn meal
Fought the fierce tusky boar—a shivering wretch!
Aghast and comfortless when the bleak north,   60
With winter charged, let the mixed tempest fly,
Hail, rain, and snow, and bitter-breathing frost.
Then to the shelter of the hut he fled,
And the wild season, sordid, pined away;
For home he had not: home is the resort   65
Of love, of joy, of peace and plenty, where,
Supporting and supported, polished friends
And dear relations mingle into bliss.
But this the rugged savage never felt,
Even desolate in crowds; and thus his days   70
Rolled heavy, dark, and unenjoyed along—
A waste of time! till Industry approached,
And roused him from his miserable sloth;
His faculties unfolded; pointed out
Where lavish Nature the directing hand   75
Of Art demanded; showed him how to raise
His feeble force by the mechanic powers,
To dig the mineral from the vaulted earth,
On what to turn the piercing rage of fire,
On what the torrent, and the gathered blast;   80
Gave the tall ancient forest to his axe;
Taught him to chip the wood, and hew the stone,
Till by degrees the finished fabric rose;
Tore from his limbs the blood-polluted fur,
And wrapped them in the woolly vestment warm,   85
Or bright in glossy silk, and flowing lawn;
With wholesome viands filled his table, poured
The generous glass around, inspired to wake
The life-refining soul of decent wit;
Nor stopped at barren bare necessity;   90
But, still advancing bolder, led him on
To pomp, to pleasure, elegance, and grace;
And, breathing high ambition through his soul,
Set science, wisdom, glory in his view,
And bade him be the lord of all below.   95

Then gathering men their natural powers combined,
And formed a public; to the general good
Submitting, aiming, and conducting all.
For this the patriot-council met, the full,
The free, and fairly represented whole;   100
For this they planned the holy guardian laws,
Distinguished orders, animated arts,
And, with joint force Oppression chaining, set
Imperial Justice at the helm, yet still
To them accountable: nor slavish dreamed   105
That toiling millions must resign their weal
And all the honey of their search to such
As for themselves alone themselves have raised.

   Hence every form of cultivated life
In order set, protected, and inspired   110
Into perfection wrought. Uniting all,
Society grew numerous, high, polite,
And happy. Nurse of art, the city reared
In beauteous pride her tower-encircled head;
And, stretching street on street, by thousands drew,   115
From twining woody haunts, or the tough yew
To bows strong-straining, her aspiring sons.

   Then Commerce brought into the public walk
The busy merchant; the big warehouse built;
Raised the strong crane; choked up the loaded street   120
With foreign plenty; and thy stream, O Thames,
Large, gentle, deep, majestic, king of floods!
Chose for his grand resort. On either hand,
Like a long wintry forest, groves of masts
Shot up their spires; the bellying sheet between   125
Possessed the breezy void; the sooty hulk
Steered sluggish on; the splendid barge along
Rowed regular to harmony; around,
The boat light-skimming stretched its oary wings;
While deep the various voice of fervent toil   130
From bank to bank increased; whence, ribbed with oak
To bear the British thunder, black, and bold,
The roaring vessel rushed into the main.[n]

   Then too the pillared dome magnific heaved

97 *public*: community or commonwealth.   125 *sheet*: sail, cf. *Su.* 1465.
134 *magnific*: magnificent, cf. *P.L.* X.354.

Its ample roof; and Luxury within   135
Poured out her glittering stores. The canvas smooth,
With glowing life protuberant, to the view
Embodied rose; the statue seemed to breathe
And soften into flesh beneath the touch
Of forming art, imagination-flushed.   140
    All is the gift of Industry,—whate'er
Exalts, embellishes, and renders life
Delightful. Pensive Winter, cheered by him,
Sits at the social fire, and happy hears
The excluded tempest idly rave along;   145
His hardened fingers deck the gaudy Spring;
Without him Summer were an arid waste;
Nor to the Autumnal months could thus transmit
Those full, mature, immeasurable stores
That, waving round, recall my wandering song.[n]   150
    Soon as the morning trembles o'er the sky,
And unperceived unfolds the spreading day,
Before the ripened field the reapers stand
In fair array, each by the lass he loves,
To bear the rougher part and mitigate   155
By nameless gentle offices her toil.
At once they stoop, and swell the lusty sheaves;
While through their cheerful band the rural talk,
The rural scandal, and the rural jest
Fly harmless, to deceive the tedious time   160
And steal unfelt the sultry hours away.
Behind the master walks, builds up the shocks,
And, conscious, glancing oft on every side
His sated eye, feels his heart heave with joy.
The gleaners spread around, and here and there,   165
Spike after spike, their sparing harvest pick.
Be not too narrow, husbandmen! but fling
From the full sheaf with charitable stealth
The liberal handful.[n] Think, oh! grateful think
How good the God of harvest is to you,   170
Who pours abundance o'er your flowing fields,
While these unhappy partners of your kind
Wide-hover round you, like the fowls of heaven,
And ask their humble dole. The various turns

---

157 *lusty*: full of vigorous growth.   166 *spike*: ear of grain, Lat. *spica*.

Of fortune ponder; that your sons may want   175
What now with hard reluctance faint ye give.

    The lovely young Lavinia once had friends;
And fortune smiled deceitful on her birth.
For, in her helpless years deprived of all,
Of every stay save innocence and Heaven,   180
She, with her widowed mother, feeble, old,
And poor, lived in a cottage far retired
Among the windings of a woody vale;
By solitude and deep surrounding shades,
But more by bashful modesty, concealed.   185
Together thus they shunned the cruel scorn
Which virtue, sunk to poverty, would meet
From giddy fashion and low-minded pride;
Almost on Nature's common bounty fed,
Like the gay birds that sung them to repose,   190
Content, and careless of to-morrow's fare.[n]
Her form was fresher than the morning-rose
When the dew wets its leaves; unstained and pure
As is the lily or the mountain-snow.
The modest virtues mingled in her eyes,   195
Still on the ground dejected, darting all
Their humid beams into the blooming flowers:
Or when the mournful tale her mother told,
Of what her faithless fortune promised once,
Thrilled in her thought, they, like the dewy star   200
Of evening, shone in tears. A native grace
Sat fair-proportioned on her polished limbs,
Veiled in a simple robe, their best attire,
Beyond the pomp of dress, for loveliness
Needs not the foreign aid of ornament,   205
But is when unadorned adorned the most.
Thoughtless of beauty, she was beauty's self,
Recluse amid the close-embowering woods.
As in the hollow breast of Apennine,
Beneath the shelter of encircling hills,   210
A myrtle rises, far from human eye,

176 *faint*: half-heartedly.
189 *Nature's common bounty*: nuts, berries, etc., growing on common or waste
    land.
196 *dejected*: thrown down, cf. *Su.* 1066.

And breathes its balmy fragrance o'er the wild—[n]
So flourished blooming, and unseen by all,
The sweet Lavinia; till at length, compelled
By strong necessity's supreme command,   215
With smiling patience in her looks she went
To glean Palemon's fields. The pride of swains
Palemon was, the generous and the rich,
Who led the rural life in all its joy
And elegance, such as Arcadian song   220
Transmits from ancient uncorrupted times,
When tyrant custom had not shackled man,
But free to follow Nature was the mode.[n]
He then, his fancy with autumnal scenes
Amusing, chanced beside his reaper-train   225
To walk, when poor Lavinia drew his eye;
Unconscious of her power, and turning quick
With unaffected blushes from his gaze—
He saw her charming, but he saw not half
The charms her downcast modesty concealed.   230
That very moment love and chaste desire
Sprung in his bosom, to himself unknown;
For still the world prevailed, and its dread laugh,
Which scarce the firm philosopher can scorn,
Should his heart own a gleaner in the field;   235
And thus in secret to his soul he sighed:
'What pity that so delicate a form,
By beauty kindled, where enlivening sense
And more than vulgar goodness seem to dwell,
Should be devoted to the rude embrace   240
Of some indecent clown! She looks, methinks,
Of old Acasto's line; and to my mind
Recalls that patron of my happy life,
From whom my liberal fortune took its rise,—
Now to the dust gone down, his houses, lands,   245
And once fair-spreading family dissolved.
'Tis said that in some lone, obscure retreat,
Urged by remembrance sad and decent pride,
Far from those scenes which knew their better days,
His aged widow and his daughter live;   250
Whom yet my fruitless search could never find.
Romantic wish, would this the daughter were!'
    When, strict inquiring, from herself he found

She was the same, the daughter of his friend,
Of bountiful Acasto, who can speak   255
The mingled passions that surprised his heart
And through his nerves in shivering transport ran?
Then blazed his smothered flame, avowed and bold
And, as he viewed her ardent o'er and o'er,
Love, gratitude, and pity wept at once.   260
Confused and frightened at his sudden tears,
Her rising beauties flushed a higher bloom,
As thus Palemon, passionate and just,
Poured out the pious rapture of his soul:
'And art thou then Acasto's dear remains?   265
She whom my restless gratitude has sought
So long in vain? O yes! the very same,
The softened image of my noble friend,
Alive his every feature, every look,
More elegantly touched. Sweeter than Spring!   270
Thou sole surviving blossom from the root
That nourished up my fortune! say, ah where,
In what sequestered desert, hast thou drawn
The kindest aspect of delighted Heaven?
Into such beauty spread, and blown so fair?   275
Though poverty's cold wind and crushing rain
Beat keen and heavy on thy tender years.
Oh, let me now into a richer soil
Transplant thee safe, where vernal suns and showers
Diffuse their warmest, largest influence;   280
And of my garden be the pride and joy!
It ill befits thee, oh, it ill befits
Acasto's daughter—his, whose open stores,
Though vast, were little to his ampler heart,
The father of a country—thus to pick   285
The very refuse of those harvest-fields
Which from his bounteous friendship I enjoy.
Then throw that shameful pittance from thy hand,
But ill applied to such a rugged task,
The fields, the master, all, my fair, are thine;   290
If, to the various blessings which thy house
Has on me lavished, thou wilt add that bliss,
That dearest bliss, the power of blessing thee!'
     Here ceased the youth: yet still his speaking eye
Expressed the sacred triumph of his soul,   295

With conscious virtue, gratitude, and love
Above the vulgar joy divinely raised.
Nor waited he reply. Won by the charm
Of goodness irresistible, and all
In sweet disorder lost, she blushed consent.   300
The news immediate to her mother brought,
While, pierced with anxious thought, she pined away
The lonely moments for Lavinia's fate;
Amazed, and scarce believing what she heard,
Joy seized her withered veins, and one bright gleam   305
Of setting life shone on her evening hours,—
Not less enraptured than the happy pair;
Who flourished long in tender bliss, and reared
A numerous offspring, lovely like themselves,
And good, the grace of all the country round.   310

   Defeating oft the labours of the year,
The sultry South collects a potent blast.
At first, the groves are scarcely seen to stir
Their trembling tops; and a still murmur runs
Along the soft-inclining fields of corn.   315
But, as the aerial tempest fuller swells,
And in one mighty stream, invisible,
Immense, the whole excited atmosphere
Impetuous rushes o'er the sounding world—
Strained to the root, the stooping forest pours   320
A rustling shower of yet untimely leaves.
High-beat, the circling mountains eddy in,
From the bare wild, the dissipated storm,
And send it in a torrent down the vale.
Exposed, and naked to its utmost rage,   325
Through all the sea of harvest^n rolling round,
The billowy plain floats wide; nor can evade,
Though pliant to the blast, its seizing force—
Or whirled in air or into vacant chaff
Shook waste. And sometimes too a burst of rain,   330
Swept from the black horizon, broad descends
In one continuous flood. Still over head
The mingling tempest weaves its gloom, and still
The deluge deepens; till the fields around
Lie sunk and flatted in the sordid wave.   335

322 *eddy in*: whirl round in eddies.

Sudden the ditches swell; the meadows swim.
Red from the hills innumerable streams
Tumultuous roar, and high above its banks
The river lift—before whose rushing tide
Herds, flocks, and harvests, cottages, and swains   340
Roll mingled down; all that the winds had spared
In one wild moment ruined, the big hopes
And well-earned treasures of the painful year.
Fled to some eminence, the husbandman
Helpless beholds the miserable wreck   345
Driving along; his drowning ox, at once .
Descending with his labours scattered round,
He sees; and instant o'er his shivering thought
Comes winter unprovided, and a train
Of clamant children dear. Ye masters, then   350
Be mindful of the rough laborious hand
That sinks you soft in elegance and ease;
Be mindful of those limbs in russet clad
Whose toil to yours is warmth and graceful pride;
And oh, be mindful of that sparing board   355
Which covers yours with luxury profuse,
Makes your glass sparkle, and your sense rejoice;
Nor cruelly demand what the deep rains
And all-involving winds have swept away!

  Here the rude clamour of the sportsman's joy,   360
The gun fast-thundering and the winded horn,
Would tempt the Muse to sing the rural game,—
How, in his mid career, the spaniel, struck
Stiff by the tainted gale, with open nose
Outstretched and finely sensible, draws full,   365
Fearful, and cautious on the latent prey;
As in the sun the circling covey bask
Their varied plumes, and, watchful every way,
Through the rough stubble turn the secret eye.
Caught in the meshy snare, in vain they beat   370
Their idle wings, entangled more and more:[n]
Nor, on the surges of the boundless air
Though borne triumphant, are they safe; the gun,

337 *Red*: muddy. T. may have in mind the red soil of the Cheviot region.
364 *tainted gale*: light breeze imbued with the scent of an animal; cf. Pope,
  Windsor Forest 101.
365 *draws*: inhales.   366 *prey*: partridge.

Glanced just, and sudden, from the fowler's eye,
O'ertakes their sounding pinions, and again 375
Immediate brings them from the towering wing
Dead to the ground;[n] or drives them wide-dispersed,
Wounded and wheeling various down the wind.
    These are not subjects for the peaceful Muse,
Nor will she stain with such her spotless song— 380
Then most delighted when she social sees
The whole mixed animal creation round
Alive and happy. 'Tis not joy to her,
This falsely cheerful barbarous game of death,
This rage of pleasure which the restless youth 385
Awakes, impatient, with the gleaming morn;
When beasts of prey retire that all night long,
Urged by necessity, had ranged the dark,
As if their conscious ravage shunned the light
Ashamed. Not so the steady tyrant, man, 390
Who, with the thoughtless insolence of power
Inflamed beyond the most infuriate wrath
Of the worst monster that e'er roamed the waste,
For sport alone pursues the cruel chase
Amid the beamings of the gentle days. 395
Upbraid, ye ravening tribes, our wanton rage,
For hunger kindles you, and lawless want;
But lavish fed, in Nature's bounty rolled,
To joy at anguish, and delight in blood,
Is what your horrid bosoms never knew. 400
    Poor is the triumph o'er the timid hare!
Scared from the corn, and now to some lone seat
Retired—the rushy fen, the ragged furze
Stretched o'er the stony heath, the stubble chapped,
The thistly lawn, the thick entangled broom, 405
Of the same friendly hue the withered fern,
The fallow ground laid open to the sun
Concoctive, and the nodding sandy bank
Hung o'er the mazes of the mountain brook.
Vain is her best precaution; though she sits 410

395 *gentle days*: days of calm weather—not during the gales described at *Au.*
311–59. 'Never take out your hounds on a very windy, or bad day' (Peter
Beckford, *Thoughts on Hunting* (1781), letter ix).
404 *chapped*: cut short.
408 *concoctive*: ripening by heat, cf. *Su.* 909, *Au.* 7.

Concealed with folded ears, unsleeping eyes
By Nature raised to take the horizon in,[n]
And head couched close betwixt her hairy feet
In act to spring away. The scented dew
Betrays her early labyrinth; and deep,   415
In scattered sullen openings, far behind,
With every breeze she hears the coming storm;
But, nearer and more frequent as it loads
The sighing gale, she springs amazed, and all
The savage soul of game is up at once—   420
The pack full-opening various, the shrill horn
Resounded from the hills, the neighing steed
Wild for the chase, and the loud hunter's shout—
O'er a weak, harmless, flying creature, all
Mixed in mad tumult and discordant joy.   425
    The stag, too, singled from the herd, where long
He ranged the branching monarch of the shades,
Before the tempest drives. At first, in speed
He sprightly puts his faith, and, roused by fear,
Gives all his swift aerial soul to flight.   430
Against the breeze he darts, that way the more
To leave the lessening murderous cry behind.
Deception short! though, fleeter than the winds
Blown o'er the keen-aired mountain by the North,
He bursts the thickets, glances through the glades,   435
And plunges deep into the wildest wood.
If slow, yet sure, adhesive to the track
Hot-steaming, up behind him come again
The inhuman rout, and from the shady depth
Expel him, circling through his every shift.   440
He sweeps the forest oft; and sobbing sees
The glades, mild opening to the golden day,
Where in kind contest with his butting friends
He wont to struggle, or his loves enjoy.
Oft in the full-descending flood he tries   445
To lose the scent, and lave his burning sides—
Oft seeks the herd; the watchful herd, alarmed,
With selfish care avoid a brother's woe.
What shall he do? His once so vivid nerves,

416 *sullen openings*: deep-toned barking of dogs, cf. *Sp.* 266.
427 *branching*: antlered.
440 *circling through*: sweeping in a circle to pick up the scent again.

So full of buoyant spirit, now no more 450
Inspire the course; but fainting, breathless toil
Sick seizes on his heart: he stands at bay,
And puts his last weak refuge in despair.
The big round tears run down his dappled face;
He groans in anguish; while the growling pack, 455
Blood-happy, hang at his fair jutting chest,
And mark his beauteous chequered sides with gore.
    Of this enough. But, if the sylvan youth,
Whose fervent blood boils into violence,
Must have the chase, behold, despising flight, 460
The roused up lion, resolute and slow,
Advancing full on the protended spear
And coward band that circling wheel aloof.
Slunk from the cavern and the troubled wood,
See the grim wolf; on him his shaggy foe 465
Vindictive fix, and let the ruffian die:
Or, growling horrid, as the brindled boar
Grins fell destruction, to the monster's heart
Let the dart lighten from the nervous arm.
    These Britain knows not; give, ye Britons, then 470
Your sportive fury pitiless to pour
Loose on the nightly robber of the fold.
Him, from his craggy winding haunts unearthed,
Let all the thunder of the chase pursue.
Throw the broad ditch behind you; o'er the hedge 475
High bound resistless; nor the deep morass
Refuse, but through the shaking wilderness
Pick your nice way; into the perilous flood
Bear fearless, of the raging instinct full;
And, as you ride the torrent, to the banks 480
Your triumph sound sonorous, running round
From rock to rock, in circling echo tossed;
Then scale the mountains to their woody tops;
Rush down the dangerous steep; and o'er the lawn,
In fancy swallowing up the space between, 485
Pour all your speed into the rapid game.

---

462 *protended*: held out in front, cf. Pope, *Iliad* XV.888.
465 *shaggy foe*: wolfhound. Wolves disappeared from Scotland in 1740 and
    from Ireland about 1770 (Harrison Matthews, *British Mammals* (1952), p. 219).
    In 1730 they were still hunted regularly in many parts of Europe, cf. *Wi* 389–413.
469 *lighten*: glance like lightning.   472 *nightly robber*: fox.

For happy he who tops the wheeling chase;
Has every maze evolved, and every guile
Disclosed; who knows the merits of the pack;
Who saw the villain seized, and dying hard   490
Without complaint, though by an hundred mouths
Relentless torn:ⁿ O glorious he beyond
His daring peers, when the retreating horn
Calls them to ghostly halls of grey renown,
With woodland honours graced—the fox's fur   495
Depending decent from the roof, and spread
Round the drear walls, with antique figures fierce,
The stag's large front: he then is loudest heard
When the night staggers with severer toils,
With feats Thessalian Centaurs never knew,   500
And their repeated wonders shake the dome.
      But first the fuelled chimney blazes wide;
The tankards foam; and the strong table groans
Beneath the smoking sirloin, stretched immense
From side to side, in which with desperate knife   505
They deep incision make, and talk the while
Of England's glory, ne'er to be defaced
While hence they borrow vigour; or, amain
Into the pasty plunged, at intervals,
If stomach keen can intervals allow,   510
Relating all the glories of the chase.
Then sated Hunger bids his brother Thirst
Produce the mighty bowl: the mighty bowl,
Swelled high with fiery juice, steams liberal round
A potent gale, delicious as the breath   515
Of Maia to the love-sick shepherdess
On violets diffused, while soft she hears
Her panting shepherd stealing to her arms.
Nor wanting is the brown October,ⁿ drawn
Mature and perfect from his dark retreat   520

488 *evolved*: unrolled or made clear.
494 *ghostly halls of grey renown*: old-fashioned houses.
496 *decent*: fittingly (like 'graced' the word is used ironically).
497 *figures*: portraits.
500 *Thessalian Centaurs*: fabulous creatures combining the body and legs of a
    horse with the torso, head and arms of a man. Their legendary battle with the
    Lapithae occurred at a banquet after heavy drinking. Thessaly is the part of
    N.E. Greece south of Macedonia.
516 *Maia*: Roman goddess of May, the growing month.
517 *diffused*: stretched out, cf. *Su*. 707.

Of thirty years; and now his honest front
Flames in the light refulgent, not afraid
Even with the vineyard's best produce to vie.
To cheat the thirsty moments, Whist a while
Walks his grave round[n] beneath a cloud of smoke,   525
Wreathed fragrant from the pipe; or the quick dice,
In thunder leaping from the box, awake
The sounding gammon; while romp-loving miss
Is hauled about in gallantry robust.
   At last these puling idlenesses laid   530
Aside, frequent and full, the dry divan[n]
Close in firm circle; and set ardent in
For serious drinking. Nor evasion sly
Nor sober shift is to the puking wretch
Indulged apart; but earnest brimming bowls   535
Lave every soul, the table floating round,
And pavement faithless to the fuddled foot.
Thus as they swim in mutual swill, the talk,
Vociferous at once from twenty tongues,
Reels fast from theme to theme—from horses, hounds,   540
To church or mistress, politics or ghost—
In endless mazes, intricate, perplexed.
Meantime, with sudden interruption, loud
The impatient catch bursts from the joyous heart.
That moment touched is each congenial soul;   545
And, opening in a full-mouthed cry of joy,
The laugh, the slap, the jocund curse goes round;
While, from their slumbers shook, the kennelled hounds
Mix in the music of the day again.
As when the tempest, that has vexed the deep   550
The dark night long, with fainter murmurs falls;
So gradual sinks their mirth. Their feeble tongues,
Unable to take up the cumbrous word,
Lie quite dissolved. Before their maudlin eyes,
Seen dim and blue, the double tapers dance,[n]   555
Like the sun wading through the misty sky.
Then, sliding soft, they drop. Confused above,
Glasses and bottles, pipes and gazetteers,
As if the table even itself was drunk,
Lie a wet broken scene: and wide, below,   560

521 *front*: forehead (as usual in T.), cf. *Su.* 490; the ale is personified.
528 *gammon*: the game of backgammon.   558 *gazetteers*: newspapers.

Is heaped the social slaughter—where astride
The Lubber Power[n] in filthy triumph sits,
Slumbrous, inclining still from side to side,
And steeps them drenched in potent sleep till morn.
Perhaps some doctor of tremendous paunch,   565
Awful and deep, a black abyss of drink,
Outlives them all; and, from his buried flock
Retiring, full of rumination sad,
Laments the weakness of these latter times.
        But if the rougher sex by this fierce sport   570
Is hurried wild, let not such horrid joy
E'er stain the bosom of the British fair.
Far be the spirit of the chase from them!
Uncomely courage, unbeseeming skill,
To spring the fence, to rein the prancing steed,   575
The cap, the whip, the masculine attire
In which they roughen to the sense and all
The winning softness of their sex is lost.
In them 'tis graceful to dissolve at woe;
With every motion, every word, to wave   580
Quick o'er the kindling cheek the ready blush;
And from the smallest violence to shrink
Unequal, then the loveliest in their fears;
And, by this silent adulation soft,
To their protection more engaging man.   585
O may their eyes no miserable sight,
Save weeping lovers, see! a nobler game,
Through love's enchanting wiles pursued, yet fled,
In chase ambiguous. May their tender limbs
Float in the loose simplicity of dress![n]   590
And, fashioned all to harmony, alone
Know they to seize the captivated soul,
In rapture warbled from love-breathing lips;
To teach the lute to languish; with smooth step,
Disclosing motion in its every charm,   595
To swim along and swell the mazy dance;
To train the foliage o'er the snowy lawn;
To guide the pencil, turn the tuneful page;

566 *black*: i.e. the colour of the clergyman's dress.
595: disclosing charm in every motion.
597: to embroider, cf. Cowper, *Task* IV.150–3.
598 *tuneful page*: music score.

To lend new flavour to the fruitful year,
And heighten nature's dainties; in their race   600
To rear their graces into second life;
To give society its highest taste;
Well-ordered home man's best delight to make;
And, by submissive wisdom, modest skill,
With every gentle care-eluding art,   605
To raise the virtues, animate the bliss,
Even charm the pains to something more than joy,
And sweeten all the toils of human life:
This be the female dignity and praise.[n]

Ye swains, now hasten to the hazel-bank,   610
Where down yon dale the wildly-winding brook
Falls hoarse from steep to steep. In close array,
Fit for the thickets and the tangling shrub,
Ye virgins, come. For you their latest song
The woodlands raise; the clustering nuts for you   615
The lover finds amid the secret shade;
And, where they burnish on the topmost bough,
With active vigour crushes down the tree;
Or shakes them ripe from the resigning husk,
A glossy shower and of an ardent brown   620
As are the ringlets of Melinda's hair—
Melinda! formed with every grace complete,
Yet these neglecting, above beauty wise,
And far transcending such a vulgar praise.

Hence from the busy joy-resounding fields,   625
In cheerful error let us tread the maze
Of Autumn unconfined; and taste, revived,
The breath of orchard[n] big with bending fruit.
Obedient to the breeze and beating ray,
From the deep-loaded bough a mellow shower   630
Incessant melts away. The juicy pear
Lies in a soft profusion scattered round.

599 *To lend . . . dainties*: preserve fruit and make jams.
601 *in their race . . . second life*: educate their daughters.
612 *close array*: close-fitting dress.
620 *ardent*: shining, cf. *Au.* 691.
621 *Melinda*: identity unknown. In Sept. 1729 T. wrote affectionately of some unnamed woman, a neighbour of David Mallet's at Shawford near Winchester; see *Letters and Documents*, pp. 65–6.
626 *error*: wandering, cf. *P.L.* IV.239.

A various sweetness swells the gentle race,
By Nature's all-refining hand prepared,
Of tempered sun, and water, earth, and air,   635
In ever-changing composition mixed.
Such, falling frequent through the chiller night,
The fragrant stores, the wide-projected heaps
Of apples, which the lusty-handed year
Innumerous o'er the blushing orchard shakes.   640
A various spirit, fresh, delicious, keen,
Dwells in their gelid pores, and active points
The piercing cider for the thirsty tongue—
Thy native theme, and boon inspirer too,
Phillips, Pomona's bard! the second thou   645
Who nobly durst in rhyme-unfettered verse
With British freedom sing the British song—
How from Silurian vats high-sparkling wines
Foam in transparent floods, some strong to cheer
The wintry revels of the labouring hind,   650
And tasteful some to cool the summer hours.[n]

In this glad season, while his sweetest beams
The Sun sheds equal o'er the meekened day,
Oh, lose me in the green delightful walks
Of, Dodington,[n] thy seat, serene and plain;   655
Where simple Nature reigns; and every view
Diffusive spreads the pure Dorsetian downs
In boundless prospect—yonder shagged with wood,
Here rich with harvest, and there white with flocks!
Meantime the grandeur of thy lofty dome   660
Far-splendid seizes on the ravished eye.
New beauties rise with each revolving day;
New columns swell; and still the fresh Spring finds
New plants to quicken, and new groves to green.
Full of thy genius all, the Muses' seat!   665
Where, in the secret bower and winding walk,
For virtuous Young[n] and thee they twine the bay.
Here wandering oft, fired with the restless thirst

645 *Pomona*: see *Su.* 663 fn.
648 *Silurian*: Herefordshire; referring to the Silures, a British tribe who lived west
   of the River Severn in Roman Britain.
653 *equal*: moderately; cf. *Au.* 24 fn.
660 *dome*: house (Eastbury had no 'dome' in the modern sense); cf. *Sp.* 650, *Au.*
   1182, and Johnson, *London*, 203, *Vanity of Human Wishes*, 139.

Of thy applause, I solitary court
The inspiring breeze, and meditate the book   670
Of Nature, ever open, aiming thence
Warm from the heart to learn the moral song.[n]
And, as I steal along the sunny wall,
Where Autumn basks, with fruit empurpled deep,
My pleasing theme continual prompts my thought—   675
Presents the downy peach, the shining plum
With a fine bluish mist of animals
Clouded, the ruddy nectarine, and dark
Beneath his ample leaf the luscious fig.
The vine too here her curling tendrils shoots,   680
Hangs out her clusters glowing to the south,
And scarcely wishes for a warmer sky.[n]

Turn we a moment fancy's rapid flight
To vigorous soils and climes of fair extent,
Where, by the potent sun elated high,   685
The vineyard swells refulgent on the day,
Spreads o'er the vale, or up the mountain climbs
Profuse, and drinks amid the sunny rocks,
From cliff to cliff increased, the heightened blaze.
Low bend the weighty boughs. The clusters clear,   690
Half through the foliage seen, or ardent flame
Or shine transparent; while perfection breathes
White o'er the turgent film the living dew.
As thus they brighten with exalted juice,
Touched into flavour by the mingling ray,[n]   695
The rural youth and virgins o'er the field,
Each fond for each to cull the autumnal prime,
Exulting rove, and speak the vintage nigh.
Then comes the crushing swain; the country floats,
And foams unbounded with the mashy flood,   700
That, by degrees fermented, and refined,
Round the raised nations pours the cup of joy—
The claret smooth, red as the lip we press
In sparkling fancy while we drain the bowl,
The mellow-tasted burgundy, and, quick   705
As is the wit it gives, the gay champagne.

670 *meditate*: (trans.), cf. *Su.* 1248.   674 *empurpled*: see *Sp.* 110 fn.
691 *ardent*: shining, cf. *Au.* 620.   693 *turgent film*: swelling skin.
693 *living dew*: bloom.   702 *raised*: excited.

Now, by the cool declining year condensed,
Descend the copious exhalations, checked
As up the middle sky unseen they stole,
And roll the doubling fogs around the hill.[n]   710
No more the mountain, horrid, vast, sublime,[n]
Who pours a sweep of rivers from his sides,
And high between contending kingdoms rears
The rocky long division, fills the view
With great variety; but in a night   715
Of gathering vapour, from the baffled sense
Sinks dark and dreary. Thence expanding far,
The huge dusk gradual swallows up the plain:
Vanish the woods: the dim-seen river seems,
Sullen and slow, to roll the misty wave.   720
Even in the height of noon oppressed, the sun
Sheds, weak and blunt, his wide-refracted ray;
Whence glaring oft, with many a broadened orb,
He frights the nations. Indistinct on earth,
Seen through the turbid air, beyond the life   725
Objects appear, and, wildered, o'er the waste
The shepherd stalks gigantic;[n] till at last,
Wreathed dun around, in deeper circles still
Successive closing, sits the general fog
Unbounded o'er the world, and, mingling thick,   730
A formless grey confusion covers all.
As when of old (so sung the Hebrew bard)
Light, uncollected, through the Chaos urged
Its infant way, nor order yet had drawn
His lovely train from out the dubious gloom.   735
     These roving mists, that constant now begin
To smoke along the hilly country, these,
With weighty rains and melted Alpine snows,
The mountain-cisterns fill—those ample stores
Of water, scooped among the hollow rocks,   740
Whence gush the streams, the ceaseless fountains play,

708 *exhalations*: evaporations, cf. Virgil, *Georgics* II.217.
709 *middle sky*: see *Su.* 768 fn.
726 *wildered*: straying.
732 *Hebrew bard*: Moses, who was inspired on mountain tops (cf. Exod. 3, 19,
   P.L. I.6–10). T. implies that such divine inspiration was somehow linked with
   his experience of light and mist among mountains.
733 *uncollected*: i.e. by the sun. Light was created on the first day, the sun on the
   fourth; cf. Gen. 1:1–19.

And their unfailing wealth the rivers draw.
Some sages say, that, where the numerous wave
For ever lashes the resounding shore,
Drilled through the sandy stratum, every way,   745
The waters with the sandy stratum rise;
Amid whose angles infinitely strained,
They joyful leave their jaggy salts behind,
And clear and sweeten as they soak along.
Nor stops the restless fluid, mounting still,   750
Though oft amidst the irriguous vale it springs;
But, to the mountain courted by the sand,
That leads it darkling on in faithful maze,
Far from the parent main, it boils again
Fresh into day, and all the glittering hill   755
Is bright with spouting rills. But hence this vain
Amusive dream! why should the waters love
To take so far a journey to the hills,
When the sweet valleys offer to their toil
Inviting quiet and a nearer bed?   760
Or if, by blind ambition led astray,
They must aspire, why should they sudden stop
Among the broken mountain's rushy dells.
And, ere they gain its highest peak, desert
The attractive sand that charmed their course so long?   765
Besides, the hard agglomerating salts,
The spoil of ages, would impervious choke
Their secret channels, or by slow degrees,
High as the hills, protrude the swelling vales:
Old ocean too, sucked through the porous globe,   770
Had long ere now forsook his horrid bed,
And brought Deucalion's watery times again.
   Say, then, where lurk the vast eternal springs
That, like creating Nature, lie concealed
From mortal eye, yet with their lavish stores   775
Refresh the globe and all its joyous tribes?
O thou pervading genius, given to man
To trace the secrets of the dark abyss!
Oh! lay the mountains bare, and wide display
Their hidden structure to the astonished view;   780

772 *Deucalion*: in Greek mythology a Titan who, like Noah, built a boat and saved himself and his wife from a flood sent by Zeus to destroy the whole race of sinful men; cf. Ovid, *Metamorphoses* I.262–347.

Strip from the branching Alps their piny load,
The huge incumbrance of horrific woods
From Asian Taurus, from Imaus stretched
Athwart the roving Tartar's sullen bounds;
Give opening Haemus to my searching eye,   785
And high Olympus pouring many a stream!
Oh, from the sounding summits of the north,
The Dofrine Hills, through Scandinavia rolled
To farthest Lapland and the frozen main;
From lofty Caucasus, far seen by those   790
Who in the Caspian and black Euxine toil;
From cold Riphaean rocks, which the wild Russ
Believes the stony girdle of the world;
And all the dreadful mountains wrapped in storm
Whence wide Siberia draws her lonely floods;   795
Oh, sweep the eternal snows! Hung o'er the deep,
That ever works beneath his sounding base,
Bid Atlas, propping heaven, as poets feign,
His subterranean wonders spread! Unveil
The miny caverns, blazing on the day,   800
Of Abyssinia's cloud-compelling cliffs,
And of the bending Mountains of the Moon![n]
O'ertopping all these giant-sons of earth,
Let the dire Andes, from the radiant line

783 *Taurus*: mountains running from S.W. Asia Minor to Armenia.
783 *Imaus*: a mountain range of central Asia mentioned by classical geographers
   and perhaps to be located in the Hindu Kush; cf. *P.L.* III.431–2.
784 *sullen*: dismal, cf. Pope, *Rape of the Lock* IV.19.
785 *Haemus*: see *Au.* 1318 fn.
786 *Olympus*: 'The mountain called by that name in the lesser Asia [i.e. Asia
   Minor].' (T.)
788 *Dofrine Hills*: the Dovrefjell on the borders of Norway and Sweden.
790 *Caucasus*: mountains of the Caucasus provided landmarks for sailors on the
   Caspian and the Black (or Euxine) Seas.
793 *stony girdle of the world*: 'The Moscovites call the Riphean mountains Weliki
   Camenypoys, that is, the great stony girdle; because they suppose them to
   encompass the whole Earth.' (T.) Ancient geographers located the Riphaean
   mountains in northernmost Scythia, i.e. modern Siberia; cf. Virgil, *Georgics*
   I.240.
798 *Atlas*: mountains in N. Africa; cf. Herodotus, *History* IV.184, for the identi-
   fication of these mountains with the Titan who was condemned by Zeus to
   bear heaven on his head and hands.
800 *miny*: subterranean.
801 *compelling*: driving or forcing together, Lat. *compellere* (cloud-compelling is
   a Homeric epithet for Zeus).
804 *dire*: because subject to earthquakes.   804 *line*: Equator.

Stretched to the stormy seas that thunder round   805
The Southern Pole, their hideous deeps unfold!
Amazing scene! Behold! the glooms disclose!
I see the rivers in their infant beds!
Deep, deep I hear them labouring to get free!
I see the leaning strata, artful ranged;   810
The gaping fissures, to receive the rains,
The melting snows, and ever-dripping fogs.
Strowed bibulous above I see the sands,
The pebbly gravel next, the layers then
Of mingled moulds, of more retentive earths,   815
The guttered rocks and mazy-running clefts,
That, while the stealing moisture they transmit,
Retard its motion, and forbid its waste.
Beneath the incessant weeping of these drains,
I see the rocky siphons stretched immense,   820
The mighty reservoirs, of hardened chalk
Or stiff compacted clay capacious formed:
O'erflowing thence, the congregated stores,
The crystal treasures of the liquid world,
Through the stirred sands a bubbling passage burst,   825
And, welling out around the middle steep
Or from the bottoms of the bosomed hills
In pure effusion flow. United thus,
The exhaling sun, the vapour-burdened air,
The gelid mountains, that to rain condensed   830
These vapours in continual current draw,
And send them o'er the fair-divided earth
In bounteous rivers to the deep again,
A social commerce hold, and firm support
The full-adjusted harmony of things.[n]   835

When Autumn scatters his departing gleams,
Warned of approaching Winter, gathered, play
The swallow-people; and, tossed wide around,
O'er the calm sky in convolution swift
The feathered eddy floats, rejoicing once   840
Ere to their wintry slumbers they retire,
In clusters clung beneath the mouldering bank,

816 *guttered*: worn into channels by the action of water.
832 *fair-divided*: (by rivers).
838 *swallow-people*: swallows, swifts, martins.

And where, unpierced by frost, the cavern sweats:
Or rather, into warmer climes conveyed,
With other kindred birds of season, there   845
They twitter cheerful, till the vernal months
Invite them welcome back—for thronging now
Innumerous wings are in commotion all.[n]
    Where the Rhine loses his majestic force
In Belgian plains, won from the raging deep   850
By diligence amazing and the strong
Unconquerable hand of liberty,[n]
The stork-assembly meets, for many a day
Consulting deep and various ere they take
Their arduous voyage through the liquid sky.   855
And now, their route designed, their leaders chose,
Their tribes adjusted, cleaned their vigorous wings,
And many a circle, many a short essay,
Wheeled round and round, in congregation full
The figured flight ascends, and, riding high   860
The aerial billows, mixes with the clouds.[n]
    Or, where the Northern Ocean in vast whirls
Boils round the naked melancholy isles
Of farthest Thulè, and the Atlantic surge
Pours in among the stormy Hebrides,   865
Who can recount what transmigrations there
Are annual made ? what nations come and go ?
And how the living clouds on clouds arise,
Infinite wings ! till all the plume-dark air
And rude resounding shore are one wild cry ?   870
    Here the plain harmless native his small flock
And herd diminutive of many hues
Tends on the little island's verdant swell
The shepherd's sea-girt reign; or, to the rocks
Dire-clinging, gathers his ovarious food;[n]   875
Or sweeps the fishy shore; or treasures up
The plumage, rising full, to form the bed
Of luxury. And here a while the muse,
High hovering o'er the broad cerulean scene,
Sees Caledonia in romantic view—[n]   880

855 *liquid*: clear, cf. Pope, *Windsor Forest* 186.
860 *figured*: in (wedge) formation.   864 *Thulè*: see *Su*. 1168 fn.
867 *nations*: of birds.   877 *plumage*: eider-down.
880 *Caledonia*: Roman name for North Britain, i.e. Scotland.

Her airy mountains from the waving main
Invested with a keen diffusive sky,
Breathing the soul acute; her forests huge,
Incult, robust, and tall, by Nature's hand
Planted of old; her azure lakes between,   885
Poured out extensive, and of watery wealth
Full; winding deep and green, her fertile vales,
With many a cool translucent brimming flood
Washed lovely, from the Tweed (pure parent-stream,
Whose pastoral banks first heard my Doric reed,   890
With, silvan Jed, thy tributary brook)[n]
To where the north-inflated tempest foams
O'er Orca's or Betubium's highest peak—
Nurse of a people, in misfortune's school
Trained up to hardy deeds, soon visited   895
By Learning, when before the Gothic rage
She took her western flight; a manly race
Of unsubmitting spirit, wise, and brave,
Who still through bleeding ages struggled hard
(As well unhappy Wallace can attest,   900
Great patriot-hero! ill requited chief!)
To hold a generous undiminished state,
Too much in vain! Hence, of unequal bounds
Impatient, and by tempting glory borne
O'er every land, for every land their life   905
Has flowed profuse, their piercing genius planned,

---

882 *diffusive*: spreading widely (cf. *Su.* 851, 1752, *Wi.* 681) or, perhaps, shedding rain (drawn from the 'waving main', *Au.* 881).

883 *Breathing the soul acute*: manifesting the keen spirit of its people.

884 *Incult*: not planted or cultivated by man.

886 *watery wealth*: fish. On periphrases see *Sp.* 132 end-note.

890 *Doric reed*: see *Au.* 3 end-note.

893 *Orca, Betubium*: two of the northernmost promontories of the Scottish mainland were named Orcas and Berubium by the ancient geographer Ptolemy, and identified in Camden's *Britannia* (trans. Gibson, 1720) as Howburn and Urdehead.

896 *Learning*: Columba, Aidan, Cuthbert and other evangelists of the sixth and seventh centuries.

896 *Gothic rage*: barbarian invasions of the fifth century—particularly the sack of Rome in 410.

900 *Wallace*: Sir William Wallace, the Scottish statesman and general who successfully resisted Edward I's attempts to subdue Scotland, but was betrayed and hanged, drawn, and quartered in 1305.

903 *unequal bounds*: unjustly narrow territorial boundaries. Scotland had for ages supplied the world with large numbers of emigrants and mercenary soldiers, and would long continue to do this.

And swelled the pomp of peace their faithful toil:
As from their own clear north in radiant streams
Bright over Europe bursts the boreal morn.
    Oh! is there not some patriot in whose power   910
That best, that godlike luxury is placed,
Of blessing thousands, thousands yet unborn,
Through late posterity? some, large of soul,
To cheer dejected Industry, to give
A double harvest to the pining swain,   915
And teach the labouring hand the sweets of toil?
How, by the finest art, the native robe
To weave; how, white as Hyperborean snow,
To form the lucid lawn; with venturous oar
How to dash wide the billow; nor look on,   920
Shamefully passive, while Batavian fleets
Defraud us of the glittering finny swarms
That heave our friths and crowd upon our shores;
How all-enlivening trade to rouse, and wing
The prosperous sail from every growing port,   925
Uninjured, round the sea-encircled globe;
And thus, in soul united as in name,
Bid Britain reign the mistress of the deep?[n]
    Yes, there are such. And full on thee, Argyll,[n]
Her hope, her stay, her darling, and her boast,   930
From her first patriots and her heroes sprung,
Thy fond imploring country turns her eye;
In thee, with all a mother's triumph, sees
Her every virtue, every grace combined,
Her genius, wisdom, her engaging turn,   935
Her pride of honour, and her courage tried,
Calm and intrepid, in the very throat
Of sulphurous war, on Tenier's dreadful field.

909 *boreal morn*: aurora borealis, cf. *Au.* 1108–37.
913 *late*: distant, cf. *Su.* 1520.
918 *Hyperborean*: of the far north, cf. Virgil, *Georgics* IV.517; according to ancient geographers the Hyperboreans lived north of the Riphaean mountains, cf. *Au.* 792.
921 *Batavian*: Dutch; the Batavi were an ancient people living in part of what is now Holland.
922 *finny swarms*: fish. On periphrases see *Sp.* 132 end-note.
927 *soul*: national spirit.
938 *Tenier*: Taisniere, the name of a wood near Malplaquet in Flanders where the Duke of Argyll commanded the right wing in the battle of 11 Sept. 1709 and fought with great courage.

Nor less the palm of peace enwreathes thy brow:
For, powerful as thy sword, from thy rich tongue   940
Persuasion flows, and wins the high debate;
While mixed in thee combine the charm of youth,
The force of manhood, and the depth of age.
Thee, Forbes,[n] too, whom every worth attends,
As truth sincere, as weeping friendship kind,   945
Thee, truly generous, and in silence great,
Thy country feels through her reviving arts,
Planned by thy wisdom, by thy soul informed;
And seldom has she felt a friend like thee.[n]

But see the fading many-coloured woods,   950
Shade deepening over shade, the country round
Imbrown; a crowded umbrage, dusk and dun,
Of every hue from wan declining green
To sooty dark. These now the lonesome muse,
Low-whispering, lead into their leaf-strown walks,   955
And give the season in its latest view.
    Meantime, light shadowing all, a sober calm
Fleeces unbounded ether; whose least wave
Stands tremulous, uncertain where to turn
The gentle current; while, illumined wide,   960
The dewy-skirted clouds imbibe the sun,
And through their lucid veil his softened force
Shed o'er the peaceful world.[n] Then is the time
For those whom Wisdom and whom Nature charm
To steal themselves from the degenerate crowd,   965
And soar above this little scene of things—
To tread low-thoughted Vice beneath their feet,
To soothe the throbbing passions into peace,
And woo lone Quiet in her silent walks.
    Thus solitary, and in pensive guise,   970
Oft let me wander o'er the russet mead,
And through the saddened grove, where scarce is heard
One dying strain to cheer the woodman's toil.
Haply some widowed songster pours his plaint
Far in faint warblings through the tawny copse;[n]   975
While congregated thrushes, linnets, larks,
And each wild throat whose artless strains so late

---

952 *Imbrown*: make dark, cf. *P.L.* IV.246.
952 *dusk*: dusky, cf. *P.L.* XI.741.   957 *light*: lightly.

Swelled all the music of the swarming shades,
Robbed of their tuneful souls, now shivering sit
On the dead tree, a dull despondent flock,   980
With not a brightness waving o'er their plumes,
And naught save chattering discord in their note.
Oh, let not, aimed from some inhuman eye,
The gun the music of the coming year
Destroy, and harmless, unsuspecting harm,   985
Lay the weak tribes, a miserable prey !
In mingled murder fluttering on the ground !
    The pale descending year, yet pleasing still,
A gentler mood inspires; for now the leaf
Incessant rustles from the mournful grove,   990
Oft startling such as studious walk below,
And slowly circles through the waving air.
But, should a quicker breeze amid the boughs
Sob, o'er the sky the leafy deluge streams;
Till, choked and matted with the dreary shower,   995
The forest-walks, at every rising gale,
Roll wide the withered waste, and whistle bleak.
Fled is the blasted verdure of the fields;.
And, shrunk into their beds, the flowery race
Their sunny robes resign. Even what remained   1000
Of bolder fruits falls from the naked tree;
And—woods, fields, gardens, orchards all around—
The desolated prospect thrills the soul.
    He comes ! he comes ! in every breeze the Power
Of Philosophic Melancholy[n] comes !   1005
His near approach the sudden-starting tear,
The glowing cheek, the mild dejected air,
The softened feature, and the beating heart,
Pierced deep with many a virtuous pang, declare.
O'er all the soul his sacred influence breathes;   1010
Inflames imagination; through the breast
Infuses every tenderness; and far
Beyond dim earth exalts the swelling thought.
Ten thousand thousand fleet ideas, such
As never mingled with the vulgar dream,   1015
Crowd fast into the mind's creative eye.
As fast the correspondent passions rise,
As varied, and as high—devotion raised
To rapture, and divine astonishment;

The love of nature unconfined, and, chief,   1020
Of human race; the large ambitious wish
To make them blest; the sigh for suffering worth
Lost in obscurity; the noble scorn
Of tyrant pride; the fearless great resolve;
The wonder which the dying patriot draws,   1025
Inspiring glory through remotest time;
The awakened throb for virtue and for fame;
The sympathies of love and friendship dear,
With all the social offspring of the heart.[n]

   Oh! bear me then to vast embowering shades,   1030
To twilight groves, and visionary vales,
To weeping grottoes, and prophetic glooms;
Where angel forms athwart the solemn dusk,
Tremendous, sweep, or seem to sweep along;
And voices more than human, through the void   1035
Deep-sounding, seize the enthusiastic ear.[n]

   Or is this gloom too much? Then lead, ye Powers
That o'er the garden and the rural seat
Preside, which, shining through the cheerful land
In countless numbers, blest Britannia sees—[n]   1040
Oh! lead me to the wide extended walks,
The fair majestic paradise of Stowe![n]
Not Persian Cyrus on Ionia's shore[n]
E'er saw such sylvan scenes, such various art
By genius fired, such ardent genius tamed   1045
By cool judicious art, that in the strife
All-beauteous Nature fears to be outdone.
And there, O Pitt![n] thy country's early boast,
There let me sit beneath the sheltered slopes,
Or in that Temple[n] where, in future times,   1050
Thou well shalt merit a distinguished name,
And, with thy converse blest, catch the last smiles
Of Autumn beaming o'er the yellow woods.
While there with thee the enchanted round I walk,
The regulated wild, gay fancy then   1055
Will tread in thought the groves of Attic land;
Will from thy standard taste refine her own,

1031 *visionary*: where visions will be seen.
1043 *Cyrus*: Cyrus the younger (d. 401 B.C.); and see end-note.
1048 *Pitt*: William Pitt the Elder (1708–78); and see end-note.
1056 *Attic land*: Attica, the part of Greece around Athens.

Correct her pencil to the purest truth
Of Nature, or, the unimpassioned shades
Forsaking, raise it to the human mind.[n]   1060
Oh, if hereafter she with juster hand
Shall draw the tragic scene, instruct her thou
To mark the varied movements of the heart,
What every decent character requires,
And every passion speaks! Oh, through her strain   1065
Breathe thy pathetic eloquence, that moulds
The attentive senate, charms, persuades, exalts,
Of honest zeal the indignant lightning throws,
And shakes Corruption on her venal throne![n]
While thus we talk, and through Elysian vales[n]   1070
Delighted rove, perhaps a sigh escapes—
What pity, Cobham![n] thou thy verdant files
Of ordered trees shouldst here inglorious range,
Instead of squadrons flaming o'er the field,
And long-embattled hosts! when the proud foe,   1075
The faithless vain disturber of mankind,
Insulting Gaul, has roused the world to war;
When keen, once more, within their bounds to press
Those polished robbers, those ambitious slaves,
The British youth would hail thy wise command,   1080
Thy tempered ardour and thy veteran skill.[n]

The western sun withdraws the shortened day;
And humid evening, gliding o'er the sky,
In her chill progress, to the ground condensed
The vapours throws. Where creeping waters ooze,   1085
Where marshes stagnate, and where rivers wind,
Cluster the rolling fogs, and swim along
The dusky-mantled lawn. Meanwhile the moon,
Full-orbed and breaking through the scattered clouds,
Shows her broad visage in the crimsoned east.   1090
Turned to the sun direct, her spotted disc
(Where mountains rise, umbrageous dales descend,
And caverns deep, as optic tube descries)
A smaller earth, gives all his blaze again,
Void of its flame, and sheds a softer day.   1095

1064 *decent*: appropriate to rank or dignity, cf. *Au.* 496.
1072 *Cobham*: Sir Richard Temple, Viscount Cobham (1669–1749); and see end-note.
1093 *optic tube*: telescope, cf. *P.L.* I.288.

Now through the passing cloud she seems to stoop,
Now up the pure cerulean rides sublime.
Wide the pale deluge floats, and streaming mild
O'er the skied mountain to the shadowy vale,
While rocks and floods reflect the quivering gleam,   1100
The whole air whitens with a boundless tide
Of silver radiance trembling round the world.[n]
  But when, half blotted from the sky, her light
Fainting, permits the starry fires to burn
With keener lustre through the depth of heaven;   1105
Or quite extinct her deadened orb appears,
And scarce appears, of sickly beamless white;
Oft in this season, silent from the north
A blaze of meteors shoots—ensweeping first
The lower skies, they all at once converge   1110
High to the crown of heaven, and, all at once
Relapsing quick, as quickly re-ascend,
And mix and thwart, extinguish and renew,
All ether coursing in a maze of light.
  From look to look, contagious through the crowd,   1115
The panic runs, and into wondrous shapes
The appearance throws—armies in meet array,
Thronged with aerial spears and steeds of fire;
Till, the long lines of full-extended war
In bleeding fight commixed, the sanguine flood   1120
Rolls a broad slaughter o'er the plains of heaven.
As thus they scan the visionary scene,
On all sides swells the superstitious din,
Incontinent; and busy frenzy talks
Of blood and battle; cities overturned,   1125
And late at night in swallowing earthquake sunk,
Or hideous wrapped in fierce ascending flame;
Of sallow famine, inundation, storm;
Of pestilence, and every great distress;
Empires subversed, when ruling fate has struck   1130
The unalterable hour: even Nature's self
Is deemed to totter on the brink of time.
Not so the man of philosophic eye
And inspect sage: the waving brightness he
Curious surveys, inquisitive to know   1135

1099 *skied*: seeming to touch the sky.   1113 *thwart*: cross, cf. *Su.* 343.
1114 *ether*: see *Sp.* 148 fn.   1134 *inspect sage*: wise insight.

The causes and materials, yet unfixed,
Of this appearance beautiful and new.[n]

Now black and deep the night begins to fall,
A shade immense! Sunk in the quenching gloom,
Magnificent and vast, are heaven and earth.   1140
Order confounded lies, all beauty void,
Distinction lost, and gay variety
One universal blot—such the fair power
Of light to kindle and create the whole.
Drear is the state of the benighted wretch   1145
Who then bewildered wanders through the dark
Full of pale fancies and chimeras huge;
Nor visited by one directive ray
From cottage streaming or from airy hall.
Perhaps, impatient as he stumbles on,   1150
Struck from the root of slimy rushes, blue
The wild-fire scatters round, or, gathered, trails
A length of flame deceitful o'er the moss;
Whither decoyed by the fantastic blaze,
Now lost and now renewed, he sinks absorbed,   1155
Rider and horse, amid the miry gulf—
While still, from day to day, his pining wife
And plaintive children his return await,
In wild conjecture lost. At other times,
Sent by the better genius of the night,   1160
Innoxious, gleaming on the horse's mane,
The meteor sits, and shows the narrow path
That winding leads through pits of death, or else
Instructs him how to take the dangerous ford.[n]

The lengthened night elapsed, the morning shines   1165
Serene, in all her dewy beauty bright,
Unfolding fair the last autumnal day.
And now the mounting sun dispels the fog;
The rigid hoar-frost melts before his beam;
And, hung on every spray, on every blade   1170
Of grass, the myriad dew-drops twinkle round.
Ah, see where, robbed and murdered, in that pit
Lies the still-heaving hive! at evening snatched,
Beneath the cloud of guilt-concealing night,
And fixed o'er sulphur—while, not dreaming ill,   1175

1136 *unfixed*: unexplained by man.

The happy people in their waxen cells
Sat tending public cares and planning schemes
Of temperance for Winter poor; rejoiced
To mark, full-flowing round, their copious stores.
Sudden the dark oppressive steam ascends;   1180
And, used to milder scents, the tender race
By thousands tumbles from their honeyed domes,
Convolved and agonizing in the dust.
And was it then for this you roamed the Spring,
Intent from flower to flower ? for this you toiled   1185
Ceaseless the burning summer-heats away ?
For this in Autumn searched the blooming waste,
Nor lost one sunny gleam ? for this sad fate ?
O man ! tyrannic lord ! how long, how long
Shall prostrate nature groan beneath your rage,   1190
Awaiting renovation ? When obliged,
Must you destroy ? Of their ambrosial food
Can you not borrow, and in just return
Afford them shelter from the wintry winds ?
Or, as the sharp year pinches, with their own   1195
Again regale them on some smiling day ?
See where the stony bottom of their town
Looks desolate and wild,—with here and there
A helpless number, who the ruined state
Survive, lamenting weak, cast out to death !ⁿ   1200
Thus a proud city, populous and rich,
Full of the works of peace, and high in joy,
At theatre or feast, or sunk in sleep
(As late, Palermo, was thy fate) is seized
By some dread earthquake, and convulsive hurled   1205
Sheer from the black foundation, stench-involved,
Into a gulf of blue sulphureous flame.

    Hence every harsher sight ! for now the day,
O'er heaven and earth diffused, grows warm and high;
Infinite splendour ! wide-investing all.   1210
How still the breeze ! save what the filmy threads
Of dew evaporate brushes from the plain.

1182 *domes*: houses, but also alluding to the domed shape of beehives; cf. Virgil, *Georgics* II.159, *Au.* 660 fn.

1201 *Thus a proud city* . . .: Cf. *P.L.* I.230–7. Palermo in Sicily was shaken by a violent earthquake on the night of 1 Sept. 1726.

1212 *save what . . . brushes from the plain*: save what breeze brushes the filmy threads of evaporated dew from the fields.

How clear the cloudless sky ! how deeply tinged
With a peculiar blue ! the ethereal arch
How swelled immense ! amid whose azure throned,   1215
The radiant sun how gay ! how calm below
The gilded earth ! the harvest-treasures all
Now, gathered in, beyond the rage of storms,
Sure to the swain; the circling fence shut up;
And instant Winter's utmost rage defied—   1220
While, loose to festive joy, the country round
Laughs with the loud sincerity of mirth,
Shook to the wind their cares. The toil-strung youth,
By the quick sense of music taught alone,
Leaps wildly graceful in the lively dance.   1225
Her every charm abroad, the village-toast,
Young, buxom, warm, in native beauty rich,
Darts not-unmeaning looks; and, where her eye
Points an approving smile, with double force
The cudgel rattles, and the wrestler twines.   1230
Age too shines out; and, garrulous, recounts
The feats of youth. Thus they rejoice; nor think
That with to-morrow's sun their annual toil
Begins again the never-ceasing round.

Oh, knew he but his happiness, of men   1235
The happiest he ! who far from public rage
Deep in the vale, with a choice few retired.
Drinks the pure pleasures of the rural life.[n]
What though the dome be wanting, whose proud gate
Each morning vomits out the sneaking crowd   1240
Of flatterers false, and in their turn abused ?
Vile intercourse ! What though the glittering robe,
Of every hue reflected light can give,
Or floating loose or stiff with mazy gold,
The pride and gaze of fools, oppress him not ?   1245
What though, from utmost land and sea purveyed,
For him each rarer tributary life
Bleeds not, and his insatiate table heaps
With luxury and death ? What though his bowl
Flames not with costly juice; nor, sunk in beds   1250

1214 *ethereal arch*: upper sky, distinguished from 'sky' (1213), cf. *Sp.* 148 fn.
1220 *instant*: imminent, cf. *Su.* 1195.
1223 *toil-strung*: given vigour by toil, cf. Dryden, *To John Driden* 89.
1244 *mazy*: intricately embroidered.

Oft of gay care, he tosses out the night,
Or melts the thoughtless hours in idle state ?
What though he knows not those fantastic joys
That still amuse the wanton, still deceive;
A face of pleasure, but a heart of pain;   1255
Their hollow moments undelighted all ?
Sure peace is his; a solid life, estranged
To disappointment and fallacious hope—
Rich in content, in Nature's bounty rich,
In herbs and fruits; whatever greens the Spring   1260
When heaven descends in showers, or bends the bough
When Summer reddens and when Autumn beams,
Or in the wintry glebe whatever lies
Concealed and fattens with the richest sap:
These are not wanting; nor the milky drove,   1265
Luxuriant spread o'er all the lowing vale;
Nor bleating mountains; nor the chide of streams
And hum of bees, inviting sleep sincere
Into the guiltless breast beneath the shade,
Or thrown at large amid the fragrant hay;   1270
Nor aught besides of prospect, grove, or song,
Dim grottoes, gleaming lakes, and fountain clear.
Here too dwells simple truth, plain innocence,
Unsullied beauty, sound unbroken youth
Patient of labour—with a little pleased,   1275
Health ever-blooming, unambitious toil,
Calm contemplation, and poetic ease.

    Let others brave the flood in quest of gain,
And beat for joyless months the gloomy wave.
Let such as deem it glory to destroy   1280
Rush into blood, the sack of cities seek—
Unpierced, exulting in the widow's wail,
The virgin's shriek, and infant's trembling cry.
Let some, far distant from their native soil,
Urged or by want or hardened avarice,   1285
Find other lands beneath another sun.[n]
Let this through cities work his eager way
By legal outrage and established guile,

1265 *milky drove*: cattle (both elements in the periphrasis emphasize the cow's relation to man. On periphrases see *Sp.* 132 end-note).
1267 *chide*: confused noise.
1286 *another sun*: cf. *Wi.* 893 fn.

The social sense extinct; and that ferment
Mad into tumult the seditious herd,   12⁹0
Or melt them down to slavery. Let these
Ensnare the wretched in the toils of law,
Fomenting discord, and perplexing right,
An iron race ! and those of fairer front,
But equal inhumanity, in courts,   1295
Delusive pomp, and dark cabals delight;
Wreathe the deep bow, diffuse the lying smile,
And tread the weary labyrinth of state.
While he, from all the stormy passions free
That restless men involve, hears, and but hears,   1300
At distance safe, the human tempest roar,
Wrapped close in conscious peace. The fall of kings,
The rage of nations, and the crush of states
Move not the man who, from the world escaped,
In still retreats and flowery solitudes   1305
To Nature's voice attends from month to month,
And day to day, through the revolving year—
Admiring, sees her in her every shape;
Feels all her sweet emotions at his heart;
Takes what she liberal gives, nor thinks of more.   1310
He, when young Spring protrudes the bursting gems,
Marks the first bud, and sucks the healthful gale
Into his freshened soul; her genial hours
He full enjoys; and not a beauty blows
And not an opening blossom breathes in vain.   1315
In Summer he, beneath the living shade,
Such as o'er frigid Tempe wont to wave,
Or Haemus cool, reads what the muse, of these
Perhaps, has in immortal numbers sung;
Or what she dictates writes; and oft, an eye   1320
Shot round, rejoices in the vigorous year.
When Autumn's yellow lustre gilds the world
And tempts the sickled swain into the field,
Seized by the general joy his heart distends,
With gentle throes; and, through the tepid gleams   1325

1294 *iron race*: people living in an Iron Age (cf. *Sp.* 242–74 end-note); T. implies
    that the contented country-dweller lives in something comparable to the Golden
    Age (cf. *Au.* 1349–51).
1311 *gems*: see *Sp.* 196 fn.   1317 *Tempe*: see *Sp.* 909 fn.
1318 *Haemus*: a mountain in Thessaly celebrated by classical poets. Virgil refers
    to its cool, enclosed valleys, *Georgics* II.488; cf. *Au.* 785.

Deep musing, then he best exerts his song.
Even Winter wild to him is full of bliss.
The mighty tempest, and the hoary waste
Abrupt and deep, stretched o'er the buried earth,
Awake to solemn thought. At night the skies,   1330
Disclosed and kindled by refining frost,
Pour every lustre on the exalted eye.
A friend, a book the stealing hours secure,
And mark them down for wisdom. With swift wing,
O'er land and sea imagination roams;   1335
Or truth, divinely breaking on his mind,
Elates his being, and unfolds his powers;
Or in his breast heroic virtue burns.
The touch of kindred, too, and love he feels—
The modest eye whose beams on his alone   1340
Ecstatic shine, the little strong embrace
Of prattling children, twined around his neck,
And emulous to please him, calling forth
The fond parental soul. Nor purpose gay,
Amusement, dance, or song, he sternly scorns: 1345
For happiness and true philosophy
Are of the social still and smiling kind.
This is the life which those who fret in guilt
And guilty cities never knew—the life
Led by primeval ages uncorrupt   1350
When angels dwelt, and God himself, with man!
    O Nature! all-sufficient! over all
Enrich me with the knowledge of thy works;
Snatch me to heaven; thy rolling wonders there,
World beyond world, in infinite extent   1355
Profusely scattered o'er the blue immense,
Show me; their motions, periods, and their laws
Give me to scan; through the disclosing deep
Light my blind way: the mineral strata there;
Thrust blooming thence the vegetable world;   1360
O'er that the rising system, more complex,
Of animals; and, higher still, the mind,
The varied scene of quick-compounded thought,
And where the mixing passions endless shift;
These ever open to my ravished eye—   1365

1329 *hoary waste Abrupt*: sudden snowfall.

A search, the flight of time can ne'er exhaust!
But, if to that unequal—if the blood
In sluggish streams about my heart forbid
That best ambition—under closing shades
Inglorious lay me by the lowly brook,   1370
And whisper to my dreams. From thee begin,
Dwell all on thee, with thee conclude my song;
And let me never, never stray from thee![n]

1367 *if the blood . . . forbid*: The ancients thought that slowness of intellect might
    be caused by coldness of blood about the heart; cf. Virgil, *Georgics* II.483–4.
1370 *Inglorious*: humble, cf. *Au.* 1073.

W. Kent. inv et del.

H. Tardieu Scul.

Winter

Winter

THE ARGUMENT

The subject proposed. Address to the Earl of Wilmington. First approach
of Winter. According to the natural course of the season, various storms
described. Rain. Wind. Snow. The driving of the snows: a man perishing
among them; whence reflections of the wants and miseries of human life.
The wolves descending from the Alps and Apennines. A winter evening
described: as spent by philosophers; by the country people; in the city.
Frost. A view of Winter within the polar circle. A thaw. The whole con-
cluding with moral reflections on a future state.

SEE, Winter comes to rule the varied year,
Sullen and sad, with all his rising train—
Vapours, and clouds, and storms. Be these my theme;
These, that exalt the soul to solemn thought
And heavenly musing. Welcome, kindred glooms!   5
Cogenial horrors, hail! With frequent foot,
Pleased have I, in my cheerful morn of life,
When nursed by careless solitude I lived
And sung of Nature with unceasing joy,
Pleased have I wandered through your rough domain;   10
Trod the pure virgin-snows, myself as pure;
Heard the winds roar, and the big torrent burst;
Or seen the deep-fermenting tempest brewed
In the grim evening-sky. Thus passed the time,
Till through the lucid chambers of the south   15
Looked out the joyous Spring—looked out and smiled.[n]

To thee, the patron of this first essay,
The Muse, O Wilmington! renews her song.
Since has she rounded the revolving year:
Skimmed the gay Spring; on eagle-pinions borne,   20
Attempted through the Summer-blaze to rise;
Then swept o'er Autumn with the shadowy gale.
And now among the Wintry clouds again,
Rolled in the doubling storm, she tries to soar,

6 *Cogenial*: Congenial.
15 *chambers of the south*: the southern sky, cf. Job 9:9.

To swell her note with all the rushing winds,   25
To suit her sounding cadence to the floods;
As is her theme, her numbers wildly great.
Thrice happy, could she fill thy judging ear
With bold description and with manly thought!
Nor art thou skilled in awful schemes alone,   30
And how to make a mighty people thrive;
But equal goodness, sound integrity,
A firm, unshaken, uncorrupted soul
Amid a sliding age, and burning strong,
Not vainly blazing, for thy country's weal,   35
A steady spirit, regularly free—
These, each exalting each, the statesman light
Into the patriot; these, the public hope
And eye to thee converting, bid the Muse
Record what envy dares not flattery call.[n]   40

    Now, when the cheerless empire of the sky
To Capricorn the Centaur-Archer yields,
And fierce Aquarius stains the inverted year—
Hung o'er the farthest verge of heaven, the sun
Scarce spreads o'er ether the dejected day.
Faint are his gleams, and ineffectual shoot   45
His struggling rays in horizontal lines
Through the thick air; as clothed in cloudy storm,
Weak, wan, and broad, he skirts the southern sky;[n]
And, soon descending, to the long dark night,   50
Wide-shading all, the prostrate world resigns.
Nor is the night unwished; while vital heat,
Light, life, and joy the dubious day forsake.
Meantime, in sable cincture, shadows vast,
Deep-tinged and damp, and congregated clouds,   55
And all the vapoury turbulence of heaven
Involve the face of things. Thus Winter falls,
A heavy gloom oppressive o'er the world,
Through Nature shedding influence malign,

---

42 *Capricorn*: the Goat, the tenth sign of the zodiac, into which the sun enters at
the winter solstice (21 or 22 Dec.).
42 *Centaur-Archer*: Sagittarius, the ninth sign of the zodiac, into which the sun
enters about 22 Nov. For Centaur see *Au.* 500 fn.
43 *Aquarius*: the Water-Carrier, the eleventh sign of the zodiac, into which the
sun enters on 21 Jan.; cf. Virgil, *Georgics* III.304, and, for 'inverted year',
Horace, *Satires* I.i.36.

And rouses up the seeds of dark disease.[n]   60
The soul of man dies in him, loathing life,
And black with more than melancholy views.
The cattle droop; and o'er the furrowed land,
Fresh from the plough, the dun discoloured flocks,
Untended spreading, crop the wholesome root.[n]   65
Along the woods, along the moorish fens,
Sighs the sad genius of the coming storm;[n]
And up among the loose disjointed cliffs
And fractured mountains wild, the brawling brook
And cave, presageful, send a hollow moan,   70
Resounding long in listening fancy's ear.
    Then comes the Father of the tempest forth,
Wrapped in black glooms. First, joyless rains obscure
Drive through the mingling skies with vapour foul,
Dash on the mountain's brow, and shake the woods   75
That grumbling wave below. The unsightly plain
Lies a brown deluge; as the low-bent clouds
Pour flood on flood, yet unexhausted still
Combine, and, deepening into night, shut up
The day's fair face.[n] The wanderers of heaven,   80
Each to his home, retire; save those that love
To take their pastime in the troubled air,
Or skimming flutter round the dimply pool.
The cattle from the untasted fields return
And ask, with meaning low, their wonted stalls,   85
Or ruminate in the contiguous shade.
Thither the household feathery people crowd,
The crested cock, with all his female train,
Pensive and dripping; while the cottage-hind
Hangs o'er the enlivening blaze, and taleful there 90
Recounts his simple frolic: much he talks,
And much he laughs, nor recks the storm that blows
Without, and rattles on his humble roof.
    Wide o'er the brim, with many a torrent swelled,
And the mixed ruin of its banks o'erspread,   95
At last the roused-up river pours along:
Resistless, roaring, dreadful, down it comes,
From the rude mountain and the mossy wild,
Tumbling through rocks abrupt, and sounding far;

80 *wanderers of heaven*: wild birds, as distinguished from 'household feathery people' (*Wi.* 87). On periphrases see *Sp.* 132 end-note.

Then o'er the sanded valley floating spreads,   100
Calm, sluggish, silent; till again, constrained
Between two meeting hills, it bursts a way
Where rocks and woods o'erhang the turbid stream;
There, gathering triple force, rapid and deep,
It boils, and wheels, and foams, and thunders through.   105

Nature! great Parent! whose unceasing hand
Rolls round the Seasons of the changeful year,
How mighty, how majestic are thy works!
With what a pleasing dread they swell the soul,
That sees astonished, and astonished sings!   110
Ye too, ye winds! that now begin to blow
With boisterous sweep, I raise my voice to you.
Where are your stores, ye powerful beings! say,
Where your aerial magazines reserved
To swell the brooding terrors of the storm?   115
In what far-distant region of the sky,
Hushed in deep silence, sleep you when 'tis calm?[n]

When from the pallid sky the Sun descends,
With many a spot, that o'er his glaring orb
Uncertain wanders, stained; red fiery streaks   120
Begin to flush around. The reeling clouds
Stagger with dizzy poise, as doubting yet
Which master to obey; while, rising slow,
Blank in the leaden-coloured east, the moon
Wears a wan circle round her blunted horns.   125
Seen through the turbid, fluctuating air,
The stars obtuse emit a shivering ray;
Or frequent seem to shoot athwart the gloom,
And long behind them trail the whitening blaze.
Snatched in short eddies, plays the withered leaf;   130
And on the flood the dancing feather floats.
With broadened nostrils to the sky upturned,
The conscious heifer snuffs the stormy gale.
Even, as the matron, at her nightly task,
With pensive labour draws the flaxen thread,   135
The wasted taper and the crackling flame
Foretell the blast. But chief the plumy race,
The tenants of the sky, its changes speak.

---

124 *Blank*: white.
138 *plumy race, tenants of the sky*: birds. On periphrases see *Sp.* 132 end-note.

Retiring from the downs, where all day long
They picked their scanty fare, a blackening train   140
Of clamorous rooks thick-urge their weary flight,
And seek the closing shelter of the grove.
Assiduous, in his bower, the wailing owl
Plies his sad song. The cormorant on high
Wheels from the deep, and screams along the land.   145
Loud shrieks the soaring hern; and with wild wing
The circling sea-fowl cleave the flaky clouds.
Ocean, unequal pressed, with broken tide
And blind commotion heaves; while from the shore,
Eat into caverns by the restless wave,   150
And forest-rustling mountain comes a voice
That, solemn-sounding, bids the world prepare.[n]
Then issues forth the storm with sudden burst,
And hurls the whole precipitated air
Down in a torrent. On the passive main   155
Descends the ethereal force, and with strong gust
Turns from its bottom the discoloured deep.
Through the black night that sits immense around,
Lashed into foam, the fierce-conflicting brine
Seems o'er a thousand raging waves to burn.   160
Meantime the mountain-billows, to the clouds
In dreadful tumult swelled, surge above surge,
Burst into chaos with tremendous roar,
And anchored navies from their stations drive
Wild as the winds, across the howling waste   165
Of mighty waters: now the inflated wave
Straining they scale, and now impetuous shoot
Into the secret chambers of the deep,
The wintry Baltic thundering o'er their head.
Emerging thence again, before the breath   170
Of full-exerted heaven they wing their course,
And dart on distant coasts—if some sharp rock
Or shoal insidious break not their career,
And in loose fragments fling them floating round.
   Nor less at land the loosened tempest reigns.   175
The mountain thunders, and its sturdy sons
Stoop to the bottom of the rocks they shade.
Lone on the midnight steep, and all aghast,

146 *hern*: heron.　　176 *sturdy sons*: trees.

The dark wayfaring stranger breathless toils,
And often falling, climbs against the blast.   180
Low waves the rooted forest, vexed, and sheds
What of its tarnished honours yet remain—
Dashed down and scattered, by the tearing wind's
Assiduous fury, its gigantic limbs.
Thus struggling through the dissipated grove,   185
The whirling tempest raves along the plain;
And, on the cottage thatched or lordly roof
Keen-fastening, shakes them to the solid base.
Sleep frighted flies; and round the rocking dome,
For entrance eager, howls the savage blast.   190
Then too, they say, through all the burdened air
Long groans are heard, shrill sounds, and distant sighs,
That, uttered by the demon[n] of the night,
Warn the devoted wretch of woe and death.
  Huge uproar lords it wide. The clouds, commixed   195
With stars swift-gliding, sweep along the sky.
All Nature reels: till Nature's King, who oft
Amid tempestuous darkness dwells alone,
And on the wings of the careering wind
Walks dreadfully serene, commands a calm;   200
Then straight air, sea, and earth are hushed at once.
  As yet 'tis midnight deep. The weary clouds,
Slow-meeting, mingle into solid gloom.
Now, while the drowsy world lies lost in sleep,
Let me associate with the serious Night,   205
And Contemplation, her sedate compeer;
Let me shake off the intrusive cares of day,
And lay the meddling senses all aside.
  Where now, ye lying vanities of life!
Ye ever-tempting, ever-cheating train!   210
Where are you now? and what is your amount?
Vexation, disappointment, and remorse.
Sad, sickening thought! and yet deluded man,
A scene of crude disjointed visions past,
And broken slumbers, rises still resolved,   215
With new-flushed hopes, to run the giddy round.
  Father of light and life! thou Good Supreme!
O teach me what is good! teach me Thyself!

182 *honours*: foliage, cf. Virgil, *Georgics* II. 404.
194 *devoted*: consigned to destruction, cf. *P.L.* V.890.

Save me from folly, vanity, and vice,
From every low pursuit; and feed my soul   220
With knowledge, conscious peace, and virtue pure—
Sacred, substantial, never-fading bliss!
    The keener tempests come: and, fuming dun
From all the livid east or piercing north,
Thick clouds ascend, in whose capacious womb   225
A vapoury deluge lies, to snow congealed.
Heavy they roll their fleecy world along,
And the sky saddens with the gathered storm.
Through the hushed air the whitening shower descends,
At first thin-wavering; till at last the flakes   230
Fall broad and wide and fast, dimming the day
With a continual flow. The cherished fields
Put on their winter-robe of purest white.
'Tis brightness all; save where the new snow melts
Along the mazy current. Low the woods   235
Bow their hoar head; and, ere the languid sun
Faint from the west emits his evening ray,
Earth's universal face, deep-hid and chill,
Is one wild dazzling waste, that buries wide
The works of man. Drooping, the labourer-ox   240
Stands covered o'er with snow, and then demands
The fruit of all his toil. The fowls of heaven,
Tamed by the cruel season, crowd around
The winnowing store,[n] and claim the little boon
Which Providence assigns them. One alone,   245
The redbreast, sacred to the household gods,
Wisely regardful of the embroiling sky,
In joyless fields and thorny thickets leaves
His shivering mates, and pays to trusted man
His annual visit. Half afraid, he first   250
Against the window beats; then brisk alights
On the warm hearth; then, hopping o'er the floor,
Eyes all the smiling family askance,
And pecks, and starts, and wonders where he is—
Till, more familiar grown, the table-crumbs   255
Attract his slender feet. The foodless wilds
Pour forth their brown inhabitants. The hare,
Though timorous of heart, and hard beset
By death in various forms, dark snares, and dogs,
And more unpitying men, the garden seeks,   260

Urged on by fearless want. The bleating kind
Eye the bleak heaven, and next the glistening earth,
With looks of dumb despair; then, sad-dispersed,
Dig for the withered herb through heaps of snow.
 Now, shepherds, to your helpless charge be kind: 265
Baffle the raging year, and fill their pens
With food at will; lodge them below the storm,
And watch them strict: for, from the bellowing east,
In this dire season, oft the whirlwind's wing
Sweeps up the burden of whole wintry plains   270
In one wide waft, and o'er the hapless flocks,
Hid in the hollow of two neighbouring hills,
The billowy tempest whelms; till, upward urged,
The valley to a shining mountain swells,
Tipped with a wreath high-curling in the sky.   275
 As thus the snows arise, and, foul and fierce,
All Winter drives along the darkened air,
In his own loose-revolving fields the swain
Disastered stands; sees other hills ascend,
Of unknown joyless brow; and other scenes,   280
Of horrid prospect, shag the trackless plain;
Nor finds the river nor the forest, hid
Beneath the formless wild; but wanders on
From hill to dale, still more and more astray—
Impatient flouncing through the drifted heaps,   285
Stung with the thoughts of home: the thoughts of home
Rush on his nerves and call their vigour forth
In many a vain attempt. How sinks his soul!
What black despair, what horror fills his heart,
When, for the dusky spot which fancy feigned   290
His tufted cottage rising through the snow,
He meets the roughness of the middle waste,
Far from the track and blest abode of man;
While round him night resistless closes fast,
And every tempest, howling o'er his head,   295

261 *bleating kind*: sheep. On periphrases see *Sp.* 132 end-note.
271 *waft*: act of wafting or carrying off.
273 *o'er the hapless flocks ... whelms*: the tempest overwhelms the flocks.
275 *wreath*: plume of powdery snow blown by the strong wind.
279 *disastered*: stricken by calamity, cf. *Hamlet* I.i.117.
281 *shag*: make rough, cf. *Sp.* 910.
291 *tufted*: perhaps turf-roofed, or with grass growing on its thatch, or surroun-
 ded by trees.

Renders the savage wilderness more wild.
Then throng the busy shapes into his mind
Of covered pits, unfathomably deep,
A dire descent! beyond the power of frost;
Of faithless bogs; of precipices huge,   300
Smoothed up with snow; and (what is land unknown,
What water) of the still unfrozen spring,
In the loose marsh or solitary lake,
Where the fresh fountain from the bottom boils.
These check his fearful steps; and down he sinks   305
Beneath the shelter of the shapeless drift,
Thinking o'er all the bitterness of death,
Mixed with the tender anguish nature shoots
Through the wrung bosom of the dying man—
His wife, his children, and his friends unseen.   310
In vain for him the officious wife prepares
The fire fair-blazing and the vestment warm;
In vain his little children, peeping out
Into the mingling storm, demand their sire
With tears of artless innocence. Alas!   315
Nor wife nor children more shall he behold,
Nor friends, nor sacred home. On every nerve
The deadly Winter seizes, shuts up sense,
And o'er his inmost vitals creeping cold,
Lays him along the snows a stiffened corse,   320
Stretched out, and bleaching in the northern blast.
    Ah! little think the gay licentious proud,
Whom pleasure, power, and affluence surround—
They, who their thoughtless hours in giddy mirth,
And wanton, often cruel, riot waste—   325
Ah! little think they, while they dance along,
How many feel, this very moment, death
And all the sad variety of pain;
How many sink in the devouring flood,
Or more devouring flame; how many bleed,   330
By shameful variance betwixt man and man;
How many pine in want, and dungeon-glooms,
Shut from the common air and common use
Of their own limbs; how many drink the cup

299 *beyond the power of frost*: unfrozen and so capable of drowning him
311 *officious*: obliging.

Of baleful grief, or eat the bitter bread   335
Of misery; sore pierced by wintry winds,
How many shrink into the sordid hut
Of cheerless poverty; how many shake
With all the fiercer tortures of the mind,
Unbounded passion, madness, guilt, remorse—   340
Whence, tumbled headlong from the height of life,
They furnish matter for the tragic muse;
Even in the vale, where wisdom loves to dwell,
With friendship, peace, and contemplation joined,
How many, racked with honest passions, droop   345
In deep retired distress; how many stand
Around the death-bed of their dearest friends,
And point the parting anguish! Thought fond man
Of these, and all the thousand nameless ills
That one incessant struggle render life,   350
One scene of toil, of suffering, and of fate,
Vice in his high career would stand appalled,
And heedless rambling Impulse learn to think;
The conscious heart of Charity would warm,
And her wide wish Benevolence dilate;   355
The social tear would rise, the social sigh;
And, into clear perfection, gradual bliss,
Refining still, the social passions[n] work.
     And here can I forget the generous band[n]
Who, touched with human woe, redressive searched   360
Into the horrors of the gloomy jail?
Unpitied and unheard where misery moans,
Where sickness pines, where thirst and hunger burn,
And poor misfortune feels the lash of vice;
While in the land of liberty—the land   365
Whose every street and public meeting glow
With open freedom—little tyrants raged,
Snatched the lean morsel from the starving mouth,
Tore from cold wintry limbs the tattered weed,
Even robbed them of the last of comforts, sleep,   370
The free-born Briton to the dungeon chained
Or, as the lust of cruelty prevailed,
At pleasure marked him with inglorious stripes,
And crushed out lives, by secret barbarous ways,
That for their country would have toiled or bled.   375
O great design! if executed well,

With patient care and wisdom-tempered zeal.
Ye sons of mercy! yet resume the search;
Drag forth the legal monsters into light,
Wrench from their hands Oppression's iron rod,   380
And bid the cruel feel the pains they give.
Much still untouched remains; in this rank age,
Much is the patriot's weeding hand required.
The toils of law—what dark insidious men
Have cumbrous added to perplex the truth   385
And lengthen simple justice into trade—
How glorious were the day that saw these broke,
And every man within the reach of right!

By wintry famine roused, from all the tract
Of horrid mountains which the shining Alps,   390
And wavy Apennines, and Pyrenees
Branch out stupendous into distant lands,
Cruel as death, and hungry as the grave!
Burning for blood, bony, and gaunt, and grim!
Assembling wolves in raging troops descend;   395
And, pouring o'er the country, bear along,
Keen as the north-wind sweeps the glossy snow.
All is their prize. They fasten on the steed,
Press him to earth, and pierce his mighty heart.
Nor can the bull his awful front defend,   400
Or shake the murdering savages away.
Rapacious, at the mother's throat they fly,
And tear the screaming infant from her breast.
The godlike face of man avails him naught.
Even Beauty, force divine! at whose bright glance   405
The generous lion stands in softened gaze,[n]
Here bleeds, a hapless undistinguished prey.
But if, apprised of the severe attack,
The country be shut up, lured by the scent,
On churchyards drear (inhuman to relate!)   410
The disappointed prowlers fall, and dig
The shrouded body from the grave; o'er which,
Mixed with foul shades and frighted ghosts, they howl.

Among those hilly regions, where, embraced
In peaceful vales, the happy Grisons dwell,   415

384 *toils*: snares, cf. *Au.* 1292.
415 *Grisons*: inhabitants of the mountainous eastern canton of Switzerland.

Oft, rushing sudden from the loaded cliffs,
Mountains of snow their gathering terrors roll.
From steep to steep, loud thundering, down they come,
A wintry waste in dire commotion all;
And herds, and flocks, and travellers, and swains,   420
And sometimes whole brigades of marching troops,
Or hamlets sleeping in the dead of night,
Are deep beneath the smothering ruin whelmed.[n]

Now, all amid the rigours of the year,
In the wild depth of winter, while without   425
The ceaseless winds blow ice, be my retreat,
Between the groaning forest and the shore,
Beat by the boundless multitude of waves,
A rural, sheltered solitary scene;
Where ruddy fire and beaming tapers join   430
To cheer the gloom. There studious let me sit,
And hold high converse with the mighty dead—
Sages of ancient time, as gods revered,
As gods beneficent, who blessed mankind
With arts and arms, and humanized a world.   435
Roused at the inspiring thought, I throw aside
The long-lived volume, and deep-musing hail
The sacred shades that slowly rising pass
Before my wondering eyes. First Socrates,[n]
Who, firmly good in a corrupted state,   440
Against the rage of tyrants single stood,
Invincible! calm reason's holy law,
That voice of God within the attentive mind,
Obeying, fearless or in life or death:
Great moral teacher! wisest of mankind!   445
Solon[n] the next, who built his commonweal
On equity's wide base; by tender laws
A lively people curbing, yet undamped
Preserving still that quick peculiar fire,
Whence in the laurelled field of finer arts,   450
And of bold freedom, they unequalled shone,
The pride of smiling Greece and human-kind.
Lycurgus[n] then, who bowed beneath the force

---

437 *long-lived volume*: probably Plutarch's Parallel *Lives* of Greeks and Romans.
11 of the 14 Greeks and 5 of the 11 Romans in T.'s catalogue of worthies (*Wi.*
439–540) are in Plutarch's *Lives*.
452 *smiling*: rich, cf. *Sp.* 84 end-note.

Of strictest discipline, severely wise,
All human passions. Following him I see,   455
As at Thermopylae he glorious fell,
The firm devoted chief,[n] who proved by deeds
The hardest lesson which the other taught.
Then Aristides lifts his honest front;
Spotless of heart, to whom the unflattering voice   460
Of freedom gave the noblest name of Just;
In pure majestic poverty revered;
Who, even his glory to his country's weal
Submitting, swelled a haughty rival's[n] fame.
Reared by his care, of softer ray appears   465
Cimon,[n] sweet-souled; whose genius, rising strong,
Shook off the load of young debauch; abroad
The scourge of Persian pride, at home the friend
Of every worth and every splendid art;
Modest and simple in the pomp of wealth.   470
Then the last worthies of declining Greece,
Late-called to glory, in unequal times,
Pensive appear. The fair Corinthian boast,
Timoleon,[n] tempered happy, mild, and firm,
Who wept the brother while the tyrant bled;   475
And, equal to the best, the Theban pair,[n]
Whose virtues, in heroic concord joined,
Their country raised to freedom, empire, fame.
He too, with whom Athenian honour sunk,
And left a mass of sordid lees behind,—   480
Phocion the Good;[n] in public life severe,
To virtue still inexorably firm;
But when, beneath his low illustrious roof,
Sweet peace and happy wisdom smoothed his brow,
Not friendship softer was, nor love more kind.   485
And he, the last of old Lycurgus' sons,
The generous victim to that vain attempt
To save a rotten state—Agis,[n] who saw
Even Sparta's self to servile avarice sunk.
The two Achaean heroes close the train—   490
Aratus,[n] who a while relumed the soul

457 *The firm devoted chief*: 'Leonidas' (T.) and see end-note.
459 *Aristides*: see *Su.* 1491 end-note.
464 *a haughty rival*: 'Themistocles' (T.); and see end-note.
476 *Theban pair*: 'Pelopidas and Epaminondas' (T.); and see end-note.

Of fondly lingering liberty in Greece;
And he, her darling, as her latest hope,
The gallant Philopoemen,[n] who to arms
Turned the luxurious pomp he could not cure,   495
Or toiling in his farm, a simple swain,
Or bold and skilful thundering in the field.
    Of rougher front, a mighty people come,
A race of heroes! in those virtuous times
Which knew no stain, save that with partial flame   500
Their dearest country they too fondly loved.
Her better founder first, the Light of Rome,
Numa,[n] who softened her rapacious sons;
Servius,[n] the king who laid the solid base
On which o'er earth the vast republic spread.   505
Then the great consuls venerable rise:
The public father[n] who the private quelled,
As on the dread tribunal, sternly sad;
He, whom his thankless country could not lose,
Camillus,[n] only vengeful to her foes;   510
Fabricius,[n] scorner of all-conquering gold,
And Cincinnatus, awful from the plough;
Thy willing victim,[n] Carthage! bursting loose
From all that pleading Nature could oppose,
From a whole city's tears, by rigid faith   515
Imperious called, and honour's dire command;
Scipio,[n] the gentle chief, humanely brave,
Who soon the race of spotless glory ran,
And, warm in youth, to the poetic shade
With friendship and philosophy retired;   520
Tully,[n] whose powerful eloquence a while
Restrained the rapid fate of rushing Rome;
Unconquered Cato, virtuous in extreme;
And thou, unhappy Brutus, kind of heart,
Whose steady arm, by awful virtue urged,   525
Lifted the Roman steel against thy friend.

499 *virtuous times*: of the first Roman kings and the early Roman Republic.
507 *The public father*: 'Marcus Junius Brutus' (T.)—an error; see end-note.
512 *Cincinnatus*: see *Su.* 1492 end-note.
513 *willing victim*: 'Regulus' (T.); and see end-note.
522 *rushing*: rapidly declining.
523 *Cato*: of Utica; see *Su.* 954 end-note.
524 *Brutus*: Marcus Junius Brutus (78–42 B.C.) the idealist republican—friend and
murderer of Julius Caesar.

Thousands besides the tribute of a verse
Demand; but who can count the stars of heaven ?
Who sing their influence on this lower world ?
    Behold, who yonder comes ! in sober state,   530
Fair, mild, and strong as is a vernal sun:
'Tis Phoebus' self, or else the Mantuan swain !
Great Homer too appears, of daring wing,
Parent of song ! and equal by his side,
The British Muse; joined hand in hand they walk,   535
Darkling, full up the middle steep to fame.
Nor absent are those shades, whose skilful touch
Pathetic drew the impassioned heart, and charmed
Transported Athens with the moral scene;
Nor those who, tuneful, waked the enchanting lyre.[n]   540
    First of your kind ! society divine !
Still visit thus my nights, for you reserved,
And mount my soaring soul to thoughts like yours.
Silence, thou lonely power ! the door be thine;
See on the hallowed hour that none intrude,   545
Save a few chosen friends, who sometimes deign
To bless my humble roof, with sense refined,
Learning digested well, exalted faith,
Unstudied wit, and humour ever gay.
Or from the Muses' hill will Pope descend,   550
To raise the sacred hour, to bid it smile,
And with the social spirit warm the heart;
For, though not sweeter his own Homer sings,
Yet is his life the more endearing song.[n]
    Where art thou, Hammond ?[n] thou the darling pride,   555
The friend and lover of the tuneful throng !
Ah ! why, dear youth, in all the blooming prime
Of vernal genius, where, disclosing fast,
Each active worth, each manly virtue lay,
Why wert thou ravished from our hope so soon ?   560

---

532 *Phoebus*: Phoebus Apollo, in Roman mythology the god of healing, oracles, and prophecy. He appears in Virgil's *Eclogues* as patron of poetry and music. Cf. *Wi.* 660, *Cas. Ind.* I.vii.4.
532 *Mantuan swain*: Virgil, cf. *Sp.* 456.
534 *Parent of song*: Homer was thought to have been the first poet.
535 *British Muse*: Milton, cf. *Su.* 1567–71.
536 *Darkling*: in the dark, cf. *Au.* 753. Milton was blind and Homer reputedly so.
537 *those shades*: the Greek dramatists and lyric poets.

What now avails that noble thirst of fame,
Which stung thy fervent breast? that treasured store
Of knowledge, early gained? that eager zeal
To serve thy country, glowing in the band
Of youthful patriots who sustain her name?   565
What now, alas! that life-diffusing charm
Of sprightly wit? that rapture for the muse,
That heart of friendship, and that soul of joy,
Which bade with softest light thy virtues smile?
Ah! only showed to check our fond pursuits,   570
And teach our humbled hopes that life is vain.
  Thus in some deep retirement would I pass
The winter-glooms with friends of pliant soul,
Or blithe or solemn, as the theme inspired:
With them would search if nature's boundless frame   575
Was called, late-rising, from the void of night,
Or sprung eternal from the Eternal Mind;[n]
Its life, its laws, its progress, and its end.
Hence larger prospects of the beauteous whole
Would gradual open on our opening minds;   580
And each diffusive harmony unite
In full perfection to the astonished eye.[n]
Then would we try to scan the moral world,
Which, though to us it seems embroiled, moves on
In higher order, fitted and impelled   585
By Wisdom's finest hand, and issuing all
In general good.[n] The sage historic Muse
Should next conduct us through the deeps of time,
Show us how empire grew, declined, and fell
In scattered states; what makes the nations smile,   590
Improves their soil, and gives them double suns;
And why they pine beneath the brightest skies
In nature's richest lap.[n] As thus we talked,
Our hearts would burn within us, would inhale
That portion of divinity, that ray   595
Of purest heaven, which lights the public soul
Of patriots and of heroes. But, if doomed
In powerless humble fortune to repress
These ardent risings of the kindling soul,

587 *historic Muse*: Clio, chief of the nine muses, who presided over history.
595 *portion of divinity*: awareness of immortality; 'the divinity that stirs within us' (Addison, *Cato* V.i.7).

Then, even superior to ambition, we   600
Would learn the private virtues—how to glide
Through shades and plains along the smoothest stream
Of rural life: or, snatched away by hope
Through the dim spaces of futurity,
With earnest eye anticipate those scenes   605
Of happiness and wonder, where the mind,
In endless growth and infinite ascent,
Rises from state to state, and world to world.[n]
But, when with these the serious thought is foiled,
We, shifting for relief, would play the shapes   610
Of frolic fancy; and incessant form
Those rapid pictures, that assembled train
Of fleet ideas, never joined before,
Whence lively Wit excites to gay surprise,
Or folly-painting Humour, grave himself,   615
Calls laughter forth, deep-shaking every nerve.[n]

   Meantime the village rouses up the fire;
While, well attested, and as well believed,
Heard solemn, goes the goblin-story round,
Till superstitious horror creeps o'er all,   620
Or frequent in the sounding hall they wake
The rural gambol. Rustic mirth goes round—
The simple joke that takes the shepherd's heart,
Easily pleased; the long loud laugh sincere;
The kiss, snatched hasty from the sidelong maid   625
On purpose guardless, or pretending sleep;
The leap, the slap, the haul; and, shook to notes
Of native music, the respondent dance.
Thus jocund fleets with them the winter-night.
   The city swarms intense. The public haunt,   630
Full of each theme and warm with mixed discourse,
Hums indistinct. The sons of riot flow
Down the loose stream of false enchanted joy
To swift destruction. On the rankled soul
The gaming fury falls; and in one gulf   635
Of total ruin, honour, virtue, peace,
Friends, families, and fortune headlong sink.
Up springs the dance along the lighted dome,

628 *respondent*: in which the dancers arrange themselves in two facing rows.
630 *intense*: with strenuous effort.

Mixed and evolved a thousand sprightly ways.
The glittering court effuses every pomp; 640
The circle deepens; beamed from gaudy robes,
Tapers, and sparkling gems, and radiant eyes,
A soft effulgence o'er the palace waves—
While, a gay insect in his summer shine,
The fop, light-fluttering, spreads his mealy wings.[n] 645
    Dread o'er the scene the ghost of Hamlet stalks;
Othello rages; poor Monimia mourns;
And Belvidera pours her soul in love.
Terror alarms the breast; the comely tear
Steals o'er the cheek: or else the comic muse 650
Holds to the world a picture of itself,
And raises sly the fair impartial laugh.
Sometimes she lifts her strain, and paints the scenes
Of beauteous life—whate'er can deck mankind,
Or charm the heart, in generous Bevil showed.[n] 655

    O thou, whose wisdom, solid yet refined,
Whose patriot virtues, and consummate skill
To touch the finer springs that move the world,
Joined to whate'er the Graces can bestow,
And all Apollo's animating fire 660
Give thee with pleasing dignity to shine
At once the guardian, ornament, and joy
Of polished life—permit the Rural Muse,
O Chesterfield,[n] to grace with thee her song.
Ere to the shades again she humbly flies, 665
Indulge her fond ambition, in thy train
(For every muse has in thy train a place)
To mark thy various full-accomplished mind—
To mark that spirit which with British scorn
Rejects the allurements of corrupted power; 670
That elegant politeness which excels,

645 *mealy*: powdered, cf. *Sp.* 537.
647 *Monimia*: the heroine of Thomas Otway's tragedy *The Orphan* (acted 1680).
648 *Belvidera*: the heroine of Otway's tragedy *Venice Preserved* (acted 1682).
655 *Bevil*: 'A character in *The Conscious Lovers*, written by Sir Richard Steele' (T.). 'Conscious' indicates that the lovers were full of refined sensibility; the play (acted 1722) was part of the eighteenth century reaction against what was thought to be the grossness of Restoration drama.
659 *Graces*: in Greek mythology three goddesses who personify loveliness or grace.
660 *Apollo*: in Greek mythology the god of prophecy and light, cf. *Wi.* 532.

Even in the judgement of presumptuous France,
The boasted manners of her shining court;
That wit, the vivid energy of sense,
The truth of nature, which with Attic point,   675
And kind well-tempered satire, smoothly keen,
Steals through the soul and without pain corrects.
Or, rising thence with yet a brighter flame,
O let me hail thee on some glorious day,
When to the listening senate ardent crowd   680
Britannia's sons to hear her pleaded cause!
Then, dressed by thee, more amiably fair,
Truth the soft robe of mild persuasion wears;
Thou to assenting reason givest again
Her own enlightened thoughts; called from the heart,   685
The obedient passions on thy voice attend;
And even reluctant party feels a while
Thy gracious power, as through the varied maze
Of eloquence, now smooth, now quick, now strong,
Profound and clear, you roll the copious flood.   690

    To thy loved haunt return, my happy Muse:
For now, behold! the joyous Winter days,
Frosty, succeed; and through the blue serene,
For sight too fine, the ethereal nitre[n] flies,
Killing infectious damps, and the spent air   695
Storing afresh with elemental life.
Close crowds the shining atmosphere; and binds
Our strengthened bodies in its cold embrace,
Constringent; feeds, and animates our blood;
Refines our spirits, through the new-strung nerves   700
In swifter sallies darting to the brain—
Where sits the soul, intense, collected, cool,
Bright as the skies, and as the season keen.
All nature feels the renovating force
Of Winter—only to the thoughtless eye   705
In ruin seen.[n] The frost-concocted glebe
Draws in abundant vegetable soul,

---

675 *Attic point*: Attic wit—from the keenness of the ancient Athenians as talkers.
687 *party*: the political faction opposed to Chesterfield.
693 *blue serene*: calm sky.
706 *concocted*: solidified (but hinting, too, at the other meaning—'ripened', 'perfected', cf. *Su.* 909, *Au.* 7,—and so indicating the fruitful part played by frost in the harmony of Nature).

And gathers vigour for the coming year;
A stronger glow sits on the lively cheek
Of ruddy fire; and luculent along   710
The purer rivers flow:[n] their sullen deeps,
Transparent, open to the shepherd's gaze,
And murmur hoarser at the fixing frost.
    What art thou, frost? and whence are thy keen stores
Derived, thou secret all-invading power,   715
Whom even the illusive fluid[n] cannot fly?
Is not thy potent energy, unseen,
Myriads of little salts, or hooked, or shaped
Like double wedges, and diffused immense
Through water, earth, and ether?[n] Hence at eve,   720
Steamed eager from the red horizon round,
With the fierce rage of Winter deep suffused,
An icy gale, oft shifting, o'er the pool
Breathes a blue film, and in its mid-career
Arrests the bickering stream. The loosened ice,   725
Let down the flood and half dissolved by day,
Rustles no more; but to the sedgy bank
Fast grows, or gathers round the pointed stone,
A crystal pavement, by the breath of heaven
Cemented firm; till, seized from shore to shore,   730
The whole imprisoned river growls below.
Loud rings the frozen earth, and hard reflects
A double noise; while, at his evening watch,
The village-dog deters the nightly thief;
The heifer lows; the distant waterfall   735
Swells in the breeze; and with the hasty tread
Of traveller the hollow-sounding plain
Shakes from afar. The full ethereal round,
Infinite worlds disclosing to the view,
Shines out intensely keen, and, all one cope   740
Of starry glitter, glows from pole to pole.
From pole to pole the rigid influence falls
Through the still night incessant, heavy, strong,
And seizes nature fast. It freezes on,
Till morn, late-rising o'er the drooping world,   745
Lifts her pale eye unjoyous. Then appears
The various labour of the silent night—

716 *illusive fluid*: spirit of wine, used in thermometers; and see end-note.
721 *steamed*: blown.

Prone from the dripping eave, and dumb cascade,
Whose idle torrents only seem to roar,
The pendent icicle; the frost-work fair,   750
Where transient hues and fancied figures rise;
Wide-spouted o'er the hill the frozen brook,
A livid tract, cold-gleaming on the morn;
The forest bent beneath the plumy wave;
And by the frost refined the whiter snow   755
Incrusted hard, and sounding to the tread
Of early shepherd, as he pensive seeks
His pining flock, or from the mountain top,
Pleased with the slippery surface, swift descends.
   On blithesome frolics bent, the youthful swains,   760
While every work of man is laid at rest,
Fond o'er the river crowd, in various sport
And revelry dissolved; where, mixing glad,
Happiest of all the train! the raptured boy
Lashes the whirling top. Or, where the Rhine   765
Branched out in many a long canal extends,
From every province swarming, void of care,
Batavia rushes forth; and, as they sweep
On sounding skates a thousand different ways
In circling poise swift as the winds along,   770
The then gay land is maddened all to joy.
Nor less the northern courts, wide o'er the snow,
Pour a new pomp. Eager, on rapid sleds,
Their vigorous youth in bold contention wheel
The long-resounding course. Meantime, to raise   775
The manly strife, with highly blooming charms,
Flushed by the season, Scandinavia's dames
Or Russia's buxom daughters glow around.
   Pure, quick, and sportful is the wholesome day;
But soon elapsed. The horizontal sun   780
Broad o'er the south hangs at his utmost noon;[n]
And ineffectual strikes the gelid cliff.
His azure gloss the mountain still maintains,
Nor feels the feeble touch. Perhaps the vale
Relents awhile to the reflected ray;   785

754 *plumy wave*: frost-coated trees having the appearance of feathers.
763 *dissolved*: dispersed, cf. *P.L.* II.506.
768 *Batavia*: Holland, cf. *Au.* 921 fn.
771 *then gay*: because the Dutch were proverbially dull.

Or from the forest falls the clustered snow,
Myriads of gems, that in the waving gleam
Gay-twinkle as they scatter. Thick around
Thunders the sport of those who with the gun,
And dog impatient bounding at the shot,   790
Worse than the season desolate the fields,
And, adding to the ruins of the year,
Distress the footed or the feathered game.[n]
    But what is this ? Our infant Winter sinks
Divested of his grandeur should our eye   795
Astonished shoot into the frigid zone,
Where for relentless months continual night
Holds o'er the glittering waste her starry reign.
There, through the prison of unbounded wilds,
Barred by the hand of nature from escape,   800
Wide roams the Russian exile. Naught around
Strikes his sad eye but deserts lost in snow,
And heavy-loaded groves, and solid floods
That stretch athwart the solitary vast
Their icy horrors to the frozen main,   805
And cheerless towns far distant—never blessed,
Save when its annual course the caravan
Bends to the golden coast of rich Cathay,
With news of human-kind. Yet there life glows;
Yet, cherished there, beneath the shining waste   810
The furry nations harbour—tipped with jet,
Fair ermines spotless as the snows they press;
Sables of glossy black; and, dark-embrowned,
Or beauteous freaked with many a mingled hue,[n]
Thousands besides, the costly pride of courts.   815
There, warm together pressed, the trooping deer
Sleep on the new-fallen snows; and, scarce his head
Raised o'er the heapy wreath, the branching elk
Lies slumbering sullen in the white abyss.
The ruthless hunter wants nor dogs nor toils,   820
Nor with the dread of sounding bows he drives
The fearful flying race—with ponderous clubs,
As weak against the mountain-heaps they push
Their beating breast in vain, and piteous bray,
He lays them quivering on the ensanguined snows,   825

---

808 *Cathay*: 'The old name for China' (T.).

And with loud shouts rejoicing bears them home.
There, through the piny forest half-absorbed,
Rough tenant of these shades, the shapeless bear,
With dangling ice all horrid, stalks forlorn;
Slow-paced, and sourer as the storms increase,   830
He makes his bed beneath the inclement drift,
And, with stern patience, scorning weak complaint,
Hardens his heart against assailing want.
    Wide o'er the spacious regions of the north,
That see Boötes urge his tardy wain,   835
A boisterous race, by frosty Caurus pierced,
Who little pleasure know and fear no pain,
Prolific swarm. They once relumed the flame
Of lost mankind in polished slavery sunk;
Drove martial horde on horde,[n] with dreadful sweep   840
Resistless rushing o'er the enfeebled south,
And gave the vanquished world another form.
Not such the sons of Lapland: wisely they
Despise the insensate barbarous trade of war;
They ask no more than simple Nature gives,   845
They love their mountains and enjoy their storms.
No false desires, no pride-created wants,
Disturb the peaceful current of their time,
And through the restless ever-tortured maze
Of pleasure or ambition bid it rage.[n]   850
Their reindeer form their riches. These their tents,
Their robes, their beds, and all their homely wealth
Supply, their wholesome fare, and cheerful cups.
Obsequious at their call, the docile tribe
Yield to the sled their necks, and whirl them swift   855
O'er hill and dale,[n] heaped into one expanse
Of marbled snow, or, far as eye can sweep,
With a blue crust of ice unbounded glazed.
By dancing meteors then, that ceaseless shake
A waving blaze refracted o'er the heavens,   860
And vivid moons, and stars that keener play
With doubled lustre from the radiant waste,

---

835 *Boötes*: the Waggoner, a bright star whose apparent position in the heavens
is close to the Great Bear or Charles's Wain. As that constellation describes only
a small circle around the pole it appears to move slowly.
836 *Caurus*: 'The north-west wind' (T.); cf. Virgil, *Georgics* III.356, *Cas. Ind.*
II.lxxviii.4.   857 *marbled*: hard, or perhaps smoothed.

Even in the depth of polar night they find
A wondrous day[n]—enough to light the chase
Or guide their daring steps to Finland fairs.   865
Wished spring returns; and from the hazy south,
While dim Aurora slowly moves before,
The welcome Sun, just verging up at first,
By small degrees extends the swelling curve;
Till, seen at last for gay rejoicing months,   870
Still round and round his spiral course he winds,
And, as he nearly dips his flaming orb,
Wheels up again and re-ascends the sky.
In that glad season, from the lakes and floods,
Where pure Niëmi's fairy mountains rise,   875
And fringed with roses Tenglio rolls his stream,[n]
They draw the copious fry. With these at eve
They cheerful-loaded to their tents repair,
Where, all day long in useful cares employed,
Their kind unblemished wives the fire prepare.   880
Thrice happy race! by poverty secured
From legal plunder and rapacious power,
In whom fell interest never yet has sown
The seeds of vice, whose spotless swains ne'er knew
Injurious deed, nor, blasted by the breath   885
Of faithless love, their blooming daughters woe.
   Still pressing on, beyond Tornea's lake,
And Hecla flaming through a waste of snow,
And farthest Greenland, to the pole itself,
Where, failing gradual, life at length goes out,   890
The muse expands her solitary flight;
And, hovering o'er the wild stupendous scene,
Beholds new seas beneath another sky.
Throned in his palace of cerulean ice,
Here Winter holds his unrejoicing court;   895
And through his airy hall the loud misrule
Of driving tempest is for ever heard:
Here the grim tyrant meditates his wrath;

---

867 *Aurora*: See *Su.* 1327 fn.
871 *spiral*: circular. During the summer months in the polar regions the sun
   never sets, as in the winter it never rises, cf. *Wi.* 797–8.
887 *Tornea's lake*: Torne Lake in northern Sweden, near the border with Norway
   and at the head of the Tornio river which divides Sweden and Finland.
888 *Hecla*: the volcano in Iceland.
893 *beneath another sky*: 'The other hemisphere' (T.).

Here arms his winds with all-subduing frost;
Moulds his fierce hail, and treasures up his snows,   900
With which he now oppresses half the globe.[n]
    Thence winding eastward to the Tartar's coast,
She sweeps the howling margin of the main;
Where, undissolving from the first of time,
Snows swell on snows amazing to the sky;   905
And icy mountains high on mountains piled
Seem to the shivering sailor from afar,
Shapeless and white, an atmosphere of clouds.
Projected huge and horrid o'er the surge,
Alps frown on Alps; or, rushing hideous down,   910
As if old Chaos was again returned,
Wide-rend the deep and shake the solid pole.[n]
Ocean itself no longer can resist
The binding fury; but, in all its rage
Of tempest taken by the boundless frost,   915
Is many a fathom to the bottom chained,
And bid to roar no more—a bleak expanse
Shagged o'er with wavy rocks, cheerless, and void
Of every life, that from the dreary months
Flies conscious southward. Miserable they!   920
Who, here entangled in the gathering ice,
Take their last look of the descending sun;
While, full of death and fierce with tenfold frost,
The long long night, incumbent o'er their heads,
Falls horrible! Such was the Briton's fate,[n]   925
As with first prow (what have not Britons dared?)
He for the passage sought, attempted since
So much in vain, and seeming to be shut
By jealous Nature with eternal bars.
In these fell regions, in Arzina caught,   930
And to the stony deep his idle ship
Immediate sealed, he with his hapless crew,
Each full exerted at his several task,
Froze into statues—to the cordage glued
The sailor, and the pilot to the helm.   935
    Hard by these shores, where scarce his freezing stream
Rolls the wild Oby, live the last of men;

902 *Tartar's coast*: northern Siberia.
918 *shagged*: made rough, cf. *Sp.* 910.   918 *wavy rocks*: frozen waves.
937 *Oby*: the river rising near the borders of Russia and Mongolia, and flowing
to the Arctic Ocean.

And, half enlivened by the distant sun,
That rears and ripens man as well as plants,
Here human nature wears its rudest form.   940
Deep from the piercing season sunk in caves,
Here by dull fires and with unjoyous cheer
They waste the tedious gloom: immersed in furs
Doze the gross race—nor sprightly jest, nor song,
Nor tenderness they know, nor aught of life   945
Beyond the kindred bears that stalk without—
Till Morn at length, her roses drooping all,
Sheds a long twilight brightening o'er their fields
And calls the quivered savage to the chase.[n]
        What cannot active government perform,   950
New-moulding man ? Wide-stretching from these shores,
A people savage from remotest time,
A huge neglected empire, one vast mind
By heaven inspired from Gothic darkness called.
Immortal Peter ![n] first of monarchs ! He   955
His stubborn country tamed,—her rocks, her fens,
Her floods, her seas, her ill-submitting sons;
And, while the fierce barbarian he subdued,
To more exalted soul he raised the man.
Ye shades of ancient heroes, ye who toiled   960
Through long successive ages to build up
A labouring plan of state, behold at once
The wonder done ! behold the matchless prince !
Who left his native throne, where reigned till then
A mighty shadow of unreal power;   965
Who greatly spurned the slothful pomp of courts;
And, roaming every land, in every port
His sceptre laid aside, with glorious hand
Unwearied plying the mechanic tool,
Gathered the seeds of trade, of useful arts,   970
Of civil wisdom, and of martial skill.
Charged with the stores of Europe home he goes !
Then cities rise amid the illumined waste;
O'er joyless deserts smiles the rural reign;
Far-distant flood to flood is social joined;   975
The astonished Euxine hears the Baltic roar;

---

941 *Deep from the piercing season*: far from summer (on 'piercing' cf. *Sp.* 556–
71, *Su.* 141 end-notes).
954 *Gothic*: barbarian.

Proud navies ride on seas that never foamed
With daring keel before; and armies stretch
Each way their dazzling files, repressing here
The frantic Alexander of the north,   980
And awing there stern Othman's shrinking sons.
Sloth flies the land, and ignorance and vice,
Of old dishonour proud: it glows around,
Taught by the royal hand that roused the whole,
One scene of arts, of arms, of rising trade—   985
For, what his wisdom planned and power enforced,
More potent still his great example showed.[n]

Muttering, the winds at eve with blunted point
Blow hollow-blustering from the south. Subdued,
The frost resolves into a trickling thaw.   990
Spotted the mountains shine: loose sleet descends,
And floods the country round. The rivers swell,
Of bonds impatient. Sudden from the hills,
O'er rocks and woods, in broad brown cataracts,
A thousand snow-fed torrents shoot at once;   995
And, where they rush, the wide-resounding plain
Is left one slimy waste. Those sullen seas,
That washed the ungenial pole, will rest no more
Beneath the shackles of the mighty north,
But, rousing all their waves, resistless heave.   1000
And, hark! the lengthening roar continuous runs
Athwart the rifted deep: at once it bursts,
And piles a thousand mountains to the clouds.
Ill fares the bark, with trembling wretches charged,
That, tossed amid the floating fragments, moors   1005
Beneath the shelter of an icy isle,
While night o'erwhelms the sea, and horror looks
More horrible.[n] Can human force endure
The assembled mischiefs that besiege them round?—
Heart-gnawing hunger, fainting weariness,   1010
The roar of winds and waves, the crush of ice,
Now ceasing, now renewed with louder rage,
And in dire echoes bellowing round the main.

980 *Alexander of the north*: Charles XII (1682–1718), King of Sweden, the military genius who inflicted defeats in turn on Denmark, Russia, and Poland (1700–2). In 1708 he invaded Russia, but his army, severely weakened by the Russian winter, was annihilated at Pultava in 1709.
981 *Othman's ... sons*: the Turks.

More to embroil the deep, Leviathan
And his unwieldy train in dreadful sport   1015
Tempest the loosened brine; while through the gloom
Far from the bleak inhospitable shore,
Loading the winds, is heard the hungry howl
Of famished monsters, there awaiting wrecks.
Yet Providence, that ever-waking Eye,   1020
Looks down with pity on the feeble toil
Of mortals lost to hope and lights them safe
Through all this dreary labyrinth of fate.

    'Tis done! Dread Winter spreads his latest glooms,
And reigns tremendous o'er the conquered year.   1025
How dead the vegetable kingdom lies!
How dumb the tuneful! Horror wide extends
His desolate domain. Behold, fond man!
See here thy pictured life; pass some few years,
Thy flowering Spring, thy Summer's ardent strength, 1030
Thy sober Autumn fading into age,
And pale concluding Winter comes at last
And shuts the scene. Ah! whither now are fled
Those dreams of greatness? those unsolid hopes
Of happiness? those longings after fame?   1035
Those restless cares? those busy bustling days?
Those gay-spent festive nights? those veering thoughts,
Lost between good and ill, that shared thy life?
All now are vanished! Virtue sole survives—
Immortal, never-failing friend of man,   1040
His guide to happiness on high. And see!
'Tis come, the glorious morn! the second birth
Of heaven and earth! awakening Nature hears
The new-creating word, and starts to life
In every heightened form, from pain and death   1045
For ever free.[n] The great eternal scheme,
Involving all, and in a perfect whole
Uniting, as the prospect wider spreads,
To reason's eye refined clears up apace.[n]
Ye vainly wise! ye blind presumptuous! now,   1050
Confounded in the dust, adore that Power

1014 *Leviathan*: the monster in Job 41, but here, as frequently in modern litera-
ture, identified with the whale.
1016 *tempests*: agitates violently, cf. *P.L.* VII.412.
1027 *tuneful kingdom*: birds. On periphrases see *Sp.* 132 end-note.

And Wisdom—oft arraigned: see now the cause
Why unassuming Worth in secret lived
And died neglected: why the good man's share
In life was gall and bitterness of soul: 1055
Why the lone widow and her orphans pined
In starving solitude; while Luxury
In palaces lay straining her low thought
To form unreal wants: why heaven-born Truth
And Moderation fair wore the red marks   1060
Of Superstition's scourge; why licensed Pain,
That cruel spoiler, that embosomed foe,
Embittered all our bliss. Ye good distressed!
Ye noble few! who here unbending stand
Beneath life's pressure, yet bear up a while,   1065
And what your bounded view, which only saw
A little part, deemed evil is no more:
The storms of wintry time will quickly pass,
And one unbounded Spring encircle all.

A Hymn on the Seasons

THESE, as they change, Almighty Father! these
Are but the varied God. The rolling year
Is full of thee.[n] Forth in the pleasing Spring
Thy beauty walks, thy tenderness and love.
Wide flush the fields; the softening air is balm;   5
Echo the mountains round; the forest smiles;
And every sense, and every heart, is joy.
Then comes thy glory in the Summer-months,
With light and heat refulgent. Then thy Sun
Shoots full perfection through the swelling year: 10
And oft thy voice in dreadful thunder speaks,
And oft, at dawn, deep noon, or falling eve,
By brooks and groves, in hollow-whispering gales.
Thy bounty shines in Autumn unconfined,
And spreads a common feast for all that lives.   15
In Winter awful thou! with clouds and storms
Around thee thrown, tempest o'er tempest rolled,
Majestic darkness! On the whirlwind's wing
Riding sublime, thou bidst the world adore,
And humblest nature with thy northern blast.   20

    Mysterious round! what skill, what force divine,
Deep-felt in these appear! a simple train,
Yet so delightful mixed, with such kind art,
Such beauty and beneficence combined,
Shade unperceived so softening into shade,   25
And all so forming an harmonious whole[n]
That, as they still succeed, they ravish still.
But, wandering oft with brute unconscious gaze,
Man marks not thee, marks not the mighty hand
That, ever busy, wheels the silent spheres,   30
Works in the secret deep, shoots steaming thence

31 *deep*: the earth, cf. *Sp.* 79–80.

The fair profusion that o'erspreads the Spring,
Flings from the sun direct the flaming day,
Feeds every creature, hurls the tempest forth,
And, as on earth this grateful change revolves, 35
With transport touches all the springs of life.

Nature, attend! join, every living soul
Beneath the spacious temple of the sky,
In adoration join; and ardent raise
One general song! To him, ye vocal gales, 40
Breathe soft, whose spirit in your freshness breathes:
Oh! talk of him in solitary glooms,
Where, o'er the rock, the scarcely-waving pine
Fills the brown shade with a religious awe.
And ye, whose bolder note is heard afar, 45
Who shake the astonished world, lift high to Heaven
The impetuous song, and say from whom you rage.
His praise, ye brooks, attune, ye trembling rills;
And let me catch it as I muse along.
Ye headlong torrents, rapid and profound; 50
Ye softer floods, that lead the humid maze
Along the vale; and thou, majestic main,
A secret world of wonders in thyself,
Sound his stupendous praise, whose greater voice
Or bids you roar or bids your roarings fall. 55
Soft roll your incense, herbs, and fruits, and flowers,
In mingled clouds to him, whose sun exalts,
Whose breath perfumes you, and whose pencil paints.
Ye forests, bend; ye harvests, wave to him—
Breathe your still song into the reaper's heart 60
As home he goes beneath the joyous moon.
Ye that keep watch in heaven, as earth asleep
Unconscious lies, effuse your mildest beams,
Ye constellations! while your angels strike
Amid the spangled sky the silver lyre. 65
Great source of day! best image here below
Of thy Creator, ever pouring wide
From world to world the vital ocean^n round!
On nature write with every beam his praise.
The thunder rolls: be hushed the prostrate world, 70

36 *springs of life*: cf. *Sp.* 330 fn.
58 *pencil*: small brush.   66 *source of day*: the sun.

While cloud to cloud returns the solemn hymn.
Bleat out afresh, ye hills; ye mossy rocks,
Retain the sound; the broad responsive low,
Ye valleys, raise; for the Great Shepherd reigns,
And his unsuffering kingdom yet will come.   75
Ye woodlands all, awake: a boundless song
Burst from the groves; and, when the restless day,
Expiring, lays the warbling world asleep,
Sweetest of birds, sweet Philomela! charm
The listening shades, and teach the night his praise!   80
Ye, chief, for whom the whole creation smiles,
At once the head, the heart, and tongue of all,
Crown the great hymn! In swarming cities vast,
Assembled men, to the deep organ join
The long-resounding voice, oft breaking clear   85
At solemn pauses through the swelling bass;
And, as each mingling flame increases each,
In one united ardour rise to heaven.
Or, if you rather choose the rural shade,
And find a fane in every sacred grove,   90
There let the shepherd's flute, the virgin's lay,
The prompting seraph, and the poet's lyre
Still sing the God of Seasons as they roll.
For me, when I forget the darling theme,
Whether the blossom blows, the summer-ray   95
Russets the plain, inspiring autumn gleams,
Or winter rises in the blackening east,
Be my tongue mute, may fancy paint no more,
And, dead to joy, forget my heart to beat!

  Should fate command me to the farthest verge   100
Of the green earth, to distant barbarous climes,
Rivers unknown to song, where first the sun
Gilds Indian mountains, or his setting beam
Flames on the Atlantic isles, 'tis nought to me;
Since God is ever present, ever felt,   105
In the void waste as in the city full,
And where he vital spreads^n there must be joy.
When even at last the solemn hour shall come,

79 *Philomela*: see *Sp.* 601 fn.
81 *chief*: man.
96 *russets the plain*: parches the grass brown, cf. *Cas. Ind.* I.ii.7.
96 *gleams*: with light reflected from ripe corn.

And wing my mystic flight to future worlds,
I cheerful will obey; there, with new powers,   110
Will rising wonders sing: I cannot go
Where Universal Love not smiles around,[n]
Sustaining all yon orbs and all their sons;
From seeming evil still educing good,
And better thence again, and better still,   115
In infinite progression. But I lose
Myself in him, in light ineffable ![n]
Come then, expressive Silence, muse his praise.

113 *sons*: inhabitants, cf. *Su*. 107 end-note.

The Castle of Indolence

An Allegorical Poem,
Written in Imitation of Spenser

ADVERTISEMENT

This poem being writ in the manner of Spenser, the obsolete words, and a simplicity of diction in some of the lines which borders on the ludicrous, were necessary to make the imitation more perfect. And the style of that admirable poet, as well as the measure in which he wrote, are as it were appropriated by custom to all allegorical poems writ in our language—just as in French the style of Marot, who lived under Francis I, has been used in tales and familiar epistles by the politest writers of the age of Louis XIV.

Marot: Clément Marot (1495–1544) was imitated by Spenser (cf. Argument of 'November' in *The Shepheardes Calender*). Boileau advised his contemporaries in the later seventeenth century 'Imitez de Marot l'élégant badinage.'

The Castle of Indolence

The Castle hight^e of Indolence,
And its false luxury;
Where for a little time, alas!
We lived right jollily.

I

O MORTAL man, who livest here by toil,
Do not complain of this thy hard estate;
That like an emmet thou must ever moil^e
Is a sad sentence of an ancient date:ⁿ
And, certes,^e there is for it reason great;
For though sometimes it makes thee weep and wail,
And curse thy stars, and early drudge and late,
Withouten that would come an heavier bale,^e
Loose life, unruly passions, and diseases pale.

II

In lowly dale, fast by a river's side,
With woody hill o'er hill encompassed round,
A most enchanting wizard did abide,
Than whom a fiend more fell is nowhere found.
It was, I ween,^e a lovely spot of ground;
And there a season atween^e June and May,
Half prankt with spring, with summer half imbrowned,
A listless climate made, where, sooth^e to say,
No living wight could work, ne^e carèd even for play.

III

Was nought around but images of rest:
Sleep-soothing groves, and quiet lawns between;
And flowery beds that slumbrous influence kest,^e
From poppies breathed; and beds of pleasant green,

Where never yet was creeping creature seen.
Meantime unnumbered glittering streamlets played,
And hurlèd everywhere their waters sheen;[e]
That, as they bickered through the sunny glade,
Though restless still themselves, a lulling murmur made.

                            IV

Joined to the prattle of the purling rills,
Were heard the lowing herds along the vale,
And flocks loud-bleating from the distant hills,
And vacant shepherds piping in the dale:
And now and then sweet Philomel would wail,
Or stock-doves plain amid the forest deep,
That drowsy rustled to the sighing gale;
And still a coil the grasshopper did keep:
Yet all these sounds yblent[e] inclinèd all to sleep.

                             V

Full in the passage of the vale, above,
A sable, silent, solemn forest stood;
Where nought but shadowy forms were seen to move,
As Idless[e] fancied in her dreaming mood.
And up the hills, on either side, a wood
Of blackening pines, ay waving to and fro,
Sent forth a sleepy horror through the blood;
And where this valley winded out, below,
The murmuring main was heard, and scarcely heard, to flow.

                            VI

A pleasing land of drowsyhed it was:
Of dreams that wave before the half-shut eye;
And of gay castles in the clouds that pass,
For ever flushing round a summer sky:
There eke the soft delights, that witchingly
Instil a wanton sweetness through the breast,
And the calm pleasures always hovered nigh;
But whate'er smacked of noyance,[e] or unrest,
Was far far off expelled from this delicious nest.[n]

---

iv *vacant*: carefree.   iv *Philomel*: see *Sp*. 601 fn.
iv *coil*: disturbance.   v *ay*: aye, ever.
vi *drowsyhed*: drowsiness, cf. *F.Q*.I.ii.7.5.

VII

The landskip such, inspiring perfect ease;
Where Indolence (for so the wizard hight)ᵉ
Close-hid his castle mid embowering trees,
That half shut out the beams of Phoebus bright,
And made a kind of checkered day and night.
Meanwhile, unceasing at the massy gate,
Beneath a spacious palm, the wicked wight
Was placed; and, to his lute, of cruel fate
And labour harsh complained, lamenting man's estate.

VIII

Thither continual pilgrims crowded still
From all the roads of earth that pass there by:
For, as they chaunced to breathe on neighbouring hill,
The freshness of this valley smote their eye,
And drew them ever and anon more nigh,
Till clustering round the enchanter false they hung,
Ymoltenᵉ with his syren melody;
While o'er th' enfeebling lute his hand he flung,
And to the trembling chord these tempting verses sung:

IX

'Behold! ye pilgrims of this earth, behold!
See all but man with unearned pleasure gay.
See her bright robes the butterfly unfold,
Broke from her wintry tomb in prime of May.
What youthful bride can equal her array?
Who can with her for easy pleasure vie?
From mead to mead with gentle wing to stray,
From flower to flower on balmy gales to fly,
Is all she has to do beneath the radiant sky.

vii *landskip*: landscape.
vii *Phoebus*: Phoebus (i.e. 'the bright') Apollo was, in Greek mythology, some-
   times identified with the sun, cf. *Wi.* 532, 660.
viii *breathe*: pause to catch breath, cf. *F.Q.* IV.ii.18.7.
viii *syren*: siren, cf. *Sp.* 994 fn.
ix *tomb*: chrysalis, cf. *Su.* 245.

X

'Behold the merry minstrels of the morn,
The swarming songsters of the careless grove,
Ten thousand throats that, from the flowering thorn,
Hymn their good God, and carol sweet of love,
Such grateful kindly raptures them emove!
They neither plough nor sow; ne, fit for flail,
E'er to the barn the nodding sheaves they drove;
Yet theirs each harvest dancing in the gale,
Whatever crowns the hill, or smiles along the vale.

XI

'Outcast of Nature, man! the wretched thrall
Of bitter-dropping sweat, of sweltry^e pain,
Of cares that eat away thy heart with gall,
And of the vices, an inhuman train,
That all proceed from savage thirst of gain:
For when hard-hearted Interest first began
To poison earth, Astraea left the plain;
Guile, Violence, and Murder seized on man,
And, for soft milky streams, with blood the rivers ran.

XII

'Come, ye, who still the cumbrous load of life
Push hard up hill; but, as the farthest steep
You trust to gain, and put an end to strife,
Down thunders back the stone with mighty sweep,
And hurls your labours to the valley deep,
Forever vain: come, and withouten fee
I in oblivion will your sorrows steep,
Your cares, your toils; will steep you in a sea
Of full delight: O come, ye weary wights, to me!^{n}

x *merry minstrels . . . swarming songsters*: birds. On periphrases see *Sp.* 132
   end-note.
x *emove*: affect with emotion.
x *fit for flail*: ready for threshing.
xi *Interest*: self-interest.
xi *Astraea*: the constellation Virgo (cf. *Au.* 23), identified by the Romans with
   Justice. In the Golden Age (cf. *Sp.* 242–74 end-note) she lived on earth ('the
   plain'), but owing to man's wickedness she fled to the skies. Cf. Virgil, *Eclogues*
   IV.6; *Georgics* II.473–4.
xi *for*: instead of. (In the Golden Age the rivers ran with milk and honey, cf.
   Ovid, *Metamorphoses*, I.111.)

XIII

'With me, you need not rise at early dawn,
To pass the joyless day in various stounds;[e]
Or, louting[e] low, on upstart fortune fawn,
And sell fair honour for some paltry pounds;
Or through the city take your dirty rounds
To cheat, and dun, and lie, and visit pay,
Now flattering base, now giving secret wounds;
Or prowl in courts of law for human prey,
In venal senate thieve, or rob on broad highway.[n]

XIV

'No cocks, with me, to rustic labour call,
From village on to village sounding clear;
To tardy swain no shrill-voiced matrons squall;
No dogs, no babes, no wives to stun your ear;
No hammers thump; no horrid blacksmith sear,[e]
Ne noisy tradesmen your sweet slumbers start
With sounds that are a misery to hear:
But all is calm as would delight the heart
Of Sybarite[n] of old, all Nature, and all Art.

XV

'Here nought but candour reigns, indulgent ease,
Good-natured lounging, sauntering up and down:
They who are pleased themselves must always please;
On others' ways they never squint a frown,
Nor heed what haps in hamlet or in town.
Thus, from the source of tender Indolence,
With milky blood the heart is overflown,
Is soothed and sweetened by the social sense;[n]
For interest, envy, pride, and strife are banished hence.

XVI

'What, what is virtue but repose of mind?
A pure ethereal calm that knows no storm,
Above the reach of wild ambition's wind,
Above those passions that this world deform,
And torture man, a proud malignant worm!

xv *candour*: kindliness.   xv *milky*: gentle.

But here, instead, soft gales of passion play,
And gently stir the heart, thereby to form
A quicker sense of joy; as breezes stray
Across the enlivened skies, and make them still more gay.

XVII

'The best of men have ever loved repose:
They hate to mingle in the filthy fray;
Where the soul sours, and gradual rancour grows,
Imbittered more from peevish day to day.
Even those whom fame has lent her fairest ray,
The most renowned of worthy wights of yore,
From a base world at last have stolen away:
So Scipio, to the soft Cumaean shore
Retiring, tasted joy he never knew before.

XVIII

'But if a little exercise you chuse,
Some zest for ease, 'tis not forbidden here.
Amid the groves you may indulge the Muse,
Or tend the blooms, and deck the vernal year;
Or softly stealing, with your watery gear,⁰
Along the brooks, the crimson-spotted fry
You may delude: the whilst, amused, you hear
Now the hoarse stream, and now the zephyr's sigh,
Attunèd to the birds, and woodland melody.

XIX

'O grievous folly! to heap up estate,
Losing the days you see beneath the sun;
When, sudden, comes blind unrelenting Fate,
And gives the untasted portion you have won
With ruthless toil, and many a wretch undone,

---

xvii *Scipio*: Scipio Africanus Major (236–184 B.C.) the Roman Consul and general
who defeated the Carthaginians at Zama in 204 B.C. After being accused of
bribery he retired to his estate at Liternum near Cumae and Naples. Cf. *Wi.*
517.
xviii *amused*: musing.   xix *blind*: undiscriminating.
xix *Fate*: in classical mythology Fate or the Fates (usually represented as three
old women) allotted a new-born child's portion of life and so determined
the moment of his death. Cf. *Lycidas*, 75, where Milton identifies Fates with
Furies (as the Greeks sometimes did, cf. Hesiod, *Theogony*, 217–22).

To those who mock you gone to Pluto's reign,
There with sad ghosts to pine, and shadows dun:
But sure it is of vanities most vain,
To toil for what you here untoiling may obtain.'ⁿ

XX

He ceased. But still their trembling ears retained
The deep vibrations of his witching song;
That, by a kind of magic power, constrained
To enter in, pell-mell, the listening throng.
Heaps poured on heaps, and yet they slipt along
In silent ease: as when, beneath the beam
Of summer moons, the distant woods among,
Or by some flood all silvered with the gleam,
The soft-embodied fays through airy portal stream.ⁿ

XXI

By the smooth demon so it ordered was,
And here his baneful bounty first began:
Though some there were who would not further pass,
And his alluring baits suspected han.ᵉ
The wise distrust the too fair-spoken man,
Yet through the gate they cast a wishful eye:
Not to move on, perdie,ᵉ is all they can;
For, do their very best, they cannot fly,
But often each way look, and often sorely sigh.

XXII

When this the watchful wicked wizard saw,
With sudden spring he leaped upon them strait;
And, soon as touched by his unhallowed paw,
They found themselves within the cursèd gate,
Full hard to be repassed, like that of Fate.
Not stronger were of old the giant-crew,
Who sought to pull high Jove from regal state,
Though feeble wretch he seemed, of sallow hue:
Certes, who bides his grasp, will that encounter rue.

xix *Pluto's reign*: kingdom of Pluto who, in Greek mythology, ruled over the
   dead, cf. *F.Q.*II.vii.21.4.
xxii *strait*: straightway.
xxii *giant-crew*: in Greek mythology the huge sons of Ge (the Earth) who rebelled
   unsuccessfully against Zeus and the other gods.

XXIII

For whomsoe'er the villain takes in hand,
Their joints unknit, their sinews melt apace;
As lithe they grow as any willow-wand,
And of their vanished force remains no trace:
So when a maiden fair, of modest grace,
In all her buxom blooming May of charms,
Is seizèd in some losel's[e] hot embrace,
She waxeth very weakly as she warms,
Then sighing yields her up to love's delicious harms.

XXIV

Waked by the crowd, slow from his bench arose
A comely full-spread porter, swoln with sleep:
His calm, broad, thoughtless aspect breathed repose;
And in sweet torpor he was plungèd deep,
Ne could himself from ceaseless yawning keep;
While o'er his eyes the drowsy liquor ran,
Through which his half-waked soul would faintly peep.
Then, taking his black staff, he called his man,
And roused himself as much as rouse himself he can.

XXV

The lad leaped lightly at his master's call.
He was, to weet,[e] a little roguish page,
Save sleep and play who minded nought at all,
Like most the untaught striplings of his age.
This boy he kept each band to disengage,
Garters and buckles, task for him unfit,
But ill-becoming his grave personage,
And which his portly paunch would not permit.
So this same limber page to all performèd it.[n]

XXVI

Meantime the master-porter wide displayed
Great store of caps, of slippers, and of gowns,
Wherewith he those who entered in arrayed,
Loose as the breeze that plays along the downs,
And waves the summer woods when evening frowns.

O fair undress, best dress! it checks no vein,
But every flowing limb in pleasure drowns,
And heightens ease with grace. This done, right fain
Sir Porter sat him down, and turned to sleep again.

XXVII

Thus easy robed, they to the fountain sped,
That in the middle of the court up-threw
A stream, high-spouting from its liquid bed,
And falling back again in drizzly dew:
There each deep draughts, as deep he thirsted, drew;
It was a fountain of Nepenthe rare:
Whence, as Dan Homer sings, huge pleasaunce grew,
And sweet oblivion of vile earthy care,
Fair gladsome waking thoughts, and joyous dreams more fair.

XXVIII

This rite performed, all inly pleased and still,
Withouten trump was proclamation made:—
'Ye sons of Indolence, do what you will;[n]
And wander where you list, through hall or glade:
Be no man's pleasure for another's staid:
Let each as likes him best his hours employ,
And curst be he who minds his neighbour's trade!
Here dwells kind ease, and unreproving joy:
He little merits bliss who others can annoy.'

XXIX

Strait of these endless numbers, swarming round
As thick as idle motes in sunny ray,
Not one eftsoons[e] in view was to be found,
But every man strolled off his own glad way.
Wide o'er this ample court's blank area,
With all the lodges that thereto pertained,
No living creature could be seen to stray;
While solitude and perfect silence reigned:
So that to think you dreamt you almost was constrained.

---

xxvi *undress*: informal costume worn at home.
xxvii *Nepenthe*: the magic drug that makes one forget all troubles; cf. Homer, *Odyssey*, IV.220 ff., *F.Q.* IV.iii.43–5.
xxvii *Dan*: Master (often used playfully).   xxvii *pleasaunce*: pleasure.
xxix *you . . . was*: common as the second person singular form in the eighteenth century.

XXX

As when a shepherd of the Hebrid Isles,
Placed far amid the melancholy main,
(Whether it be lone fancy him beguiles,
Or that aerial beings sometimes deign
To stand embodied to our senses plain)
Sees on the naked hill, or valley low,
The whilst in ocean Phoebus dips his wain,
A vast assembly moving to and fro;
Then all at once in air dissolves the wondrous show.

XXXI

Ye gods of quiet, and of sleep profound,
Whose soft dominion o'er this castle sways,
And all the widely-silent places round,
Forgive me, if my trembling pen displays
What never yet was sung in mortal lays.
But how shall I attempt such arduous string?
I who have spent my nights and nightly days
In this soul-deadening place, loose-loitering—
Ah! how shall I for this uprear my moulted wing?[n]

XXXII

Come on, my Muse, nor stoop to low despair,
Thou imp[e] of Jove, touched by celestial fire!
Thou yet shalt sing of war, and actions fair,
Which the bold sons of Britain will inspire;
Of ancient bards thou yet shalt sweep the lyre;
Thou yet shalt tread in tragic pall the stage,
Paint love's enchanting woes, the hero's ire,
The sage's calm, the patriot's noble rage,
Dashing corruption down through every worthless age.[n]

xxx *Hebrid Isles*: 'Those islands on the western coast of Scotland, called the
    Hebrides.' (T.) Cf. *Au.* 871–80.
xxx *Phoebus dips his wain*: the sun sets, see *Cas. Ind.* I.vii.4 fn.
xxxi *nightly days*: days that have been slept through.
xxxii *imp of Jove*: the Muses were the daughters of Zeus (Jupiter, or Jove); cf.
    'imp of Phoebus' in *F.Q.* I.xi.5.

XXXIII

The doors, that knew no shrill alarming bell,
Ne cursèd knocker plied by villain's hand,
Self-opened into halls, where, who can tell
What elegance and grandeur wide expand
The pride of Turkey and of Persia land ?
Soft quilts on quilts, on carpets carpets spread,
And couches stretched around in seemly band;
And endless pillows rise to prop the head;
So that each spacious room was one full-swelling bed.

XXXIV

And everywhere huge covered tables stood,
With wines high-flavoured and rich viands crowned
Whatever sprightly juice or tastful food
On the green bosom of this Earth are found,
And all old Ocean genders in his round—[n]
Some hand unseen these silently displayed,
Even undemanded by a sign or sound;
You need but wish, and, instantly obeyed,
Fair-ranged the dishes rose, and thick the glasses played.

XXXV

Here freedom reigned without the least alloy;
Nor gossip's tale, nor ancient maiden's gall,
Nor saintly spleen durst murmur at our joy,
And with envenomed tongue our pleasures pall.
For why ? there was but one great rule for all;
To wit, that each should work his own desire,
And eat, drink, study, sleep, as it may fall,
Or melt the time in love, or wake the lyre,
And carol[e] what, unbid, the Muses might inspire.

XXXVI

The rooms with costly tapestry were hung,
Where was inwoven many a gentle tale,
Such as of old the rural poets sung

xxxiv *played*: made play of reflected light.
xxxv *saintly spleen*: Puritan disapproval.
xxxv *pall*: weaken, cf. *F.Q.* V.iv.5.9.
xxxvi *rural poets*: the classical masters of pastoral poetry; Theocritus had written
of Sicily and Virgil of Arcadia, cf. *Su.* 1301 fn.

Or of Arcadian or Sicilian vale:
Reclining lovers, in the lonely dale,
Poured forth at large the sweetly tortured heart;
Or, looking tender passion, swelled the gale,
And taught charmed echo to resound their smart;
While flocks, woods, streams around, repose and peace impart.

XXXVII

Those pleased the most, where, by a cunning hand,
Depeinten was the patriarchal age;
What time Dan Abraham left the Chaldee land,
And pastured on from verdant stage to stage,
Where fields and fountains fresh could best engage.
Toil was not then. Of nothing took they heed,
But with wild beasts the silvan war to wage,
And o'er vast plains their herds and flocks to feed:
Blest sons of Nature they! true Golden Age indeed!

XXXVIII

Sometimes the pencil, in cool airy halls,,
Bade the gay bloom of vernal landskips rise,
Or Autumn's varied shades imbrown the walls:
Now the black tempest strikes the astonished eyes;
Now down the steep the flashing torrent flies;
The trembling sun now plays o'er ocean blue,
And now rude mountains frown amid the skies;
Whate'er Lorrain light-touched with softening hue,
Or savage Rosa dashed, or learnèd Poussin drew.[n]

XXXIX

Each sound too here to languishment inclined,
Lulled the weak bosom, and inducèd ease.
Aerial music in the warbling wind,
At distance rising oft, by small degrees,
Nearer and nearer came, till o'er the trees

xxxvii *Depeiten*: painted.
xxxvii *Dan*: Master, cf. *Cas. Ind.* I.xxvii.
xxxvii *Abraham*: cf. Gen. 11:31.
xxxvii *Golden Age*: see *Sp.* 242–74 end-note.
xxxviii *pencil*: small painting brush, cf. *Hymn* 58.
xxxviii *landskips*: landscapes, cf. *Cas. Ind.* I.vii.1.

It hung, and breathed such soul-dissolving airs
As did, alas! with soft perdition please:
Entangled deep in its enchanting snares,
The listening heart forgot all duties and all cares.

XL

A certain music, never known before,
Here soothed the pensive melancholy mind;
Full easily obtained. Behoves no more,
But sidelong to the gently-waving wind
To lay the well-tuned instrument reclined;
From which, with airy flying fingers light,
Beyond each mortal touch the most refined,
The god of winds drew sounds of deep delight:
Whence, with just cause, the harp of Aeolus[n] it hight.

XLI

Ah me! what hand can touch the strings so fine?
Who up the lofty diapason roll
Such sweet, such sad, such solemn airs divine,
Then let them down again into the soul?
Now rising love they fanned; now pleasing dole
They breathed, in tender musings, through the heart;
And now a graver sacred strain they stole,
As when seraphic hands an hymn impart:
Wild warbling Nature all, above the reach of Art![n]

XLII

Such the gay splendour, the luxurious state,
Of Caliphs old, who on the Tygris' shore,
In mighty Bagdat, populous and great,
Held their bright court, where was of ladies store;
And verse, love, music still the garland wore:
When sleep was coy, the bard in waiting there
Cheered the lone midnight with the muse's lore;[n]
Composing music bade his dreams be fair,
And music lent new gladness to the morning air.

xlii *composing*: soothing.

XLIII

Near the pavilions where we slept, still ran
Soft-tinkling streams, and dashing waters fell,
And sobbing breezes sighed, and oft began
(So worked the wizard) wintry storms to swell,
As heaven and earth they would together mell:[o]
At doors and windows, threatening, seemed to call
The demons[n] of the tempest, growling fell;
Yet the least entrance found they none at all;
Whence sweeter grew our sleep, secure in massy hall.

XLIV

And hither Morpheus sent his kindest dreams,
Raising a world of gayer tinct and grace;
O'er which were shadowy cast Elysian gleams,
That played in waving lights from place to place,
And shed a roseate smile on nature's face.
Not Titian's pencil e'er could so array,
So fleece with clouds the pure ethereal space;
Ne could it e'er such melting forms display,
As loose on flowery beds all languishingly lay.

XLV

No, fair illusions! artful phantoms, no!
My Muse will not attempt your fairy-land:
She has no colours that like you can glow;
To catch your vivid scenes too gross her hand.
But sure it is, was ne'er a subtler band
Than these same guileful angel-seeming sprights,
Who thus in dreams voluptuous, soft, and bland,
Poured all the Arabian heaven upon our nights,
And blessed them oft besides with more refined delights.

xliv *Morpheus*: in Greek mythology the god of dreams; cf. *F.Q.* I.i.38–44.
xliv *Elysian*: of Elysium—in classical mythology the blessed place where those favoured by the gods enjoy a happy life after death; cf. *Au.* 1070.
xliv *Titian*: (1480–1576), the Venetian painter widely regarded as the greatest master of colour.
xliv *pencil*: small painting brush, cf. *Cas. Ind.* I.xxxviii.1.
xlv *Arabian heaven*: dreams of beautiful women (alluding to the houris or beautiful nymphs who would solace the blessed in the Mohammedan Paradise).

XLVI

They were in sooth^e a most enchanting train,
Even feigning virtue; skilful to unite
With evil good, and strew with pleasure pain.
But, for those fiends whom blood and broils delight,
Who hurl the wretch as if to hell outright
Down, down black gulfs where sullen waters sleep,
Or hold him clambering all the fearful night
On beetling cliffs, or pent in ruins deep—
They, till due time should serve, were bid far hence to keep.

XLVII

Ye guardian spirits, to whom man is dear,
From these foul demons shield the midnight gloom!
Angels of fancy and of love, be near,
And o'er the wilds of sleep diffuse a bloom;
Evoke the sacred shades of Greece and Rome,
And let them virtue with a look impart!
But chief, a while O! lend us from the tomb
Those long-lost friends for whom in love we smart,
And fill with pious awe and joy-mixt woe the heart!

XLVIII

Or are you sportive?—bid the morn of youth
Rise to new light, and beam afresh the days
Of innocence, simplicity, and truth,
To cares estranged, and manhood's thorny ways
What transport to retrace our boyish plays,
Our easy bliss, when each thing joy supplied—
The woods, the mountains, and the warbling maze
Of the wild brooks! But, fondly wandering wide,
My Muse, resume the task that yet doth thee abide.

XLIX

One great amusement of our household was—
In a huge crystal magic globe^n to spy,
Still as you turned it, all things that do pass
Upon this ant-hill earth; where constantly

---

xlvii *guardian spirits*: true guardian-angels, not the angel-seeming spirits of
I.xlv.6.
xlvii *sacred shades*: such as those evoked in *Wi.* 437–534.

Of idly-busy men the restless fry
Run bustling to and fro with foolish haste
In search of pleasures vain, that from them fly,
Or which, obtained, the caitiffs dare not taste:
When nothing is enjoyed, can there be greater waste ?

L

Of Vanity the Mirror this was called.
Here you a muckworm of the town might see
At his dull desk, amid his legers stalled,
Eat up with carking care and penurie,
Most like to carcase parched on gallow-tree.
'A penny savèd is a penny got'—
Firm to this scoundrel maxim keepeth he,
Ne of its rigour will he bate a jot,
Till it has quenched his fire, and banishèd his pot.

LI

Strait from the filth of this low grub, behold !
Comes fluttering forth a gaudy spendthrift heir,
All glossy gay, enamelled all with gold, ´
The silly tenant of the summer-air.
In folly lost, of nothing takes he care;
Pimps, lawyers, stewards, harlots, flatterers vile,
And thieving tradesmen him among them share:
His father's ghost from Limbo-lake the while
Sees this, which more damnation doth upon him pile.[n]

LII

This globe pourtrayed the race of learned men,
Still at their books, and turning o'er the page,
Backwards and forwards: oft they snatch the pen
As if inspired, and in a Thespian rage;
Then write, and blot, as would your ruth engage.
Why, authors, all this scrawl and scribbling sore ?
To lose the present, gain the future age,
Praisèd to be when you can hear no more,
And much enriched with fame when useless worldly store !

li *Limbo-lake*: the pit of Hell, cf. *F.Q.* I.ii.32.5.
lii *Thespian rage*: frenzy of dramatic inspiration. Thespis was a semi-legendary
Greek dramatic poet of the sixth century B.C.

LIII

Then would a splendid city rise to view,
With carts, and cars, and coaches roaring all:
Wide-poured abroad, behold the prowling crew;
See how they dash along from wall to wall!
At every door, hark how they thundering call!
Good Lord! what can this giddy rout excite?
Why? each on each to prey, by guile or gall;
With flattery these, with slander those to blight,
And make new tiresome parties for the coming night.

LIV

The puzzling sons of party next appeared,
In dark cabals and nightly juntos met;
And now they whispered close, now shrugging reared
The important shoulder; then, as if to get
New light, their twinkling eyes were inward set.
No sooner Lucifer recalls affairs,
Than forth they various rush in mighty fret;
When lo! pushed up to power, and crowned their cares,
In comes another set, and kicketh them down stairs.

LV

But what most showed the vanity of life
Was to behold the nations all on fire,
In cruel broils engaged, and deadly strife:
Most Christian kings, inflamed by black desire,
With honourable ruffians in their hire,
Cause war to rage, and blood around to pour.
Of this sad work when each begins to tire,
They sit them down just where they were before,
Till for new scenes of woe peace shall their force restore.

LVI

To number up the thousands dwelling here,
An useless were, and eke an endless task—
From kings, and those who at the helm appear,
To gipsies brown in summer-glades who bask.

liv *sons of party*: politicians.
liv *Lucifer*: 'The Morning Star' (T.).

Yea, many a man, perdie,[e] I could unmask,
Whose desk and table make a solemn show
With tape-tied trash, and suits of fools, that ask
For place or pension, laid in decent row;
But these I passen by, with nameless numbers moe.[e]

LVII

Of all the gentle tenants of the place,
There was a man of special grave remark:
A certain tender gloom o'erspread his face,
Pensive, not sad; in thought involved, not dark:
As soote[e] this man could sing as morning-lark,
And teach the noblest morals of the heart;
But these his talents were yburied stark;
Of the fine stores he nothing would impart,
Which or boon Nature gave or Nature-painting Art.

LVIII

To noontide shades incontinent he ran
Where purls the brook with sleep-inviting sound;
Or, when Dan Sol to slope his wheels began,
Amid the broom he basked him on the ground,
Where the wild thyme and camomil are found:
There would he linger till the latest ray
Of light sat quivering on the welkin's bound;
Then homeward through the twilight shadows stray,
Sauntering and slow. So had he passèd many a day.

LIX

Yet not in thoughtless slumber were they past:
For oft the heavenly fire, that lay concealed
Emongst the sleeping embers, mounted fast,
And all its native light anew revealed.

lvii *man of special grave remark*: William Paterson, fellow-student of T. at Edin-
burgh, and friend of his in London ('remark' is air of observation).
lviii *incontinent*: precipitately.
lviii *Dan Sol*: the sun (for 'Dan' see I.xxvii.7).
lviii *slope his wheels*: descend (the reference is to the sun's chariot, cf. I.xxx.7).

Oft as he traversed the cerulean field,
And marked the clouds that drove before the wind,
Ten thousand glorious systems would he build,
Ten thousand great ideas filled his mind;
But with the clouds they fled, and left no trace behind.

LX

With him was sometimes joined in silent walk
(Profoundly silent, for they never spoke)
One[n] shyer still, who quite detested talk:
Oft, stung by spleen, at once away he broke
To groves of pine and broad o'ershadowing oak;
There, inly thrilled, he wandered all alone,
And on himself his pensive fury wroke,
Ne[e] ever uttered word, save when first shone
The glittering star of eve—'Thank heaven! the day is done.'

LXI

Here lurked a wretch who had not crept abroad
For forty years, ne face of mortal seen—
In chamber brooding like a loathly toad;
And sure his linen was not very clean.
Through secret loophole, that had practised been
Near to his bed, his dinner vile he took;
Unkempt, and rough, of squalid face and mien,
Our castle's shame! whence, from his filthy nook,
We drove the villain out for fitter lair to look.

LXII

One day there chanced into these halls to rove
A joyous youth, who took you at first sight;
Him the wild wave of pleasure hither drove,
Before the sprightly tempest tossing light:
Certes,[e] he was a most engaging wight,
Of social glee, and wit humane though keen,
Turning the night to day and day to night:
For him the merry bells had rung, I ween,
If, in this nook of quiet, bells had ever been.

lix *cerulean field*: the sky.
lxi *wretch*: no likely original for this character has been found.
lxi *practised*: contrived.
lxii *joyous youth*: John Forbes, son of Duncan, cf. *Au.* 944 end-note.
lxii *took*: charmed.

LXIII

But not even pleasure to excess is good:
What most elates then sinks the soul as low:
When spring-tide joy pours in with copious flood,
The higher still the exulting billows flow,
The farther back again they flagging go
And leave us grovelling on the dreary shore.
Taught by this son of joy, we found it so;
Who, whilst he staid, kept in a gay uproar
Our maddened Castle all, the abode of sleep no more.

LXIV

As when in prime of June a burnished fly,
Sprung from the meads, o'er which he sweeps along,
Cheered by the breathing bloom and vital sky,
Tunes up amid these airy halls his song,
Soothing at first the gay reposing throng:
And oft he sips their bowl; or, nearly drowned,
He, thence recovering, drives their beds among,
And scares their tender sleep with trump profound;
Then out again he flies, to wing his mazy round.

LXV

Another guest there was, of sense refined,
Who felt each worth,—for every worth he had;
Serene yet warm, humane yet firm his mind,
As little touched as any man's with bad:
Him through their inmost walks the Muses lad,[e]
To him the sacred love of Nature lent;
And sometimes would he make our valley glad.
Whenas we found he would not here be pent,
To him the better sort this friendly message sent:—

LXVI

Come, dwell with us! true son of virtue, come!
But if, alas! we cannot thee persuade
To lie content beneath our peaceful dome, .
Ne[e] ever more to quit our quiet glade;

lxv *Another guest*: Lyttelton, see *Sp*. 906 end-note.

Yet, when at last thy toils, but ill apaid,
Shall dead thy fire, and damp its heavenly spark,
Thou wilt be glad to seek the rural shade,
There to indulge the muse, and nature mark:
We then a lodge for thee will rear in Hagley Park.'

LXVII

Here whilom^e ligged^e the Esopus of the age;
But, called by fame, in soul yprickèd deep,
A noble pride restored him to the stage,
And roused him like a giant from his sleep.
Even from his slumbers we advantage reap:
With double force the astonished scene he wakes,
Yet quits not Nature's bounds. He knows to keep
Each due decorum: now the heart he shakes,
And now with well-urged sense the enlightened judgement takes.

LXVIII

A bard here dwelt, more fat than bard beseemsⁿ
Who, void of envy, guile, and lust of gain,
On virtue still, and nature's pleasing themes,
Poured forth his unpremeditated strain,
The world forsaking with a calm disdain:
Here laughed he careless in his easy seat;
Here quaffed, encircled with the joyous train;
Oft moralizing sage; his ditty sweet
He loathèd much to write, ne carèd to repeat.

LXIX

Full oft by holy feet our ground was trod;
Of clerks good plenty here you mote espy.
A little, round, fat, oily man of God
Was one I chiefly marked among the fry:
He had a roguish twinkle in his eye,

---

lxvi *apaid*: repaid.   lxvi *Hagley Park*: see *Sp.* 908 end-note.
lxvii *Esopus*: Claudius Aesopus was a celebrated Roman tragic actor of the
  first century B.C. T. refers here to James Quin (1693–1766), cf. *Letters and
Documents*, pp. 200–1.
  lxix *mote*: might.
lxix *man of God*: Rev. Patrick Murdoch (d.1774), longstanding friend of T.,
  tutor to John Forbes (cf. I.lxii) and, later, T.'s biographer. One of T.'s two verse
  epistles to Murdoch was entitled 'To the incomparable soporific doctor', see
  Robertson, pp. 465, 467.

And shone all glittering with ungodly dew,
If a tight damsel chanced to trippen by;
Which when observed, he shrunk into his mew,
And straight would recollect his piety anew.

LXX

Nor be forgot a tribe who minded nought
(Old inmates of the place) but state affairs:
They looked, perdie,° as if they deeply thought;
And on their brow sat every nation's cares.
The world by them is parcelled out in shares,
When in the Hall of Smoke they congress hold,
And the sage berry sun-burnt Mocha bears
Has cleared their inward eye: then, smoke-enrolled,
Their oracles break forth, mysterious as of old.

LXXI

Here languid Beauty kept her pale-faced court:
Bevies of dainty dames of high degree
From every quarter hither made resort;
Where, from gross mortal care and business free,
They lay poured out in ease and luxury.
Or, should they a vain show of work assume,
Alas! and well-a-day! what can it be?
To knot, to twist, to range the vernal bloom;
But far is cast the distaff, spinning-wheel, and loom.

LXXII

Their only labour was to kill the time;
And labour dire it is, and weary woe.
They sit, they loll, turn o'er some idle rhyme;
Then, rising sudden, to the glass they go,
Or saunter forth with tottering step and slow:
This soon too rude an exercise they find;
Strait on the couch their limbs again they throw,
Where, hours on hours, they sighing lie reclined,
And court the vapoury god soft-breathing in the wind.

lxix *mew*: lit. a cage.
lxx *Hall of Smoke*: perhaps some meeting-place in Richmond.
lxx *sage berry*: coffee bean, cf. Pope, *Rape of the Lock* III. 117.
lxx *enrolled*: enwrapped, cf. *F.Q.* I.xi. 44.4.
lxxi *poured out*: cf. 'diffused', *Au.* 517.
lxxi *knot*: do fancy knitting or tatting; cf. Addison, *Spectator* 536, 'Knotting is
   again in fashion.'   lxxi *twist*: plait.
lxxii *vapoury god*: god of vapours or the spleen, cf. I.lxxv.7 end-note.

LXXIII

Now must I mark the villainy we found,
But ah ! too late, as shall eftsoons^e be shown.
A place here was, deep, dreary, under ground;
Where still our inmates, when unpleasing grown,
Diseased, and loathsome, privily were thrown.
Far from the light of heaven they languished there,
Unpitied, uttering many a bitter groan;
For of these wretches taken was no care:
Fierce fiends and hags of hell their only nurses were.ⁿ

LXXIV

Alas the change ! from scenes of joy and rest
To this dark den, where sickness tossed alway.
Here Lethargy, with deadly sleep opprest,
Stretched on his back a mighty lubbard lay,
Heaving his sides, and snorèd night and day:
To stir him from his traunce it was not eath,^e
And his half-opened eyne he shut straitway;
He led, I wot, the softest way to death,
And taught withouten pain and strife to yield the breath.

LXXV

Of limbs enormous, but withal unsound,
Soft-swoln, and pale, here lay the Hydropsy:
Unwieldy man ! with belly monstrous round,
For ever fed with watery supply;
For still he drank, and yet he still was dry.
And moping here did Hypochondria sit,
Mother of Spleen,ⁿ in robes of various dye,
Who vexèd was full oft with ugly fit;
And some her frantic deemed, and some her deemed a wit.

lxxiv *lubbard*: lubber, cf. *Au.* 562 end-note.
lxxiv *eyne*: eyes.   lxxiv *wot*: know.

LXXVI

A lady proud she was, of ancient blood,
Yet oft her fear her pride made crouchen low:
She felt, or fancied in her fluttering mood,
All the diseases which the spittles know,
And sought all physic which the shops bestow,
And still new leaches and new drugs would try,
Her humour ever wavering to and fro;
For sometimes she would laugh, and sometimes cry,
Then sudden waxèd wroth; and all she knew not why.

LXXVII

Fast by her side a listless maiden pined,
With aching head and squeamish heart-burnings;
Pale, bloated, cold, she seemed to hate mankind,
Yet loved in secret all forbidden things.
And here the Tertian shakes his chilling wings:
The sleepless Gout here counts the crowing cocks—
A wolf now gnaws him, now a serpent stings:
Whilst Apoplexy crammed Intemperance knocks
Down to the ground at once, as butcher felleth ox.[n]

CANTO II

The Knight of Arts *and* Industry,
And his atchievements fair;
That, by this Castle's overthrow,
Secured, and crownèd were.

I

ESCAPED the castle of the Sire of sin,
Ah! where shall I so sweet a dwelling find?
For all around without, and all within,
Nothing save what delightful was and kind,
Of goodness savouring and a tender mind,
E'er rose to view. But now another strain,
Of doleful note, alas! remains behind:
I now must sing of pleasure turned to pain,
And of the false enchanter, Indolence, complain.

lxxvi *spittles*: hospitals.   lxxvi *leaches*: physicians.

II

Is there no patron to protect the Muse,
And fence for her Parnassus' barren soil?
To every labour its reward accrues,
And they are sure of bread who swink[e] and moil;[e]
But a fell tribe the Aonian hive despoil,[n]
As ruthless wasps oft rob the painful bee:
Thus, while the laws not guard that noblest toil,
Ne for the Muses other meed decree,
They praisèd are alone, and starve right merrily.

III

I care not, fortune, what you me deny:
You cannot rob me of free nature's grace;
You cannot shut the windows of the sky,
Through which Aurora shows her brightening face:
You cannot bar my constant feet to trace
The woods and lawns by living stream at eve.
Let health my nerves and finer fibres brace,
And I their toys to the great children leave:
Of fancy, reason, virtue, nought can me bereave.[n]

IV

Come, then, my Muse, and raise a bolder song:
Come, lig[e] no more upon the bed of sloth,
Dragging the lazy languid line along,
Fond to begin, but still to finish loth,
Thy half-writ scrolls all eaten by the moth:
Arise, and sing that generous imp of fame
Who, with the sons of softness nobly wroth,
To sweep away this human lumber came,
Or in a chosen few to rouse the slumbering flame.

ii *Muse*: referring here to the poet, cf. Milton, *Lycidas* 19.
ii *Parnassus*: the mountain in Greece associated with the worship of Apollo and
the nine Muses.
ii *Aonian*: Mount Helicon, sacred to the Muses, stood in the part of Boeotia
called Aonia. The Muses were sometimes called Aonides.
iii *Aurora*: see *Su.* 828 fn.
iii *great children*: men; cf. 'Men are but children of a larger growth' (Dryden,
All for Love IV.i).

V

In Fairy-land there lived a knight of old,
Of feature stern, Selvaggio[n] well ycleped,[e]
A rough unpolished man, robust and bold,
But wondrous poor: he neither sowed nor reaped,
Ne stores in summer for cold winter heaped;
In hunting all his days away he wore;
Now scorched by June, now in November steeped,
Now pinched by biting January sore,
He still in woods pursued the libbard[e] and the boar.[n]

VI

As he one morning, long before the dawn,
Pricked[e] through the forest to dislodge his prey,
Deep in the winding bosom of a lawn,
With wood wild-fringed, he marked a taper's ray,
That from the beating rain and wintry fray
Did to a lonely cot his steps decoy:
There, up to earn the needments[e] of the day,
He found dame Poverty, nor fair nor coy;
Her he compressed, and filled her with a lusty boy.

VII

Amid the greenwood shade this boy was bred,
And grew at last a knight of muchel[e] fame,
Of active mind and vigorous lustyhed,
The Knight of Arts and Industry by name.
Earth was his bed, the boughs his roof did frame;
He knew no beverage but the flowing stream;
His tasteful well-earned food the silvan game,
Or the brown fruit with which the woodlands teem:
The same to him glad Summer or the Winter breme.

VIII

So passed his youthly morning, void of care,
Wild as the colts that through the commons run:
For him no tender parents troubled were;
He of the forest seemed to be the son,

vi *lawn*: glade.   vi *fray*: assault.
vi *compressed*: sexually embraced, cf. Pope, *Odyssey* I.95.
vii *lustyhed*: lustiness.   vii *breme*: fierce.

And certes[e] had been utterly undone
But that Minerva pity of him took,
With all the gods that love the rural wonne,[e]
That teach to tame the soil and rule the crook;
Ne[e] did the sacred Nine disdain a gentle look.

IX

Of fertile genius, him they nurtured well
In every science and in every art
By which mankind the thoughtless brutes excel,
That can or use, or joy, or grace impart,
Disclosing all the powers of head and heart:
Ne were the goodly exercises spared
That brace the nerves or make the limbs alert,
And mix elastic force with firmness hard:
Was never knight on ground mote be with him compared.

X

Sometimes, with early morn, he mounted gay
The hunter-steed, exulting o'er the dale,
And drew the roseate breath of orient day:
Sometimes, retiring to the secret vale,
Yclad[e] in steel, and bright with burnished mail,
He strained the bow, or tossed the sounding spear,
Or, darting on the goal, outstript the gale,
Or wheeled the chariot in its mid career,
Or strenuous wrestled hard with many a tough compeer.

XI

At other times he pryed through Nature's store,
Whate'er she in the ethereal round contains,
Whate'er she hides beneath her verdant floor,
The vegetable and the mineral reigns;
Or else he scanned the globe, those small domains,
Where restless mortals such a turmoil keep,
Its seas, its floods, its mountains, and its plains;
But more he searched the mind, and roused from sleep
Those moral seeds[n] whence we heroic actions reap.

viii *Minerva*: in Roman mythology the goddess of wisdom, handicrafts and war.
viii *the gods*: see *Cas. Ind.* II.xxviii.6 fnn.
viii *sacred Nine*: the Muses.   ix *mote*: might.
xi *ethereal round*: upper sky, cf. *Sp.* 148 fn.   xi *reigns*: kingdoms.

XII

Nor would he scorn to stoop from high pursuits
Of heavenly Truth, and practise what she taught.
Vain is the tree of knowledge without fruits.
Sometimes in hand the spade or plough he caught,
Forth-calling all with which boon earth is fraught;
Sometimes he plied the strong mechanic tool,
Or reared the fabric from the finest draught;
And oft he put himself to Neptune's school,
Fighting with winds and waves on the vext ocean pool.

XIII

To solace then these rougher toils he tried
To touch the kindling canvas into life;
With Nature his creating pencil vied,—
With Nature joyous at the mimic strife:
Or to such shapes as graced Pygmalion's wife
He hewed the marble; or with varied fire
He roused the trumpet and the martial fife,
Or bade the lute sweet tenderness inspire,
Or verses framed that well might wake Apollo's lyre.

XIV

Accomplished thus he from the woods issúed,
Full of great aims and bent on bold emprise;
The work which long he in his breast had brewed
Now to perform he ardent did devise,
To-wit, a barbarous world to civilize.
Earth was till then a boundless forest wild—
Nought to be seen but savage wood and skies;
No cities nourished arts, no culture smiled,
No government, no laws, no gentle manners mild.

XV

A rugged wight, the worst of brutes, was man;
On his own wretched kind he, ruthless, preyed:
The strongest still the weakest over-ran;
In every country mighty robbers swayed,
And guile and ruffian force were all their trade.

xii *Neptune*: in Roman mythology god of the sea.
xiii *Pygmalion's wife*: Pygmalion the legendary sculptor prayed to have a wife as
    beautiful as a certain statue he had carved; Aphrodite, the goddess of love,
    thereupon brought the statue to life; cf. Ovid, *Metamorphoses* X.243–97.
xiii *Apollo*: see *Wi.* 532, 660 fnn.
xiv *emprise*: enterprise, cf. *F.Q.* II.iii.35.4.

Life was not life, but rapine, want, and woe;
Which this brave knight, in noble anger, made
To swear he would the rascal rout o'erthrow,
For, by the Powers Divine, it should no more be so!

XVI

It would exceed the purport of my song
To say how this best sun, from orient climes,
Came beaming life and beauty all along,
Before him chasing indolence and crimes.
Still, as he passed, the nations he sublimes,
And calls forth arts and virtue with his ray:
Then Egypt, Greece, and Rome their golden times
Successive had; but now in ruins grey
They lie, to slavish sloth and tyranny a prey.

XVII

To crown his toils, Sir Industry then spread
The swelling sail, and made for Britain's coast.
A sylvan life till then the natives led,
In the brown shades and greenwood forest lost,
All careless rambling where it liked them most—
Their wealth the wild-deer bouncing through the glade;
They lodged at large, and lived at Nature's cost;
Save spear and bow withouten other aid;
Yet not the Roman steel their naked breast dismayed.

XVIII

He liked the soil, he liked the clement skies,
He liked the verdant hills and flowery plains:
'Be this my great, my chosen isle! (he cries)
This—whilst my labours liberty sustains—
This Queen of Ocean all assault disdains.'
Nor liked he less the genius of the land,
To freedom apt and persevering pains,
Mild to obey, and generous to command,
Tempered by forming Heaven with kindest firmest hand.

XIX

Here by degrees his master-work arose,
Whatever arts and industry can frame,
Whatever finished agriculture knows,
Fair Queen of Arts! from heaven itself who came

When Eden flourished in unspotted fame;
And still with her sweet innocence we find,
And tender peace, and joys without a name,
That, while they rapture, tranquillize the mind;
Nature and Art at once, delight and use combined.

XX

Then towns he quickened by mechanic arts,
And bade the fervent city glow with toil;
Bade social commerce raise renownèd marts,
Join land to land, and marry soil to soil,
Unite the poles, and without bloody spoil
Bring home of either Ind the gorgeous stores;
Or, should despotic rage the world embroil,
Bade tyrants tremble on remotest shores,
While o'er the encircling deep Britannia's thunder roars.

XXI

The drooping Muses then he westward called,
From the famed city by Propontis Sea,
What time the Turk the enfeebled Grecian thralled;
Thence from their cloistered walks he set them free,
And brought them to another Castalie,
Where Isis many a famous noursling breeds,
Or where old Cam soft paces o'er the lea
In pensive mood, and tunes his Doric reeds,
The whilst his flocks at large the lonely shepherd feeds.[n]

XXII

Yet the fine arts were what he finished least.
For why ? They are the quintessence of all,
The growth of labouring time, and slow increast;

xix *rapture*: enrapture.   xx *either Ind*: both the East and the West Indies.
xxi *city by Propontis Sea*: 'Constantinople' (T.). The revival of learning in western
  Europe began with the fall of Constantinople to the Turks in 1453.
xxi *Castalie*: kingdom of the Muses (from the Castalian spring on the slopes of
  Parnassus, cf. *Cas. Ind.* II.ii.2).
xxi *Isis*: River Thames at Oxford.
xxi *Cam*: the river at Cambridge. Isis and Cam here represent the two universi-
  ties. For the personification of the Cam cf. Milton, *Lycidas*, 103–7.
xxi *Doric reeds*: see *Au.* 3 end-note.

Unless, as seldom chances, it should fall
That mighty patrons the coy sisters call
Up to the sunshine of uncumbered ease,
Where no rude care the mounting thought may thrall,
And where they nothing have to do but please:
Ah! gracious God! thou knowst they ask no other fees.

XXIII

But now, alas! we live too late in time:
Our patrons now even grudge that little claim,
Except to such as sleek the soothing rhyme;
And yet, forsooth, they wear Maecenas' name,
Poor sons of puffed-up vanity, not fame.
Unbroken spirits, cheer! still, still remains
The eternal patron, Liberty; whose flame,
While she protects, inspires the noblest strains.
The best and sweetest far are toil-created gains.[n]

XXIV

Whenas the knight had framed in Britain-land
A matchless form of glorious government,
In which the sovereign laws alone command,
Laws stablished by the public free consent,
Whose majesty is to the sceptre lent—
When this great plan, with each dependent art,
Was settled firm, and to his heart's content,
Then sought he from the toilsome scene to part,
And let life's vacant eve breathe quiet through the heart.

XXV

For this he chose a farm in Deva's vale,
Where his long alleys peeped upon the main.
In this calm seat he drew the healthful gale,
Commixed the chief, the patriot, and the swain,
The happy monarch of his sylvan train!

xxii *coy sisters*: the Muses.
xxiii *Maecenas*: (c. 70–8 B.C.), the wealthy Roman who befriended Virgil,
   Horace, Propertius and other poets, and became the type of enlightened patron.
xxiv *vacant*: carefree.
xxv *Deva*: River Dee, cf. Milton, *Lycidas* 55.

Here, sided by the guardians of the fold,
He walked his rounds, and cheered his blest domain;
His days, the days of unstained nature, rolled
Replete with peace and joy, like patriarch's of old.

XXVI

Witness, ye lowing herds, who lent him milk;
Witness, ye flocks, whose woolly vestments far
Exceed soft India's cotton, or her silk;
Witness, with Autumn charged, the nodding car
That homeward came beneath sweet evening's star,
Or of September moons the radiance mild.
O hide thy head, abominable War!
Of crimes and ruffian idleness the child!
From heaven this life ysprung, from hell thy glories vild!ᵉ

XXVII

Nor from his deep retirement banished was
The amusing cares of rural industry.
Still, as with grateful change the seasons pass,
New scenes arise, new landskips strike the eye,
And all the enlivened country beautify:
Gay plains extend where marshes slept before;
O'er recent meads the exulting streamlets fly;
Dark frowning heaths grow bright with Ceres' store;
And woods imbrown the steep, or wave along the shore.

XXVIII

As nearer to his farm you made approach,
He polished nature with a finer hand:
Yet on her beauties durst not art encroach;
'Tis art's alone these beauties to expand.
In graceful dance immingled, o'er the land
Pan, Pales, Flora, and Pomona played:
Even here, sometimes, the rude wild common fand
An happy place; where, free and unafraid,
Amid the flowering brakes each coyer creature strayed.ⁿ

xxv *sided . . . fold*: accompanied by sheepdogs.
xxvi *nodding car*: swaying harvest-waggon.   xxvii *amusing*: interesting.
xxvii *Ceres' store*: corn, cf. *Su.* 863 fn.   xxviii *Pan*: see *Su.* 854 fn.
xxviii *Pales*: Roman goddess (or god) of sheepfolds and pastures.
xxviii *Flora*: see *Su.* 694 fn.   xxviii *Pomona*: see *Su.* 663 fn.
xxviii *fand*: found, i.e. provided.

XXIX

But in prime vigour what can last for ay?
That soul-enfeebling wizard, Indolence,
I whilom^e sung, wrought in his works decay:
Spread far and wide was his curst influence;
Of public virtue much he dulled the sense,
Even much of private; eat our spirit out,
And fed our rank luxurious vices: whence
The land was overlaid with many a lout;
Not, as old fame reports, wise, generous, bold, and stout.

XXX

A rage of pleasure maddened every breast;
Down to the lowest lees the ferment ran:
To his licentious wish each must be blest,
With joy be fevered,—snatch it as he can.
Thus Vice the standard reared; her arrier-ban
Corruption called, and loud she gave the word:—
'Mind, mind yourselves! why should the vulgar man,
The lacquey, be more virtuous than his lord?
Enjoy this span of life! 'tis all the gods afford.'

XXXI

The tidings reached to where in quiet hall
The good old knight enjoyed well-earned repose:
'Come, come, Sir Knight! thy children on thee call;
Come, save us yet, ere ruin round us close!
The demon Indolence thy toils o'erthrows.'
On this the noble colour stained his cheeks,
Indignant glowing through the whitening snows
Of venerable eld; his eye full-speaks
His ardent soul, and from his couch at once he breaks.

xxx *arrier-ban*: correctly 'summons to military service', but here the band so summoned.
xxx *called*: summoned.
xxxi *toils*: labours.
xxxi *eld*: old age.

XXXII

'I will (he cried), so help me God! destroy
That villain Archimage.'ᵉ—His page then strait
He to him called—a fiery-footed boy
Benemptᵉ Dispatch. 'My steed be at the gate;
My bard attend; quick, bring the net of fate.'
This net was twisted by the Sisters Three;
Which, when once cast o'er hardened wretch, too late
Repentance comes: replevy cannot be
From the strong iron grasp of vengeful destiny.

XXXIII

He came, the bard, a little Druid wight,
Of withered aspect; but his eye was keen,
With sweetness mixed. In russet brown bedight,
As is his sister of the copses green,
He crept along, unpromising of mien.
Gross he who judges so. His soul was fair;
Bright as the children of yon azure sheen,
True comeliness, which nothing can impair,
Dwells in the mind: all else is vanity and glare.

XXXIV

'Come,' quoth the knight; 'a voice has reached mine ear:
The demon Indolence threats overthrow
To all that to mankind is good and dear.
Come, Philomelus, let us instant go
O'erturn his bowers and lay his castle low.

xxxii *Archimage*: a proper name in *F.Q.*, but several 18c. imitators of Spenser before T. (Croxall, West, Cambridge, Upton) took it as a common noun. T. may be following suit; cf. p. 213, below.
xxxii *Sisters Three*: the Fates, see *Cas. Ind.* I.xix.3 fn. The weaving of a net by the Fates may be T.'s own invention, but a net is used in the capture of Acrasia in *F.Q.* II.xii.81.
xxxii *replevy*: reprieve, cf. *F.Q.* IV.xii.31.8.
xxxiii *Druid wight*: Pope, according to Joseph Warton, *Essay on the Genius and Writings of Pope* (5th edn. 1806), ii.325–6. Collins, in his *Ode* (see pp. xviii–xix above), calls T. a Druid. See *Su.* 516–63 end-note.
xxxiii *bedight*: dressed.
xxxiii *sister*: the nightingale.
xxxiii *children*: angels.
xxxiv *Philomelus*: lover of music, masc. form of Philomela the nightingale; cf. *Sp.* 601, 703 fnn.

Those men, those wretched men, who *will* be slaves,
Must drink a bitter wrathful cup of woe:
But some there be thy song, as from their graves,
Shall raise. Thrice happy he who without rigour saves!'

XXXV

Issuing forth, the knight bestrode his steed
Of ardent bay, and on whose front a star
Shone blazing bright: sprung from the generous breed
That whirl of active Day the rapid car,
He pranced along, disdaining gate or bar,
Meantime, the bard on milk-white palfrey rode;
An honest sober beast, that did not mar
His meditations, but full softly trode:
And much they moralized as thus yfere^e they yode.^e

XXXVI

They talked of virtue, and of human bliss.
What else so fit for man to settle well?
And still their long researches met in this,
This truth of truths, which nothing can refel:—
'From virtue's fount the purest joys outwell,
Sweet rills of thought that cheer the conscious soul;
While vice pours forth the troubled streams of hell,
The which, howe'er disguised, at last with dole
Will through the tortured breast their fiery torrent roll.'

XXXVII

At length it dawned, that fatal valley gay,
O'er which high wood-crowned hills their summits rear.
On the cool height awhile our palmers stay,
And spite even of themselves their senses cheer;
Then to the wizard's wonne^e their steps they steer.
Like a green isle it broad beneath them spread,
With gardens round, and wandering currents clear,
And tufted groves to shade the meadow-bed,
Sweet airs and song; and without hurry all seemed glad.

xxxiv *he who . . . saves*: the poet who delights while he teaches.
xxxv *car*: the chariot of the sun, cf. *Cas. Ind.* I.xxx.7, lviii.3.
xxxv *trode*: trod.   xxxvi *refel*: refute.   xxxvii *dawned*: came into sight.
xxxvii *palmers*: travellers (lit. pilgrims who brought back a palm branch from the
Holy Land, with particular reference here to the palmer in *F.Q.* II).

XXXVIII

'As God shall judge me, Knight! we must forgive
(The half-enraptured Philomelus cried)
The frail good man deluded here to live,
And in these groves his musing fancy hide.
Ah, nought is pure! It cannot be denied
That virtue still some tincture has of vice,
And vice of virtue. What should then betide,
But that our charity be not too nice?
Come, let us those we can to real bliss entice.'

XXXIX

'Ay, sicker,'ᵉ quoth the knight, 'all flesh is frail,
To pleasant sin and joyous dalliance bent;
But let not brutish vice of this avail,
And think to scape deservèd punishment.
Justice were cruel, weakly to relent;
From Mercy's self she got her sacred glaive.ᵉ
Grace be to those who can and will repent;
But penance long and dreary to the slave,
Who must in floods of fire his gross foul spirit lave.'

XL

Thus, holding high discourse, they came to where
The cursèd carle was at his wonted trade;
Still tempting heedless men into his snare,
In witching wise, as I before have said.
But when he saw, in goodly gear arrayed,
The grave majestic knight approaching nigh,
And by his side the bard so sage and staid,
His countenance fell; yet oft his anxious eye
Marked them, like wily fox who roosted cock doth spy.

XLI

Nathless,ᵉ with feigned respect, he bade give back
The rabble-rout, and welcomed them full kind;
Struck with the noble twain, they were not slack
His orders to obey, and fall behind.

---

xxxviii *frail good man*: victim of Indolence, but here, perhaps, especially T. himself.
xl *carle*: base fellow, cf. *F.Q.* IV.vii.18.4.

Then he resumed his song; and unconfined
Poured all his music, ran through all his strings:
With magic dustⁿ their eyne he tries to blind,
And virtue's tender airs o'er weakness flings.
What pity, base his song who so divinely sings!

XLII

Elate in thought, he counted them his own,
They listened so intent with fixed delight:
But they instead, as if transmewed^e to stone,
Marvelled he could with such sweet art unite
The lights and shades of manners, wrong and right.
Meantime the silly crowd the charm devour,
Wide-pressing to the gate. Swift on the Knight
He darted fierce to drag him to his bower,
Who backening shunned his touch, for well he knew its power.

XLIII

As in thronged amphitheatre of old
The wary retiarius trapped his foe,
Even so the Knight, returning on him bold,
At once involved him in the net of woe
Whereof I mention made not long ago.
Enraged at first, he scorned so weak a jail,
And leaped, and flew, and flouncèd to and fro;
But, when he found that nothing could avail,
He sat him felly down, and gnawed his bitter nail.

XLIV

Alarmed, the inferior demons of the place
Raised rueful shrieks and hideous yells around;
Black ruptured clouds deformed the welkin's face,
And from beneath was heard a wailing sound,
As of infernal sprights in cavern bound;

xli *eyne*: eyes.
xlii *transmewed*: transmuted, cf. *F.Q.* I.vii.35.6.
xlii *backening*: drawing back.
xliii *retiarius*: 'A gladiator who made use of a net which he threw over his adversary.' (T.)
xliii *felly*: malignantly, cf. *F.Q.* IV.viii.23.8.

A solemn sadness every creature strook,
And lightnings flashed, and horror rocked the ground:
Huge crowds on crowds outpoured, with blemished look,
As if on time's last verge this frame of things had shook.

XLV

Soon as the short-lived tempest was yspent,
Steamed from the jaws of vext Avernus' hole,
And hushed the hubbub of the rabblement,
Sir Industry the first calm moment stole:
'There must,' he cried, 'amid so vast a shoal,
Be some who are not tainted at the heart,
Not poisoned quite by this same villain's bowl:
Come, then, my bard, thy heavenly fire impart;
Touch soul with soul, till forth the latent spirit start.'

XLVI

The bard obeyed; and, taking from his side,
Where it in seemly sort depending hung,
His British harp, its speaking strings he tried,
The which with skilful touch he deftly strung,
Till tinkling in clear symphony they rung.
Then, as he felt the muses come along,
Light o'er the chords his raptured hand he flung,
And played a prelude to his rising song:
The whilst, like midnight mute, ten thousand round him throng.

XLVII

Thus, ardent, burst his strain:—'Ye hapless race,
Dire-labouring here to smother reason's ray
That lights our Maker's image in our face,
And gives us wide o'er earth unquestioned sway;
What is the adored Supreme perfection? say!
What, but eternal never-resting soul,
Almighty power, and all-directing day,
By whom each atom stirs, the planets roll;
Who fills, surrounds, informs, and agitates the whole?[n]

xlv *Avernus*: the lake near Naples, close to the point where Aeneas entered the underworld (cf. Virgil *Aeneid* VI), often—as here—identified with the underworld itself.

XLVIII

'Come, to the beaming God your hearts unfold!
Draw from its fountain life! 'Tis thence alone
We can excel. Up from unfeeling mould
To seraphs burning round the Almighty's throne,
Life rising still on life in higher tone
Perfection forms, and with perfection bliss.
In universal nature this clear shown
Not needeth proof: to prove it were, I wis,[e]
To prove the beauteous world excels the brute abyss.[n]

XLIX

'Is not the field, with lively culture green,
A sight more joyous than the dead morass?
Do not the skies, with active ether[n] clean
And fanned by sprightly zephyrs, far surpass
The foul November fogs and slumbrous mass
With which sad nature veils her drooping face?
Does not the mountain stream, as clear as glass,
Gay-dancing on, the putrid pool disgrace?
The same in all holds true, but chief in human race.

L

'It was not by vile loitering in ease
That Greece obtained the brighter palm of art;
That soft yet ardent Athens learned to please,
To keen the wit, and to sublime the heart—
In all supreme! complete in every part!
It was not thence majestic Rome arose,
And o'er the nations shook her conquering dart:
For sluggard's brow the laurel never grows;
Renown is not the child of indolent repose.

LI

'Had unambitious mortals minded nought
But in loose joy their time to wear away,
Had they alone the lap of dalliance sought,
Pleased on her pillow their dull heads to lay,
Rude nature's state had been our state to-day;

xlviii *brute abyss*: chaos.
1 *keen*: sharpen, cf. *Su.* 1259.

No cities e'er their towery fronts had raised,
No arts had made us opulent and gay,
With brother-brutes the human race had graz'd,
None e'er had soared to fame, none honoured been, none
        praised.

LII

'Great Homer's song had never fired the breast
To thirst of glory and heroic deeds;
Sweet Maro's muse, sunk in inglorious rest,
Had silent slept amid the Mincian reeds:
The wits of modern time had told their beads,
And monkish legends been their only strains;
Our Milton's Eden had lain wrapt in weeds,
Our Shakespeare strolled and laughed with Warwick swains,
Ne had my master Spenser charmed his Mulla's plains.

LIII

'Dumb, too, had been the sage historic muse,
And perished all the sons of ancient fame;
Those starry lights of virtue, that diffuse
Through the dark depth of time their vivid flame,
Had all been lost with such as have no name.
Who then had scorned his ease for others' good?
Who then had toiled, rapacious men to tame?
Who in the public breach devoted stood.
And for his country's cause been prodigal of blood?

LIV

'But, should to fame your hearts impervious be,
If right I read, you pleasure all require:
Then hear how best may be obtained this fee,
How best enjoyed this Nature's wide desire.
Toil, and be glad! let Industry inspire
Into your quickened limbs her buoyant breath!
Who does not act is dead; absorbed entire
In miry sloth, no pride, no joy he hath:
O leaden-hearted men, to be in love with death!

lii *Maro*: Virgil.
lii *Mincian reeds*: Virgil was born at Andes near Mantua on the River Mincius;
    cf. Milton, *Lycidas* 86.
liii *historic muse*: Clio.
liii *lights of virtue*: such as the worthies described in *Wi.* 439–540.

LV

'Better the toiling swain, oh happier far!
Perhaps the happiest of the sons of men!
Who vigorous plies the plough, the team, or car,
Who houghs the field, or ditches in the glen,
Delves in his garden, or secures his pen:
The tooth of avarice poisons not his peace;
He tosses not in sloth's abhorrèd den;
From vanity he has a full release;
And, rich in nature's wealth, he thinks not of increase.

LVI

'Good Lord! how keen are his sensations all!
His bread is sweeter than the glutton's cates;
The wines of France upon the palate pall
Compared with what his simple soul elates,
The native cup whose flavour thirst creates;
At one deep draught of sleep he takes the night;
And, for that heart-felt joy which nothing mates,
Of the pure nuptial bed the chaste delight,
The losel° is to him a miserable wight.

LVII

'But what avail the largest gifts of Heaven,
When drooping health and spirits go amiss?
How tasteless then whatever can be given!
Health is the vital principle of bliss,
And exercise of health. In proof of this,
Behold the wretch who slugs his life away
Soon swallowed in disease's sad abyss;
While he whom toil has braced, or manly play,
Has light as air each limb, each thought as clear as day.

LVIII

'O who can speak the vigorous joys of health?
Unclogged the body, unobscured the mind:
The morning rises gay; with pleasing stealth
The temperate evening falls serene and kind.
In health the wiser brutes true gladness find.

lv *houghs*: hoes.   lvi *native cup*: perhaps ale or cider.
lvii *slugs*: lazes, cf. *F.Q.* II.i.23.3.

See how the younglings frisk along the meads
As May comes on and wakes the balmy wind!
Rampant with life, their joy all joy exceeds:
Yet what save high-strung health this dancing pleasaunce breeds?

LIX

'But here, instead, is fostered every ill
Which or distempered minds or bodies know.
Come, then, my kindred spirits! do not spill
Your talents here. This place is but a show
Whose charms delude you to the den of woe:
Come, follow me; I will direct you right,
Where pleasure's roses, void of serpents, grow,
Sincere as sweet. Come, follow this good knight;
And you will bless the day that brought him to your sight.

LX

'Some he will lead to courts, and some to camps;
To senates some, and public sage debates,
Where, by the solemn gleam of midnight lamps,
The world is poised, and managed mighty states;
To high discovery some, that new creates
The face of earth; some to the thriving mart;
Some to the rural reign, and softer fates;
To the sweet muses some, who raise the heart:
All glory shall be yours, all Nature, and all Art.

LXI

'There are, I see, who listen to my lay,
Who wretched sigh for virtue, but despair.
"All may be done (methinks I hear them say),
Even death despised by generous actions fair;
All: but, for those who to these bowers repair,
Their every power dissolved in luxury,
To quit of torpid sluggishness the lair
And from the powerful arms of Sloth get free—
'Tis rising from the dead! Alas, it cannot be!"

LXII

'Would you then learn to dissipate the band
Of these huge threatening difficulties dire
That in the weak man's way like lions stand[n]

---

lviii *younglings*: young animals.   lviii *pleasaunce*: pleasure.

His soul appal, and damp his rising fire ?
Resolve ! resolve ! and to be men aspire !
Exert that noblest privilege, alone
Here to mankind indulged; control desire;
Let godlike reason from her sovereign throne
Speak the commanding word *I will!* and it is done.

LXIII

'Heavens ! can you, then, thus waste in shameful wise
Your few important days of trial here ?
Heirs of eternity, yborn to rise
Through endless states of being, still more near
To bliss approaching, and perfection clear—
Can you renounce a fortune so sublime,
Such glorious hopes, your backward steps to steer,
And roll, with vilest brutes, through mud and slime ?
No, no !—your heaven-touched hearts disdain the sordid crime !'[n]

LXIV

'Enough ! enough !' they cried. Strait, from the crowd
The better sort on wings of transport fly—
As, when amid the lifeless summits proud
Of Alpine cliffs, where to the gelid sky
Snows piled on snows in wintry torpor lie,
The rays divine of vernal Phoebus play,
The awakened heaps, in streamlets from on high,
Roused into action, lively leap away,
Glad-warbling through the vales, in their new being gay.

LXV

Not less the life, the vivid joy serene,
That lighted up these new-created men,
Than that which wings the exulting spirit clean,
When, just delivered from this fleshly den,
It soaring seeks its native skies agen.
How light its essence ! how unclogged its powers,
Beyond the blazon[e] of my mortal pen !
Even so we glad forsook these sinful bowers;
Even such enraptured life, such energy was ours.

lxiv *Phoebus*: see *Cas. Ind.* I.vii.4 fn.　　　lxv *agen*: again.

LXVI

But far the greater part, with rage inflamed,
Dire-muttered curses and blasphemed high Jove.
'Ye sons of hate! (they bitterly exclaimed)
What brought you to this seat of peace and love?
While with kind nature here amid the grove
We passed the harmless sabbath of our time,
What to disturb it could, fell men! emove
Your barbarous hearts? Is happiness a crime?
Then do the fiends of hell rule in yon Heaven sublime.'

LXVII

'Ye impious wretches, (quoth the Knight in wrath)
Your happiness behold!' Then strait a wand
He waved, an anti-magic power that hath
Truth from illusive falsehood to command.
Sudden the landskip sinks on every hand;
The pure quick streams are marshy puddles found;
On baleful heaths the groves all blackened stand;
And, o'er the weedy foul abhorrèd ground,
Snakes, adders, toads, each loathly creature crawls around.

LXVIII

And here and there, on trees by lightning scathed,
Unhappy wights who loathèd life yhung;
Or in fresh gore and recent murder bathed
They weltering lay; or else, infuriate flung
Into the gloomy flood, while ravens sung
The funeral dirge, they down the torrent rolled:
These, by distempered blood to madness stung,
Had doomed themselves; whence oft, when night controlled
The world, returning hither their sad spirits howled.[n]

LXIX

Meantime a moving scene was open laid.
That lazar-house, I whilom[e] in my lay
Depainten have, its horror deep-displayed,
And gave unnumbered wretches to the day,

---

lxvi *emove*: affect with emotion, cf. *Cas. Ind.* I.x.5.
lxvii *landskip*: landscape (perhaps signifying that the setting of the Castle was,
  like a painting, art—not nature; cf. *Cas. Ind.* I.vii.1, xxxviii.2).
lxix *Depainten*: painted.

Who tossing there in squalid misery lay.
Soon as of sacred light the unwonted smile
Poured on these living catacombs its ray,
Through the drear caverns stretching many a mile,
The sick up-raised their heads, and dropped their woes a while.

LXX

'O Heaven!' they cried, 'and do we once more see
Yon blessed sun, and this green earth so fair?
Are we from noisome damps of pest-house free?
And drink our souls the sweet ethereal air?
O thou, or knight or God, who holdest there
That fiend, oh keep him in eternal chains!
But what for us, the children of despair,
Brought to the brink of hell, what hope remains?
Repentance does itself but aggravate our pains.'

LXXI

The gentle knight, who saw their rueful case,
Let fall adown his silver beard some tears.
'Certes,' quoth he, 'it is not even in grace
To undo the past, and eke your broken years:
Nathless,[e] to nobler worlds repentance rears
With humble hope her eye; to her is given
A power the truly contrite heart that cheers;
She quells the brand by which the rocks are riven;
She more than merely softens, she rejoices Heaven.

LXXII

'Then patient bear the sufferings you have earned,
And by these sufferings purify the mind;
Let wisdom be by past misconduct learned:
Or pious die, with penitence resigned;
And to a life more happy and refined
Doubt not you shall, new creatures, yet arise.
Till then, you may expect in me to find
One who will wipe your sorrow from your eyes,[n]
One who will soothe your pangs, and wing you to the skies.'

lxxi *brand*: thunderbolt.

LXXIII

They silent heard, and poured their thanks in tears.
'For you (resumed the Knight, with sterner tone)
Whose hard dry hearts the obdurate demon sears—
That villain's gifts will cost you many a groan;
In dolorous mansion long you must bemoan
His fatal charms, and weep your stains away;
Till, soft and pure as infant goodness grown,
You feel a perfect change: then, who can say
What grace may yet shine forth in Heaven's eternal day?'

LXXIV

This said, his powerful wand he waved anew:
Instant, a glorious angel-train descends,
The Charities, to-wit, of rosy hue:
Sweet love their looks a gentle radiance lends,
And with seraphic flame compassion blends.
At once delighted to their charge they fly:
When lo! a goodly hospital ascends,
In which they bade each human aid be nigh,
That could the sick-bed smoothe of that unhappy fry.

LXXV

It was a worthy edifying sight,
And gives to human-kind peculiar grace,
To see kind hands attending day and night
With tender ministry from place to place.
Some prop the head; some from the pallid face
Wipe off the faint cold dews weak nature sheds;
Some reach the healing draught: the whilst, to chase
The fear supreme, around their softened beds,
Some holy man by prayer all opening heaven dispreads.

LXXVI

Attended by a glad acclaiming train
Of those he rescued had from gaping hell,
Then turned the knight; and, to his hall again
Soft-pacing, sought of Peace the mossy cell.

lxxiii *dolorous mansion*: Purgatory.
lxxv *dispreads*: opens out, cf. *F.Q.* V.xii.13.6.

Yet down his cheeks the gems of pity fell,
To see the helpless wretches that remained,
There left through delves and deserts dire to yell:
Amazed, their looks with pale dismay were stained,
And, spreading wide their hands, they meek repentance feigned.

LXXVII

But ah! their scornèd day of grace was past:
For (horrible to tell!) a desert wild
Before them stretched, bare, comfortless, and vast;
With gibbets, bones, and carcases defiled.
There nor trim field nor lively culture smiled;
Nor waving shade was seen, nor fountain fair:
But sands abrupt on sands lay loosely piled,
Through which they floundering toiled with painful care,
Whilst Phoebus smote them sore, and fired the cloudless air.

LXXVIII

Then, varying to a joyless land of bogs,
The saddened country a gray waste appeared,
Where nought but putrid streams and noisome fogs
For ever hung on drizzly Auster's beard;
Or else the ground, by piercing Caurus seared,
Was jagged with frost or heaped with glazèd snow:
Through these extremes a ceaseless round they steered,
By cruel fiends still hurried to and fro,
Gaunt Beggary, and Scorn, with many hell-hounds moe.°

LXXIX

The first was with base dunghill rags yclad,
Tainting the gale in which they fluttered light;
Of morbid hue his features, sunk and sad;
His hollow eyne shook forth a sickly light;
And o'er his lank jawbone, in piteous plight,
His black rough beard was matted rank and vile;
Direful to see! a heart-appalling sight!
Meantime foul scurf and blotches him defile;
And dogs, where'er he went, still barkèd all the while.

lxxvi *delves*: pits, cf. *F.Q.* II.vii. Argument.
lxxvii *Phoebus*: see *Cas. Ind.* I.vii.4 fn.
lxxviii *Auster*: the south wind (which, according to Virgil, *Georgics* II.462, brought rain).
lxxviii *Caurus*: see *Wi.* 836 fn.   lxxix *Tainting the gale*: see *Au.* 364 fn.
lxxix *eyne*: eyes.

LXXX

The other was a fell despightful fiend—
Hell holds none worse in baleful bower below,
By pride, and wit, and rage, and rancour keened;
Of man, alike if good or bad, the foe:
With nose upturned, he always made a show
As if he smelt some nauseous scent; his eye
Was cold and keen, like blast from boreal snow;
And taunts he casten forth most bitterly.
Such were the twain that off drove this ungodly fry.

LXXXI

Even so through Brentford[n] town, a town of mud,
An herd of bristly swine is pricked along;
The filthy beasts, that never chew the cud,
Still grunt, and squeak, and sing their troublous song,
And oft they plunge themselves the mire among;
But ay the ruthless driver goads them on,
And ay of barking dogs the bitter throng
Makes them renew their unmelodious moan;
Ne ever find they rest from their unresting fone.

lxxx *despightful*: malignant, cf. *P.L.* x.l.
lxxx *keened*: sharpened, cf. *Cas. Ind.* II.l.4.   lxxxi *fone*: foes.

EXPLANATION OF THE OBSOLETE WORDS
USED IN THIS POEM [T.]

Archimage, *the chief, or greatest of magicians or enchanters.*

Atween, *between.*

Bale, *sorrow, trouble, misfortune.*

Benempt, *named.*

Blazon, *painting, displaying.*

Carol, *to sing songs of joy.*

Certes, *certainly.*

Eath, *easy.*

Eftsoons, *immediately, often, afterwards.*

Gear (*or* Geer), *furniture, equipage, dress.*

Glaive, *sword* (Fr.).

Han, *have.*

Hight, *is named, called.*

Idless, *idleness.*

Imp, *child, or offspring; from the* Saxon *impan, to graft or plant.*

Kest, *for cast.*

Lad, *for led.*

Lea, *a piece of land, or meadow.*

Libbard, *leopard.*

Lig, *to lie.*

Losel, *a loose, idle fellow.*

Louting, *bowing, bending.*

Mell, *mingle.*

Moe, *more.*

Moil, *labour.*

Muchel (*or* Mochel), *much, great.*

Nathless, *nevertheless.*

Ne, *nor*

Needments, *necessaries.*

Noursling, *a nurse, or what is nursed.*

Noyance, *harm.*

Perdie (Fr. *par Dieu*), *an old oath.*

Prick'd through the forest, *rode through the forest.*

Sear, *dry, burnt up.*

Sheen, *bright, shining.*

Sicker, *sure, surely.*

Soote, *sweet, or sweetly.*

Sooth, *true, or truth.*

Stound, *misfortune, pang.*

Sweltry, *sultry, consuming with heat.*

Swink, *to labour.*

Transmewed, *transformed.*

Unkempt (Lat. *incomptus*), *unadorned.*

Vild, *vile.*

Ween, *to think, be of opinion.*

Weet, *to know; to weet, to wit.*

Whilom, *ere-while, formerly.*

Wis (*for* Wist), *to know, think, understand.*

Wonne (a Noun), *dwelling.*

N.B.—*The letter* Y *is frequently placed in the beginning of a word, by* Spenser, *to lengthen it a syllable.*

Yborn, *born.*

Yblent (*or* blent), *blended, mingled.*

Yclad, *clad.*

Ycleped, *called, named.*

Yfere, *together.*

Ymolten, *melted.*

Yode (*preterite tense of* yede), *went.*

Notes

The Seasons

SPRING

p. 3, 1–4 Personifications of natural phenomena (blasts, mountains, gales) and traditional mythological personifications (Spring, Winter) here, as elsewhere in *The Seasons*, convey the notion of an animated world; cf. *Sp.* 11–21, *Su.* 1–8, 46–53, *Au.* 1–3, *Wi.* 1–3, 66–73, etc.

p. 3, 5 T. was recommended to the Countess of Hertford (1699–1754) after the publication of *Winter* (1726). He enjoyed her patronage and friendship until his death, and probably wrote part of *Spring* as her guest at Marlborough Castle, Wiltshire. The story in Johnson's *Life* of T. about the poet offending the Countess is untrue. Like Pope, T. often pays tribute to his many friends among writers and their patrons; cf. *Sp.* 906, *Su.* 29, 1419–32, *Au.* 9, 655, 667, 929, 944, 1048, 1072, *Wi.* 18, 550, 555, 664, *Cas. Ind.* I.lvii–lxix.

p. 3, 22–3 'The common people are of the opinion that [the bittern] thrusts its bill into a reed, that serves as a pipe for swelling the note above its natural pitch; while others, and in this number we find Thomson the poet, imagine that the bittern puts its head under water, and then violently blowing produces its boomings.' (Goldsmith, *History of the Earth and Animated Nature* (1774), Book VI, chap. VI.)

p. 5, 32–77 See Introduction p. xi. Lines 32–43 consciously echo Virgil, *Georgics* II.330–1, I.45–6, 213, 98, but the patriotic expansion into praise of trade is typical of T.'s age. (On the mercantilist muse see Bonamy Dobrée, 'The Theme of Patriotism in the Poetry of the Early Eighteenth Century', *Proceedings of the British Academy*, xxxv (1949), 49–65.) From the Middle Ages Britain had been an exporter of wool or woollen cloth, but during the half-century to 1765 she exported large quantities of grain too.

p. 5, 84 'Smiling ... a common word in eighteenth century pastoral, may be considered the equivalent of *laetus* [joyous, abundant, etc.] which Virgil constantly applied to crops.' (G. Tillotson, *Augustan Studies* (1961), p. 37.) In T., however, the word often has devotional overtones, as implying or directly referring to the beneficent activities of God. 'Providence has imprinted so many smiles on Nature, that it is impossible for a mind which is not sunk in more gross and sensual delights to take a survey of them without several secret sensations of pleasure.' (Addison, *Spectator* 393.) Cf. *Sp.* 258, 862, 871, *Su.* 179, *Wi.* 16, Hymn 6, 81, 112, and end-note.

p. 5, 79–89 Cf. *Sp.* 184–5, 218–71, *Au.* 694. These passages upon the flow of sap in and colouring of plants draw upon Stephen Hales, *Vegetable Staticks* (1727), and upon a letter by Alexander Stuart in Richard Bradley, *New Improvements of Planting and Gardening* (1717–18). Hales described the process by which water was absorbed at the roots and, quickly or slowly according to temperature, was raised by capillary action within the plant, and was transpired from the leaves. Stuart speculated that movement of liquid produced variety of colour in vegetation. T. uses the verbs 'distil' (184) and 'ferment' (570) to describe the processes referred to by Hales and Stuart. See *McKillop* pp. 54–8. For the scientific theory that green, the central colour of the spectrum, strengthened and cherished the sight see Addison, *Spectator*, 387, and cf. *P.L.* VII.315–19.

p. 6, 102   André Deslandes in his *Nouveau Voyage d'Angleterre* (1717) noted that London was blanketed under clouds so dense that the sun was never visible, and the air so thick with coal-smoke that he could hardly draw his breath. The first notable protest against atmospheric pollution in London had been John Evelyn's *Fumifugium* (1661).

p. 6, 107   For eighteenth-century notions of synaesthesia and the 'harmony of the senses' see Addison, *Spectator* 412; cf. *Sp.* 475–7, *Au.* 627–8. For the passage 101–7 cf. *P.L.* IX.445–51.

p. 6, 111–13   T. frequently makes the point that the 'eyes' of fancy and reason see far more of Nature's beauty, order and harmony than the physical eye can. Cf. *Sp.* 183–5, 495–6, *Su.* 1730–52, *Au.* 777–835, *Wi.* 705–6, 1046–9, etc.

p. 6, 132   Throughout *The Seasons* periphrasis is used to define some particular characteristic of the natural object being described, and/or to indicate that object's place in some system or order. It is a device analagous to the terms of classification employed by seventeenth- and eighteenth-century scientists. See John Arthos, *The Language of Natural Description in Eighteenth Century Poetry* (Ann Arbor, 1949), especially Appendix B. T.'s periphrases often anthropomorphize the object. Examples of periphrasis include *Wi.* 793, 811, 822 (animals), *Sp.* 510, *Au.* 1176, 1181 (bees), 1265 (cattle), *Sp.* 546 (flowers), 395, 422, 424, *Au.* 922 (fish), *Su.* 237, 344 (insects), 378, 388, 417, *Wi.* 261 (sheep); there is a large group of periphrases for birds, most are anthropomorphic in suggestion—*Sp.* 584, 594, 597, 711, 729, 753, 789, *Su.* 737, 1121, *Wi.* 80, 87, 88, 137, 138, 793, Hymn 78, *Cas. Ind.* I.x,—but some are not—*Sp.* 617, 689, 747, *Au.* 840, *Wi.* 793.

p. 7, 114–36   Easterly winds in Spring might cause blight either by carrying insects or their eggs, or by producing the correct temperature to hatch eggs laid on plants in the previous year. The account of the causes and cures of blight comes from Richard Bradley's *New Improvements of Planting and Gardening* (1717–18), with hints from the earliest English georgic, John Philips's *Cyder* (1708), I.421–5. See *McKillop*, pp. 45–8. For insects as sons of vengeance cf. Exod. 10:13. In all editions before 1744 this passage was followed by 33 lines on microscopic Nature. In 1744 these were transferred, with alterations and omissions, to *Su.* 287–317; see *Sambrook*, pp. 9–11, 74–7.

p. 7, 143–4   Cf. Virgil, *Aeneid* I.52–4.

p. 8, 183–5   Cf. *Sp.* 79–89 and 111–13 end-notes.

p. 9, 203–12   The account of the rainbow is from Newton's *Opticks* (1704). Cf. T.'s *Poem sacred to the Memory of Sir Isaac Newton* (1727), 96–124. T., like Wordsworth (*Prelude*, (1850), III.63) was impressed above all by Newton's mind, cf. *Su.* 1560–3. For Keats it was the pre-Newtonian rainbow that was 'awful' (*Lamia* II.231).

p. 10, 242–74   According to many ancient poets the period when Saturn ruled an innocently happy world was the Golden Age; it was followed by the progressively more vicious Silver, Bronze, and Iron ages—in which last those poets and ourselves have had the misfortune to be born. The immediate source of T.'s account here is Ovid, *Metamorphoses* I.89–112, 127–50. For 'willing glebe' (247) cf. *volentia rura* (Virgil, *Georgics* II.500).

p. 11, 305   On 'social feeling' see *Sp.* 878–903 and end-note.

p. 11, 309–22 The antediluvian world was quite smooth, and, because the ecliptic and the equatorial circles coincided, perpetual spring reigned in certain favoured areas. The Flood occurred when the surface of the earth (the 'disparting orb') was suddenly fractured and fell into the great subterranean abyss ('the central waters'), throwing up a deluge that engulfed and wrecked the earth (henceforth a rough 'broken world'); at the same time, by the tilting of the earth's axis, the ecliptic became oblique and alternation of the seasons began. In T.'s day this theory was best known in the pages of Thomas Burnet's *The Sacred Theory of the Earth* (1681–9). See *McKillop*, pp. 97–106. According to the ancient poets the alternation of the seasons began in the Silver Age under the reign of Zeus; cf. Ovid, *Metamorphoses* I.116–24. Milton attributed the change of seasons to the Fall (*P.L.* X.651–707); T., at 317–22, echoes *P.L.* X.651–6 and IV.147–8.

p. 13, 336–78 The passage on vegetarianism (336–73) is based on Ovid, *Metamorphoses* XV.75–142, and perhaps influenced by the well-known *Essay on Health and Long Life* (1724) in which the physician George Cheyne had sought to introduce a more vegetarian diet to the carnivorous and scurvied English gentry. Pythagoras had advocated vegetarianism in accordance with his doctrine of the transmigration of souls between brute and man, but T. implies (374–8) that the slaughter of brutes may be to their benefit, by releasing their souls for admission into higher forms of life. This notion accords with T.'s interpretation of the great chain of being idea (cf. *Su.* 334 and end-note) in evolutionary terms, so that each being (brute, man, and angel) can step upwards for ever in the vital scale. Cf. *Su.* 1796–1805 and end-note, *Wi.* 603–8 and end-note, *Hymn* 114–18, *Cas. Ind.* II. xlviii and end-note.

p. 13, 388–93 Possibly mock-sentimental, as T.'s concern shifts from the worm to the fish ('uncomplaining wretch') and then, more realistically, to the angler's hand, but, in fishing for trout, the fly is a less cruel bait than the worm in as much as, whereas the worm is swallowed, the fly fastens in the fish's mouth in cartilage which is almost insensitive to pain. Cf. John Gay, *Rural Sports* (1720), I.265–70, and Byron's note to *Don Juan* XIII.cvi.

p. 15, 379–466 This passage was first added in the 1744 edition, revised 1746. The description of fishing is practical and didactic in the manner of the sporting georgic (cf. Gay, *Rural Sports* I.121–270), but is, perhaps, also an ironic comment on vegetarianism and 'pure perfection' (376). For the noonday reverie (458–66) cf. *Cas. Ind.* I.v–vi end-note and Introduction p. xvi. 'Imagination' (459) and 'fancy' (455) are synonymous for T.; cf. *Sp.* 469 and 473. Both words signify the power to form images in the mind: 'by the pleasures of the imagination or fancy (which I shall use promiscuously) I here mean such as arise from visible objects, either when we have them actually in our view, or when we call up their ideas into our minds.' (Addison, *Spectator* 411.)

p. 18, 563 The ether (cf. *Sp.* 148 fn.) was thought to contain substances, the most important of which was an acid which formed salt-petre or nitre (cf. *Wi.* 694 end-note), which supported vegetable life. 'The ancient philosophers supposed the ether to be igneous, and by its kind influence upon the air to be the cause of all vegetation.' (Pope, translation of the *Iliad* I.514, note; cf. *Lucretius* V. 458–9.) 'For the air is full of acid and sulphureous particles which, constantly forming in the air, are doubtless very serviceable in promoting the work of vegetation; when being imbibed by the leaves, they may not improbably be the materials out of which the more subtle and refined principles of vegetables are formed.' (Stephen Hales, *Vegetable Staticks* (1727).)

p. 18, 556–71 T. connects the universal diffusion of divine power with the penetrative force of the sun and its effect upon vegetation. For the rhapsodic manner cf. *Wi.* 106–17 and end-note; for the science cf. *Sp.* 79–89 and end-note.

p. 22, 703   I have found no classical precedent for calling birds the brothers of the Muse. In *Cas. Ind.* II.xxxiii, xxxiv, the nightingale is the sister of a Druid-bard Philomelus ('lover of music'). The Muses themselves were often represented as winged (cf. *Wi.* 18–23), and Ovid described an attempt to imprison them, *Metamorphoses* V.274–88.

p. 23, 714–28   Cf. Virgil, *Georgics* IV.511–15.

p. 24, 778–81   Cf. *P.L.* VII.438–40.

p. 25, 789–830   Cf. Virgil, *Georgics* III.212–54. T. uses the same styles as Virgil—mock love-elegiac for the bull, heroic for the horse.

p. 26, 840–8   The Iron Age earthwork now grazed by sheep is the pastoral-patriotic symbol of a Britain once primitively anarchic but now prosperous. T.'s view expands in characteristic manner; cf. *Sp.* 32–77, *Su.* 352–431, etc.

p. 26, 862   On the smiling God see *Sp.* 84 end-note.

p. 27, 878–903   God's creative bounty (879) is diffused in the form of human charity, and man, in practising charity, enjoys a God-like pleasure (901–2). 'Social love . . . is the very smile and consummation of virtue; 'tis the image of that fair perfection in the Supreme Being.' (T. to Aaron Hill, 1726, *Letters and Documents*, p. 26.) 'To have the natural, kindly or generous affections strong and powerful towards the good of the public is to have the chief means and power of self-enjoyment.' (Shaftesbury, *An Inquiry concerning Virtue or Merit* (1699), Book II, part I, conclusion.) Such social love or social feeling—so agreeable to its possessor—is a frequent theme in T.; cf. *Sp.* 305, *Su.* 1641–6, *Au.* 1006–29, *Wi.* 348–58, *Cas. Ind.* I.xv.

p. 27, 906   George, Lord Lyttelton (1709–73) was friend and patron of T., Pope, Fielding, and other writers. He courted the muse (908, 932–5); Johnson said that his poems 'have nothing to be despised, and little to be admired' (*Lives of the Poets*). He also wrote extensively on English history and on contemporary politics (926–31). A resolute opponent of Walpole, he entered the government after Walpole's fall in 1742, and became in 1744 a Lord of the Treasury. Lines 904–62 first appeared in the 1744 edition. Cf. *Cas. Ind.* I.lxv–lxvi.

p. 27, 908   Hagley Park was Lyttelton's abruptly contoured estate in Worcestershire where, in the 1740s, was created one of the most admired landscape gardens of the eighteenth century. T. first visited Hagley in 1743 (cf. *Letters and Documents*, p. 165). The description (909–16) is 'picturesque', i.e. concerned with visual relationships and harmonies.

p. 30, 996–1003   Cf. *Lucretius* IV.1133–6. I have found no model for the personification of repentance as snaky-crested; perhaps T. has in mind the snaky-haired Furies of Greek and Roman myth. The whole passage 983–1112 is rearranged, expurgated, and adapted from *Lucretius* IV.1008–1208.

p. 32, 1067–73   Cf. Virgil, *Georgics* III.258–63, in allusion to Leander who used to swim the Hellespont to visit his mistress Hero and was at last drowned.

SUMMER

p. 37, 1–8   Summer, like Spring (*Sp.* 1–4), is personified and makes a royal 'progress'; his masculine power is contrasted with Spring's feminine mildness.

p. 38, 15–20   T. took the 'hint about personizing of Inspiration' from David Mallet (*Letters and Documents*, p. 45). In this passage T. emphasizes the notion of the poet as creator; cf. *Su.* 192–6 and, perhaps *Au.* 668–72, where, 'inspiration' is not personified and T. regards the poet as imitator, and 'translator' of the 'book of Nature'.

p. 38, 29   George Bubb Dodington (1691–1762), politician, poetaster, patron, and wit, was impressed by *Winter* (1726) and invited T. to dedicate *Summer* (1727) to him. Edward Young (cf. *Au.* 667), Fielding, Glover, and Lyttelton (cf. *Sp.* 906) all made court to Dodington—as did T. who was a frequent visitor to his great house at Eastbury in Dorset (cf. *Au.* 655). Pope's sketches of Dodington's character if less charitable than T.'s are probably more faithful; cf. *Epistle to Arbuthnot* 231–48 and *Epistle to Burlington* 19–22. T. added lines 21–32 to the 1730 edition to replace a prefatory prose dedication to Dodington; he complimented Dodington also in a verse epistle *The Happy Man* (1729).

p. 38, 32–42   Cf. Gen. 1:14 and 8:22. Kepler and Newton had demonstrated that the planets are kept in their courses by a combination of transverse motion and the gravitational pull of the sun (cf. T.'s *Poem sacred to the Memory of Sir Isaac Newton* 39–42). Physico-theologians of the period argued that gravitation proceeds from 'a Divine energy and impression', and transverse motion 'can only be ascribed to the right hand of the most high God' who continues to preserve the solar system in its shape (Richard Bentley's Boyle Lectures, 1692). See *McKillop*, pp. 31–4.

p. 39, 81   The sun is personified making a royal progress, preceded by the Seasons (113, 121), the Hours (122), etc. Cf. Ps. 19:4, 5 *P.L.* VII.370–3, and the famous fresco *Aurora* (1613) by Guido Reni; see Jean Hagstrum, *The Sister Arts* (Chicago, 1958), pp. 260–1 and Plate xxix.

p. 39, 84   For the Pythagorean notion that light is material (91), descending in liquid form from that fountain of light the sun, cf. *Lucretius* V. 281–5 and *P.L.* VII,362. Cf. *Su.* 435, 453–5, 659–61, *Au.* 958, 1095–1102, *Hymn* 68.

p. 40, 90–9   Cf. *P.L.* III.1–6, VIII.122–5.

p. 40, 107   In the seventeenth and eighteenth centuries it was often claimed that there must be life on other planets. The most influential statement of this theory was by Bernard de Fontenelle whose *Plurality of Worlds* was translated into English (by Aphra Behn) in 1688, but cf. *P.L.* III.565–71, VII.621–2, VIII.140–58. For a full account of literature on the plurality of worlds see A. O. Lovejoy, *The Great Chain of Being* (Cambridge Mass., 1936), chap. IV.

p. 41, 141   T. believed that the penetrative force of the sun causes the growth and colouring of minerals. 'Minerals . . . are made in process of time, after long preparations and concoctions, by the actions of the sun within the bowels of the earth.' (Thomas Burnet, *Sacred Theory of the Earth*.) Cf. *P.L.* III.583–6, 606–12; see *McKillop*, pp. 56–7.

p. 41, 155   Newton had demonstrated that the colours of the spectrum blend into white light. T.'s description (140–59) runs through the spectrum as the colours emerge from the pure light of the diamond and return to the white light of the opal.

p. 42, 165–70   Used as a motto by Turner for his painting *Dunstanburgh Castle*, and by Constable for his *Hadleigh Castle*. T. was a favourite poet of both painters.

p. 42, 176–81   Cf. *P.L.* III.3–6. For 'smiling' (179) cf. *Sp.* 84 and end-note. The entire passage, 81–184, enforces the central significance of the sun—physically as the upholder of life, and spiritually because light is the primary power in the universe and the Creator is light himself (176, cf. *Hymn* 117).

p. 42, 185–96   T. agrees with so many eighteenth-century preachers, philosophers, and poets that 'the works of Nature everywhere sufficiently evidence a Deity' (Locke); cf. *Hymn*. Furthermore as God is the great artist or author (cf. *Sp.* 859–60) and Nature is his art (cf. *Au.* 668–72; *Hymn* 23; Browne, *Religio Medici*, Part 1, sect. 16; Pope, *Essay on Man* I.289), the best art that man can attempt—albeit a feeble best (cf. *Sp.* 468–79)—is imitation of Nature. In thus imitating God's art, in reading and translating the sacred book of Nature, the poet can follow the best paths of devotion and art.

p. 43, 216–19   That the sunflower or marigold follows the sun is a pertinacious poetic fiction; cf. Ovid, *Metamorphoses* IV.269–70.

p. 44, 267–80   Cf. John Philips. *The Splendid Shilling* (1705), 78–92. T.'s mock-heroic tone gradually becomes clearer between lines 230 and 280.

p. 45, 289–317   'Every part of matter is peopled; every green leaf swarms with inhabitants. There is scarce a single humour in the body of a man, or of any other animal, in which our glasses do not discover myriads of living creatures. The surface of animals is also covered with other animals, which are in the same manner the basis of other animals that live upon it; we find in the most solid bodies, as in marble itself, innumerable cells and cavities that are crowded with such imperceptible inhabitants as are too little for the naked eye to discover.' (Addison, *Spectator* 519, drawing on Bernard de Fontenelle's *Plurality of Worlds*; cf. *Su.* 107.) 'If the eye were so acute as to rival the finest microscopes, and to discern the smallest hair upon the leg of a gnat, it would be a curse and not a blessing to us. . . . So likewise, if our sense of hearing were exalted proportionally to the former, what a miserable condition would mankind be in ? . . . we should have no quiet or sleep in the silentest nights and most solitary places; and we must inevitably be struck deaf or dead with the noise of a clap or thunder.' (Richard Bentley, Boyle Lectures, 1692; cf. Pope, *Essay on Man* I.195–204.) These notions were often restated by eighteenth-century physico-theologians. Cf. *McKillop*, pp. 48–52.

p. 46, 318–28   This fable is from *Guardian* 70 (1713) by George Berkeley, but. T. adds the information that Ignorance is female.

p. 46, 334   The chain of beings was composed of 'an immense, or . . . infinite, number of links ranging in hierarchical order from the meagerest kind of existents, which barely escape non-existence, through "every possible" grade up to the *ens perfectissimum*—or, . . . to the highest possible kind of creature, between which and the Absolute Being the disparity was assumed to be infinite—every one of them differing from that immediately above and that immediately below it by the "least possible" degree of difference.' (A. O. Lovejoy, *The Great Chain of Being* (Cambridge, Mass., 1936), p. 59.) Lovejoy's book surveys the whole subject with great learning. For near-contemporary statements of the notion of the chain of being cf. Locke, *Essay on Human Understanding* III.vi.12, Addison,

Spectator 519, Pope, *Essay on Man* I.207–46, but the conception was Platonic and the idea prevalent in Western thought from the Middle Ages to the late eighteenth century. Cf. *Sp.* 378, *Su.* 1796–1805.

p. 46, 342–51   Cf. *Wi.* 638–47.

p. 49, 352–431   This is typical of the georgic in combining an account of husbandry with pastoral idealism (e.g. 370, 400–4) and patriotism (423-31). None of this passage appeared in the first edition; lines 352–70 were added in 1730, and 371–431 in 1744. In showing (423–31) that the farmer's activities support Britain's mercantile power T. harmonizes simple rural scenes and national grandeur; cf. *Sp.* 32–77, *Au.* 43–150.

p. 49, 453–5   For the notion of light as liquid see *Su.* 84 end-note, cf. 'dazzling deluge' (Su. 435).

p. 49, 458–63   Cf. Virgil, *Georgics* II. 487–8; 'gelid' is particularly evocative of Virgil, cf. *Su.* 208.

p. 50, 432–97   Cf. Gay, *Rural Sports* (1720), I.53–66.

p. 50, 498–505   Cf. Virgil, *Georgics* III. 146–51.

p. 51, 506–15   Cf. Job 39:19–21.

p. 52, 516–63   For T.'s claims that love of Nature refines the moral sense and may sometimes give rise to states of religious ecstasy, cf. *Sp.* 899–903, *Au.* 1004–36. The hint for the woodland spirits (539) came from David Mallet (*Letters and Documents*, p. 45), but it is not clear who exactly these spirits are. Despite the allusion to angels (525) it seems quite likely that the reference is to the Druids, about whom there was much speculation in T.'s day. The Druids were bards, they worshipped in oak groves, and so were regarded by the eighteenth century as Nature's poet-priests (555). In a MS. draft of *The Prelude* (1805), Book III, Wordsworth sees himself as a priestly poet of Nature, or

> A youthful Druid taught in shady groves
> Primeval mysteries, a Bard elect.

(*The Prelude*, ed. E. de Selincourt, second edn. rev. Helen Darbishire (Oxford, 1959), pp. 75–6 fn.). William Stukely, in *Stonehenge* (1743), regards the Druids as almost Christians and almost the equal of the Old Testament patriarchs as religious teachers. See A. L. Owen, *The Famous Druids* (Oxford, 1962) for the eighteenth-century view of the Druids. T.'s doctrine of the ascent of the soul (see *Sp.* 336–78 end-note and references there) has something in common with the Druidic belief in metempsychosis, derived from Pythagoras, and a statement of this doctrine in *Cas. Ind.* II.xlviii is put into the mouth of a Druid-bard. T. is called a Druid in Collins's famous Ode (see *Introduction*, p. xviii above). On T.'s Druidic character see J. M. S. Tompkins, 'In yonder Grave a Druid Lies', *Review of English Studies*, xxii (1946), 1–16.

p. 53, 591–606   Considerably altered in 1744 from the earlier texts—in order to make the waterfall larger and the descriptive effect more sublime; see *Sambrook*, p. 89.

p. 54, 622–8   Cf. Milton, *Il Penseroso*, 139–43.

p. 54, 641   The trade winds. 'The general breeze. Which blows constantly between the tropics from the east, or the collateral points, the north-east and south-east; caused by the pressure of the rarefied air on that before it, according to the diurnal motion of the sun from east to west.' (T.) It is not true that rarefied air can push denser air before it—as T. recognizes later in the poem, cf. *Su.* 789–90.

p. 54, 646   Because of the sun's action cf. *Su.* 141 end-note.

p. 55, 657–62   T. sees as one of the beneficent paradoxes of the harmonious natural order that tropical fruits contain cooling juices. On light as liquid ('drink . . . redoubled day', 659–61), see *Su.* 84 end-note.

p. 57, 745   The line is a quotation from Milton, 'Upon the Circumcision', 5.

p. 58, 781–3   Mount Amara 'is situate as the navel of that Ethiopian body, and centre of their Empire, under the equinoctial line where the sun may take his best view thereof, as not encountering in all his long journey with the like theatre . . . the sun himself so in love with the sight, that the first and last thing he vieweth in all those parts is this hill.' (*Purchas, his Pilgrimage* (1617), Book VII, chap. V.) Lines 747–83 are based upon several geographical descriptions derived (like Johnson's *Rasselas*) from Jesuit missionaries' accounts, but the paradisial overtones are mainly from Purchas and from *P.L.* IV.280–4, with IV.131–43. See *McKillop*, pp. 151–5.

p. 59, 788–802   Winds in the temperate zones drive clouds towards the tropics where the air is warmer and therefore less dense (789–90, cf. *Su.* 641 end-note). These clouds are condensed upon the Abyssinian, Himalayan, and other mountains to produce the monsoon rains. T.'s account is probably based on Antoine Pluche, *Spectacle de la Nature* (2nd edn. 1737), III.115–16, and *Lucretius* VI.246–322, with its notion that thunder and lightning were caused by the collision of cloud-laden winds. T., as usual, personifies natural phenomena. See *McKillop*, pp. 156–7.

p. 59, 803–5   Ancients and moderns alike had speculated about the source of the Nile; cf. Lucan, *Pharsalia* X.172–331, Pliny, *Natural History* V.x.51–4. T.'s account (806–21) refers only to the Blue Nile. The principal branch of the river is the White Nile—the source of which was determined by Speke in 1863. T. personifies the river, as usual.

p. 60, 827   'Menam's orient stream. The river that runs through Siam: on whose banks a vast multitude of those insects called fireflies make a beautiful appearance in the night.' (T.) The reference to the lantern-flies in Siam comes from John Harris, *Collection of Voyages* (1705), II.465–8; see *McKillop*, p. 159.

p. 60, 836   The native houses in trees were described in Raleigh's *Discovery of Guiana* (1596); see *McKillop*, pp. 159–60.

p. 60, 856–9   The story that the current of South American rivers carries fresh water many miles out to sea is told in *Purchas, his Pilgrimage* (1617), Book IX, chap. I, and in many other travel books. Thomson, typically, personifies ocean. For some account of all those geographical compilations—notably *Purchas* and Bernhard Varenius's *General Geography* (rev. by Isaac Newton, 1672)—which were drawn upon for this catalogue of rivers (803–59), see *McKillop*, pp. 155–60.

p. 62, 629–897   Nearly all of this long exotic excursion was first added in the 1744 edition. It sets the horrific against the paradisial aspects of the tropics, with the moral (860–97) that the civilized arts of Europe are to be preferred to the barbarous nature of the tropical regions. Cf. *Wi.* 587–93 end-note.

p. 62, 898–907   Cf. Lucan, *Pharsalia* IX.607–10. (For 898–901 cf. also Virgil, *Georgics* II.153–4.)

p. 63, 946   Cf. *P.L.* II.636–7.

p. 63, 954   Marcus Porcius Cato (95–46 B.C.), principal opponent of Julius

Caesar in the Roman Civil Wars, made a famous six-day march across the desert in 47 B.C. to join his allies at Utica, near modern Tunis, but seeing their cause was hopeless he committed suicide; cf. Lucan, *Pharsalia* IX, Addison, *Cato*.

p. 63, 960   Cf. *Su.* 993, *Wi.* 67, 193, *Cas. Ind.* I.xliii. T.'s several references to demons (or other spirits) of the storm owe suggestions both to the personifications of winds in classical mythology and to Biblical spirits; cf. Ps. 104:9–10.

p. 64, 959–77   Cf. Lucan, *Pharsalia* IX.455–92. For other accounts of sandstorms in geographical compilations known to T. see *McKillop*, pp. 161–2.

p. 64, 984–6   'The circling typhon; And dire ecnephia. Terms for particular storms or hurricanes known only between the tropics.' (T.) 'Ecnephias' is not in *N.E.D.* but is defined in Lewis and Short, *Latin Dictionary* as 'a hurricane supposed to be produced by blasts from two opposite clouds'. Pliny defines the typhoon as a whirling ecnephias (*Natural History*, II,xlix. 131–2). For the passage 980–96 cf. *Lucretius* VI.423–42; see *McKillop*, pp. 162–4.

p. 65, 1013–25   From Jean Barbot's 'Description of the Coasts of North and South Guinea' in Churchill's *Collection of Voyages*, v (1732), 225–6; see *Mc-Killop*, p. 165. T.'s lines inspired Turner's painting *The Slave Ship*.

p. 65, 1026–35   For the traditional notion that the sun draws up pestilence from swamps cf. *Lucretius* VI.1098–1102, Shakespeare, *Tempest* II.i.1.

p. 65, 1041   Admiral Vernon (1684–1757) commanded English attacks upon the Spanish West Indies in 1739–41. He earned great fame by taking Porto Bello (Panama) with only six ships, but his attempt in 1741 to take Cartagena (in what is now Colombia) failed—partly due to the onset of the plague described here by T., but mainly to the incompetence of the military officers. The siege of Cartagena is described in Smollett's *Roderick Random* (1748), chaps. xxviii–xxxiv. The whole passage 959–1051, describing tropical horrors, was first added in the 1744 edition; cf. *Su.* 629–897 end-note.

p. 66, 1055   'Ethiopia's poisoned woods. These are the causes supposed to be the first origin of the plague, in Doctor Mead's elegant book on that subject.' (T.) Richard Mead in *A Short Discourse concerning Pestilential Contagion* (8th edn., 1722) explained that the putrefaction of huge swarms of dead locusts in Africa and Asia caused plague. He argued against the policy of confining the families of plague-infected persons; cf. *Su.* 1074–7. See *McKillop*, pp. 167–8.

p. 66, 1070   'The great streets within the city . . . had grass growing in them.' (Defoe, *Journal of the Plague Year*, ed. L. A. Landa (1969), p. 101.) Cf. Pepys, *Diary*, 20 Sept. 1665. The whole passage 1070–91 draws upon Defoe's *Journal of the Plague Year*.

p. 67–8, 1092–1116   Mineral caverns contained bituminous or sulphureous exhalations (sometimes identified as firedamp) which might be ignited below ground to make earthquakes and volcanic eruptions, or be drawn into the skies and buffeted by opposing winds to cause thunder and lightning; cf. *Su.* 797–9. See *McKillop*, pp. 68–9. For 'mineral generations' (1107) cf. *Su.* 141 end-note; 'wrathful' (1106) and 'baleful' (1111) emphasize God's personality behind the storm. Lines 1108–10 echo *P.L.* VI.478–80.

p. 68, 1128   The parallel and the contrast here with *Sp.* 161–2 and *Su.* 1233 draws attention to the various emotional implications of the storms. Lines 1116–25 echo Virgil, *Georgics* I.356–9, 374–6.

p. 70, 1171–1222   The hint for this story probably comes from newspaper reports of the two rustic lovers struck dead by lightning at Stanton Harcourt, Oxfordshire, in July 1718, and by Pope's well-known epitaph upon the lovers. None of Pope's various detailed prose accounts was in print when T. published *Summer* (1727), but cf. *Correspondence of Pope*, ed. G. Sherburn (1956), i.479. T. handles the story for a devotional end, in the manner of the Book of Job, to show God's power and man's incomprehension of God's purposes; thus he makes no attempt to lessen the mystery of 'Mysterious Heaven' (1215). The unconscious irony of Celadon's confident claim (1204–14) is heightened by its echo (1208–10) of Ps. 91:5.

p. 71, 1233   See *Su.* 1128 end-note.

p. 71, 1264–8   The Roman arm may belong to Julius Caesar who, as a boy, excelled in swimming, or to Romans in general, for swimming was one of the physical exercises practised in the Iuventus—the youth movement inaugurated by Augustus to provide pre-military training. The ideal of *mens sana in corpore sano* (1267–8, cf. Juvenal, *Satires* X.356) is at least as old as the ancient Greeks, but Thomson offers unexpected—even quaint—support for it in the story of Damon and Musidora (1269–1370) which he first added in 1730 and considerably revised in 1744.

p. 73, 1304–7   Paris, son of Priam King of Troy, when guarding his sheep on Mount Ida was asked to judge which of the three goddesses Hera (Juno), Athene (Minerva), and Aphrodite (Venus) was the most beautiful. He gave his verdict to Aphrodite who had promised, in return, to give him the fairest of women. This woman was Menelaus's wife Helen, and Paris's seduction of her gave rise to the great war between Greece and Troy. In the 1730 edition of T.'s poem Damon spies upon three naked bathers, who are likened to Juno, Minerva, and Venus. The mock-epical comparison between Damon and Paris is first hinted at lines 1285–7.

p. 73, 1315–20   Not surprisingly, Musidora was painted in this pose by many English artists, including Gainsborough and Etty.

p. 74, 1371   The sun is setting. T. wrote to David Mallet, 11 Aug. 1726, about *Summer*, 'I resolved to contract the season into a day.' (*Letters and Documents*, p. 45.)

p. 76, 1418–24   'Harrington's retreat' (1419) was Petersham Lodge built in the 1720s for William Stanhope, Earl of Harrington. The pendent woods (1418) belonged to one of the very earliest English landscape gardens, laid out before 1713 by an earlier possessor of the estate—Henry Hyde, Earl of Rochester. Hyde's second daughter, Kitty, was the famous beauty and eccentric who married Charles Douglas (1698–1778), third Duke of Queensberry (referred to at line 1423). John Gay the poet lived with the Queensberrys at Ham House (cf. 1420), near Twickenham, for the last four years of his life. The Duchess also befriended Congreve, Swift, Prior, Pope, and T. Hyde's eldest son was Henry, Viscount Cornbury (1710–53—referred to at line 1424), a High Church Tory MP., author, and friend of Bolingbroke, Pope, Swift, and T. The brilliant Ham House circle was a centre of opposition to Walpole and George II.

p. 76, 1429–32   Henry Pelham (1696–1754), the Whig politician, was Secretary at War, Paymaster-General, and, from 1743 to his death, Prime Minister. His estate, Claremont (cf. 1429) at Esher on the River Mole in Surrey had one of the most famous landscape gardens of the eighteenth century—laid out by Charles Bridgeman and Vanbrugh before 1726 and later remodelled by William Kent (illustrator of the 1730 edition of *The Seasons*); cf. Pope, *Epilogue to the Satires* II.66–7.

p. 76, 1435–7   See Introduction, p. xv above. The whole passage 1371–1437 was first added in the 1744 edition, after T. had gone to live at Richmond.

p. 76, 1442   Here begins a patriotic panegyric (1442–1619) highly characteristic of the eighteenth-century English georgic; the model is Virgil's praise of fruitful, prosperous Italy—the nurse of great men—cf. *Georgics* II.138–76. Until the 1744 edition T.'s panegyric followed the line corresponding to *Su.* 628 in the present edition. Between 1727 and 1744 the panegyric was nearly doubled in length, and, though the praise of Scotsmen was transferred to *Autumn* in 1730 (cf. *Au.* 878–949 and end-note), the number of English worthies was increased gradually though various editions. In 1727 there were nine—More, Bacon, Barrow, Tillotson, Boyle, Locke, Newton, Shakespeare, and Milton. In 1738 Barrow and Tillotson the preachers were withdrawn, and Walsingham, Drake, Raleigh, Hampden, Sir Philip Sidney, Russell, and Ashley (i.e. Shaftesbury) added. In 1744 were added Alfred, the Edwards and Henrys, Algernon Sidney, Spenser, and Chaucer. The completed list of names makes up a pantheon of English patriotism, liberty, enlightenment, and humanity, but the choice of politicians (and even of philosophers) betrays a strong Whiggish bias. It is significant that eleven of the men named by T. in this list were also commemorated in the Shrine of British Worthies (cf. *Au.* 1050 end-note) which was gradually assembled at Stowe in the 1730s and early 40s.

p. 76, 1442–5   British Liberty the Queen of Arts scattering plenty—with the assistance of Property (1455) and gay Drudgery (1459)—is the political counterpart to Nature, whose liberality is referred to at, e.g., *Sp.* 98–9, 230–1, *Su.* 126–8.

p. 78, 1488   Sir Thomas More, Lord Chancellor, was convicted of high treason and executed for his refusal to accept Henry VIII as Supreme Head of the English Church. T's Protestantism emerges in the epithets 'mistaken' and 'useful'.

p. 78, 1491   T. may mean Cato the Censor (234–149 B.C.), the patriot and fearless opponent of corruption and luxury in the Roman republic but he might equally well refer to Cato of Utica, see *Su.* 954 fn.

p. 78, 1491   Aristides the Just (d. 468 B.C.), the Athenian democratic leader celebrated for rectitude, patriotism, and moderation. The intrigues of Themistocles (cf. *Wi.* 464) brought about Aristides' ostracism, but when he was allowed to return to Athens he assisted Themistocles with service and advice in the war against Persia. Cf. *Wi.* 459.

p. 78, 1492   Lucius Quinctius Cincinnatus was the traditional exemplar of early Roman pious frugality. In 458 B.C. when the Roman army was in danger of defeat he was called from the plough and made dictator; he defeated the enemy and returned to his farm. Cf. *Sp.* 60, *Wi.* 512.

p. 78, 1499–1510   Sir Walter Raleigh wrote his *History of the World* while imprisoned in the Tower of London (1603–15) on the unjust charge of high treason After the failure in 1618 of Raleigh's expedition to Guiana to find gold for the king, James I placated the Spaniards by having Raleigh executed in accordance with the sentence passed thirteen years earlier.

p. 78, 1518   Seventeenth-century Parliamentarians who sought to limit the king's prerogative claimed to be restoring a 'native freedom', i.e. the ancient Saxon liberties of the people which had been lost at the Norman Conquest. Cf. T. *Liberty* IV (1736), 689–762; see Christopher Hill, 'The Norman Yoke' in *Puritanism and the Revolution* (1958), pp. 50–122.

p. 79, 1528   Algernon Sidney (1622–83) was one of the judges at the trial of Charles I, was executed for his part in the Rye House Plot, and, like Russell, was a hero of the Whigs. Like Cassius (the murderer of Julius Caesar) he was a Republican.

p. 79, 1535   Francis Bacon (1561–1626), Lord Chancellor, was dismissed in 1621 for accepting bribes shamelessly. T. praises him as a philosopher, particularly as author of the *Novum Organum* (1620), the 'new instrument' which enunciated the inductive principles of experiment that have been the basis for most subsequent scientific investigation.

p. 79, 1549–50   T. appears to disregard the sharp line of division that Bacon drew in his *Novum Organum* between human discovery and divine revelation. For 'chain of things' cf. *Su.* 334 end-note.

p. 79, 1551   The Third Earl of Shaftesbury (1671–1713) was the moral philosopher who taught that men possessed an intuitive moral sense which naturally inclined them to act benevolently towards all creatures around them; see *Sp.* 873–903 end-note.

p. 80, 1560–3   Newton might be described as 'pure intelligence' because he sternly followed what he called the 'mathematical way' and would frame no hypotheses. His account of the system of the world in the *Principia* (1686–7) was abstract and schematic (no more and no less than a set of mathematical principles) —unlike the 'pictorial' representations of the world favoured by the so-called 'Mechanical Philosophers' of the earlier seventeenth century, Descartes, Hobbes, and Gassendi. Newton's principles were 'simple' because, as he said, 'Nature is wont to be simple, and always consonant to itself.' Cf. T., *Poem sacred to the Memory of Sir Isaac Newton*, especially lines 68–90, and Introduction, p. xiii above.

p. 80, 1566   Shakespeare's 'wildness' (what Nicholas Rowe in his *Life of Shakespeare* (1709), called his 'furor poeticus') was a commonplace of eighteenth-century criticism. Cf. Milton, *L'Allegro* 133-4.

p. 80, 1568   Dryden had declared that the powers of Homer and Virgil met and joined in Milton: 'Verses written under Mr. Milton's picture' *P.L.* (4th edn., 1688).

p. 80, 1572–5   T. praises those aspects of Spenser's verse that he sought to recapture in *The Castle of Indolence*.

p. 81, 1604–19   This description functions like a patriotic allegorical painting where—typical of this period and of T.—Public Zeal is in the foreground. Cf. the Power of Cultivation (*Su.* 1436 and Introduction p. xv above) Liberty the Queen of Arts (1442–3), Property (1455), and Drudgery (1459).

p. 81, 1619   After this line the early editions had two long passages both of which were removed in 1744. The first passage was 47 lines on the horrors of the tropics, included in the 1727 edition. The second was a 32-line account of a petrified city in the desert and was first added to the 1730 edition; though very fine it was rejected probably because T. came to believe that the story was fabulous. See *Sambrook*, pp. 93, 97, 99. and *McKillop*, pp. 145–8.

p. 82, 1641–6   See *Sp.* 878–903 end-note.

p. 83, 1681   After this line in the 1727 edition followed 14 lines on the *ignis fatuus*, transferred with alterations in 1730 to *Autumn* where they correspond to lines 1150–64 of the present edition.

p. 83, 1701   After this line in the 1727 edition followed a 37-line description of the aurora borealis, transferred with alterations in 1730 to *Autumn* where it corresponds to 1108–37 in the present edition.

p. 84, 1725–9   'The vapours which arise from the sun, the fixed stars, and the tails of the comets may meet at last with, and fall into, the atmosphere of the planets by their gravity; and there be condensed and turned into water and humid spirits. . . . So fixed stars that have been gradually wasted by the light and vapours emitted from them for a long time may be recruited by comets that fall upon them; and from this fresh supply of new fuel those old stars, acquiring new splendour, may pass for new stars.' Newton, *Principia* (trans. Andrew Motte, 1729), II.387, 385. Here Newton, most uncharacteristically, has framed hypotheses; cf. *Su.* 1560–3 end-note.

p. 84, 1735 'Heavenly airs that are played to the departed souls of good men upon their first arrival in Paradise to wear out the impression of the last agonies.' (Addison, 'Visions of Mirzah', *Spectator* 159.)

p. 85, 1744–52 Succinctly states the poet's dual interest in Nature. Cf. *Sp.* 111–13 end-note, 455 fn.

p. 85, 1753–6 These lines were engraved on the monument erected to T. in Richmond church.

p. 86, 1758–81 Cf. *Au.* 43–150 end-note.

p. 86, 1788–99 This passage draws upon Locke's *Essay concerning Human Understanding*. Our first and simplest ideas are received passively from sensations (*Essay* II.i–v). The idea of perception is the first to result from reflecting actively upon these simple ideas (*Essay* II.ix); reflecting further upon (compounding, ordering, dividing) our ideas we may build up ever more complex ideas—including false and fantastical ones (*Essay* Book II, cf. *Wi.* 609–16). However, God has set limits upon the extent of human knowledge (*Essay* IV.iii).

p. 86, 1796–1805 T. incorporates Locke's psychology—as he incorporates Pythagoras's vegetarianism and the old notion of the great chain of being—into his theory of vital ascent or spiritual evolution; cf. *Sp.* 374–8 end-note, *Su.* 344 end-note, *Wi.* 603–8 end-note.

AUTUMN

p. 89, 1–3 The book opens with the usual personification; cf. Spenser, *Mutabilitie Cantos* VII.vii.30.

p. 89, 3 The Doric dialect of ancient Greece was used by Theocritus in some of his idylls, and thereafter 'Doric' was often a synonym for the language of pastoral poetry or of country people.

p. 89, 4–5 See *Wi.* 694–6 end-note.

p. 90, 50 Cf. 'seeds of freedom', *Liberty* III.539–40; 'moral seeds', *Cas. Ind.* II.xi.9.

p. 92, 121–33 Cf. Pope, *Windsor Forest* (1713), 219–24, 385–7. Britain's naval and mercantile strength was a favourite subject for early eighteenth-century poets; cf. *Sp.* 32–77 end-note. The reference in 130–3 is to the building and launching of a ship of the line—probably the most impressive industrial spectacle of T.'s age.

p. 93, 43–150 As in *Sp.* 32–77, *Su.* 352–431, 1406–1619 a particular rural scene prompts T. to expansive, optimistic reflections on Britain's greatness—in this case in the generalized form of a Whiggish myth of progress based on *Lucretius* V.925–1457 with hints of Virgil, *Georgics* I.125-46. However, T. recognizes only the gains of progress, where Lucretius had recognized that material progress is accompanied by moral decay. The dominant verb in T.'s passage is 'raise' (47, 76, 83, 119, 138); cf. 'roused' (73), 'aspiring' (117), 'shot up' (125), 'heaved' (134), 'exalts' (142). For a contrary view of progress cf. *Sp.* 242–335, *Au.* 1235–1351.

p. 93, 167–9   The instruction of Boaz to his reapers; cf. Ruth 2:16. The story that follows, at lines 177–310, is modelled upon the Book of Ruth. The names Lavinia, Palemon, and Acasto have no reference outside T.'s poem.

p. 94, 181–3, 189–91   This comparison complements *Sp.* 680–6.

p. 95, 211–12   There are Biblical references to planting the lovely, fragrant myrtle in the wilderness; cf. Isaiah 40:19, 55:13. In classical mythology the tree was dedicated to Venus; cf. Pliny, *Natural History* XII.ii.3.

p. 95, 220–3   Cf. the chorus describing the Golden Age in Act I of Tasso's *Aminta* (1593). For Arcadia see *Su.* 1301 fn.

p. 97, 326   The watery metaphor 'sea of harvest' (cf. 'flood', *Au.* 42, 'pours', 'flowing', *Au.* 171) ironically anticipates the literal flood of 334–48.

p. 98, 363–71   The spaniel is trained to draw (365) or 'set' the game, so that the birds remain immobile watching the dog until the huntsman has been able to cast a net over them. Cf. Pope, *Windsor Forest* 99–104, Gay, 'The Setting-Dog and the Partridge' in *Fables*.

p. 99, 372–7   The rhythms convey the effect of surging flight broken by sudden death.

p. 100, 411–12   The hare 'has very prominent eyes, placed backwards in its head so that it can almost see behind it as it runs. These are never wholly closed, but as the animal is continually upon the watch it sleeps with them open.' (Goldsmith, *History of Earth and Animated Nature*, Book V, chap.II.)

p. 102, 360–492   The hunting scenes are in the tradition of the English georgic and local poem; cf. Denham, *Cooper's Hill* (1642), 241–318, Pope, *Windsor Forest* (1713), 13–119, 147–58, John Philips, *Cyder* (1708), II.169–76, Gay, *Rural Sports* (1720), 289–342, 367–87. However, in T.'s handling of this well-worn material an element of burlesque slowly emerges—to become quite plain with the mock-heroic 'O glorious he' (492) and the following drinking scene.

p. 102, 519   Strong ale brewed in October and kept for several years to become even stronger was regarded as the particular drink of those boorish, lesser country squires who were thought by many men to be the backbone of the Tory party. Defoe wrote pamphlets attacking Tory extremists under the name of the 'October Club'. Steele's *Tatler* 118 ridicules a Tory squire: 'All the hours he spent at home were in swilling himself with October and rehearsing the wonders he did in the field'; cf. Addison, *Freeholder* 22.

p. 103, 524–5   The game 'is called Whist from the silence that is to be observed in the play'. (Charles Cotton, *Complete Gamester* (1680).) Cf. 562 end-note.

p. 103, 531   'frequent and full' is quoted from *P.L.* I.797; 'divan' is a term used to describe the council in Hell in *P.L.* X.457. T.'s description continues to make mock-heroic references to the Hellish assemblies in Milton's poem; e.g. 'perplexed' (542) cf. *P.L.* II.525, and *Au.* 550-2, cf. *P.L.* II.284–90.

p. 103, 554–5 Cf. Juvenal, *Satire* VI (trans. Dryden, 1693), 422–3.

p. 104, 562   Cf. the lubber (Robin Goodfellow) lying asleep beside the fire in Milton's *L'Allegro* 110–12. T.'s Lubber (i.e. loutish) Power is the personification of drunkenness, and, after Hunger, Thirst (512), and Whist (562) makes a fitting end to an allegorical pageant—a burlesque counterpart to such set-pieces as *Su.* 1604–19.

p. 104, 589–90   The hoop-petticoat was a frequent topic of male satire; cf. Addison, *Tatler* 116 and frequently elsewhere in the *Tatler* and the *Spectator*.

p. 105, 570–609 These lines well exemplify a prevalent eighteenth-century attitude to what was called 'the fair sex', 'the weaker sex', or 'the sex'; cf. *Tatler* and *Spectator passim.*

p. 105, 627–8 Cf. *Sp.* 107 end-note.

p. 106, 644–51 *Cyder* (1708), written by John Philips (1676–1708) in imitation of Virgil's *Georgics*, described, with patriotic digressions, the cultivation of cider apples, the making and the virtues of cider. T. calls him the 'second' writer of blank verse (645–6); Milton was the first.

p. 106, 655 For Dodington see *Su.* 29 end-note. His seat was Eastbury in Dorset where a magnificent house and garden were designed by Vanbrugh; Charles Bridgeman, too, helped to design the gardens.

p. 106, 667 The phrase referring to Edward Young (1683–1765) was added in 1744 after the first five books of his moralizing blank-verse poem in nine books, *Night Thoughts* (1742–5) had been published. Young was a friend of Dodington and visitor to Eastbury; he wrote verses at that Muses' seat.

p. 107, 668–72 Cf. *Su.* 185–96 end-note.

p. 107, 675–82 'Theme' (i.e. the book of Nature) is the subject of 'presents'. The hedonistic associations of the peach, vine, etc. are perhaps, an unexpected development of 'moral song' (672), but T. found his fruits in Eden, cf. *P.L.* IV.332–4, 307. On *Au.* 676–8 cf. 'the sharpness of vinegar consists in the fierceness of the little animals that bite you by the tongue; not to name the blue on plums.' (Bernard de Fontenelle, *Plurality of Worlds*, trans. 1688.) See *McKillop*, p. 51.

p. 107, 688–95 The grapes drink the sun's light and heat which is stored and radiated by the rocky cliffs (cf. *Su.* 657–62 and end-note). The juice is exalted (694) because drawn upwards by the sun's heat (cf. *Sp.* 79–89 end-note). The reference in *Au.* 691–2 is to black grapes and white.

p. 108, 707–10 The lower part of the atmosphere contains 'exhalations' of invisible moisture drawn upwards by the sun's heat. In Autumn this moisture is drawn up more slowly than in Summer, so that it condenses gradually in the cool middle sky (cf. *Su.* 768 fn.) and is precipitated lightly as mist, rather than heavily as rain. Rate of evaporation or condensation 'reflects the sun's annual movement; for the moisture rises and falls as the sun moves in the ecliptic.' (Aristotle, *Meteorologica* I.ix.347.)

p. 108, 711 On the eighteenth-century man's new-found taste for the 'sublime' in external nature see M. H. Nicolson, *Mountain Gloom and Mountain Glory* (Ithaca, N.Y., 1959). Addison had written in *Spectator* 412 of the imagination's pleasure in 'greatness', i.e. vastness.

p. 108, 722–7 These lines describe the effects of light refracted through a dense body of mist. For 723–4 cf. *Su.* 1620 end-note, *P.L.* I.594–9; 'frights' implicitly contrasts the attitude of the fond sequacious herd with that of the enlightened few, cf. *Au.* 1103–37. Lines 725–7 refer to the magnified shadows of objects thrown by the low light of sunrise or sunset against a sheet of mist.

p. 110, 802 'A range of mountains in Africa that surround almost all Monomotapa.' (T.) Monomotapa, in the basin of the Zambezi river, was an important African empire at the time of the first Jesuit missions in the sixteenth century, but was broken up into tribal kingdoms in the mid-eighteenth century. The Mountains of the Moon were supposed, in T.'s day, to lie across the Equator in Central Africa.

p. 111, 736–835   This account of the origin of lakes and rivers was much altered during T.'s revisions to the poem. In the first edition (1730) there was a passage of 42 lines offering an elaborate version of the old percolation theory, but in 1744 this was reduced to 14 lines (743–56), when a long account of the new and correct theory (756–835) was first added. Man had long wondered whether the condensation of water vapour (the 'roving mists' of 736) could furnish enough water to fill all the world's lakes and rivers. The ancient theory (743–56) was that the salt water of the oceans percolates through sand and gravel and is drawn eventually up to the mountain springs after all salt crystals have been strained out; cf. *Lucretius* V.261–72. Milton arranged the irrigation of the Garden of Eden by such porous action, cf. *P.L.* IV.223–30. The ancient theory was still current in the early eighteenth century where it may be found, e.g. in William Derham's very widely known and often reprinted *Physico-theology* (1713), but Edmund Halley had shown as early as 1691 in his 'Account of the circulation of the watery vapours of the sea, and of the cause of springs' (*Philosophical Transactions* xvii, 468–73) that condensation could, and did, account for all the supplies of fresh water. T. takes both his objections to the percolation theory (756–72) and his account of those stratified pervious and impervious rocks which make subterranean reservoirs and conduits (807–28) from Antoine Pluche, *Spectacle de la Nature* (trans. 1733–9), iii.90–8, 117–30. T.'s versified science combines Pluche's geology with Halley's hydrography to convey his constant message—the harmony of Nature (828–35). See *McKillop*, pp. 77–85. For the repetitions of 'I see' (808–20) cf. *Sp.* 111–13, end-note.

p. 112, 836–48   Pliny (*Natural History* X.xxxiv.70–1) thought that swallows became torpid in winter like bats, and this belief persisted into the eighteenth century. Even Gilbert White (*Natural History of Selborne* (1789), Letters xii, xviii, etc.) allows the possibility that some swallows hibernate. Defoe, however, had correctly described the migration of swallows (*A Tour through Great Britain*, 1 (1724), Letter i, 'Suffolk').

p. 112, 849–52   An obstinate love of liberty among the Batavians and their descendants the Dutch was noted by many writers from Tacitus onwards. The diligence, too, of this people was emphasized in Sir William Temple's *Observations upon the United Provinces* (1673).

p. 112, 853–61   This description may be taken from Richard Bradley, *Philosophical Account of the Works of Nature* (1721), pp. 84–5; see *McKillop*, pp. 131–3; but cf. Pliny, *Natural History* X.xxxi.61–2. T. observantly contrasts the 'congregation' (859—the word is not used jocularly) of the storks with the 'convolution swift' (839) of the swallows.

p. 112, 862–75   'Some of the lesser isles [of Shetland] are so crowded with variety of sea-fowl that they darken the air when they fly in great numbers.' (Martin Martin, *A Description of the Western Isles of Scotland* (1703).) Martin wrote also of the small size and variegated colours of Hebridean cattle, sheep, and horses, and of dangerous climbs on the islands in search of birds' eggs. See *McKillop*, pp. 132–3.

p. 112, 880   Cf. *Su.* 459 and fn. T. recognizes that the 'romantic' quality attributed to the landscape is a projection of the beholder's feelings. Later poets and critics were to recognize that all our knowledge of so-called external nature is in some sense a self-projection; the world is 'half-created' as well as perceived: cf. Wordsworth, *Tintern Abbey* 105–7; Coleridge, *Biographia Literaria*, chaps. xii, xiii.

p. 113, 889–91   T. spent his youth in and near Jedburgh in Roxburghshire.

p. 114, 910–28   Many pamphlets appeared in the 1720s advocating improved agriculture, fisheries, and trade, and the development of woollen and linen manufactures in Scotland; see *McKillop*, pp. 135–6. The fortunes of the Scottish herring industry excited other poets, e.g. Defoe, *Caledonia* (1707) and John Lockman, *The Shetland Herring and Peruvian Goldmine* (1751). On that favourite early eighteenth-century poetic theme—praise of commerce—see Bonamy Dobrée, 'The Theme of Patriotism in the Poetry of the Early Eighteenth Century', *Proceedings of the British Academy*, xxxv (1949), 49–65.

p. 114, 929   John Campbell, second Duke of Argyll (1678–1743) was a distinguished soldier under Marlborough (cf. 937–8) and later commanded the forces that crushed the Jacobite rebellion of 1715. He was one of the leading Scottish promoters of the Act of Union, and after the Union a prominent spokesman in the House of Lords for Scottish interests. The many contemporary tributes to his oratory (cf. 940–1) included one by Pope, *Epilogue to the Satires* ii.86–7. Argyll is characterized in Scott's *Heart of Midlothian*.

p. 115, 944   Duncan Forbes of Culloden (1685–1747), the much-respected M.P. and Scottish judge, befriended T. when the poet first came to London in 1725. Forbes introduced improvements into Scottish agriculture and judicial process, and sought to discourage the mischievous habit of tea-drinking. His son John was a close friend of T.; see *Cas. Ind.* I.lxii–lxiv.

p. 115, 878–949   This praise of Scotland and Scotsmen was transferred to *Autumn* in 1730 and expanded from the 13 lines which appeared in the list of British worthies in *Summer* (1727); see *Su.* 1442, end-note.

p. 115, 957–63   The upper atmosphere or ether is lightly shadowed, or 'fleeced', by cirrus clouds which stretch in thin streaks in all directions ('uncertain where to turn'); this is a sign that a change in the weather is coming. There is also a lower bank of clouds which absorb the sun's light and transmit some of it. The wording of the first version of this description (*Winter* (1726)) may clarify this passage:

> Sometimes, a fleece
> Of clouds, wide-scattering, with a lucid veil,
> Soft, shadow o'er th'unruffled face of heaven;
> And, through their dewy sluices, shed the sun,
> With temper'd influence down.

For 'wave', 'current', and 'imbibe' (958–61) cf. *Su.* 84 end-note.

p. 115, 957–75   Expanded and transferred in 1730 from *Winter*.

p. 116, 1004–5   The various nervous disorders known as melancholy were thought to be found generally among men and women of high intelligence and sensitivity, so melancholy was sometimes called 'the wise disease' or even regarded as the source of wisdom; cf. Milton, *Il Penseroso* 11–12. Here the melancholy mood is prompted by the autumnal 'desolated prospect' (1003), but the lines following indicate that this 'melancholy' is compounded of moral and aesthetic sensitivity and imagination.

p. 117, 1006–29   Cf. *Sp.* 878–903 end-note.

p. 117, 1030–6   Transferred, with alterations, in 1730 from *Winter* (1726). Cf. *Su.* 516–63 end-note.

p. 117, 1039–40   The first half of the eighteenth century saw a mania, particularly among the wealthy Whig lords, for the building or rebuilding of country houses.

p. 117, 1042   By 1744 (when lines 1037–81 were first added to *Autumn*) the garden at Stowe, the Buckinghamshire estate of Lord Cobham, had been worked upon by Charles Bridgeman, Sir John Vanbrugh, James Gibbs, and William Kent. It covered over 400 acres and contained dozens of buildings, pillars, and other memorials to the persons and principles admired by Cobham's circle of opposition Whigs (cf. *Au.* 1050 end-note). The garden was much admired in the eighteenth century (cf. Pope, *Epistle to Burlington* (1731), 65–70) and often described (e.g. in Gilbert West, *Stowe, a Poem* (1732), Sarah Bridgeman, *Plans of Stowe* (1739), Anon., *A Description of Stowe* (1744)). There is a modern description in Laurence Whistler, *The Imagination of Sir John Vanbrugh and his Fellow Artists* (London, 1954), chap. 7.

p. 117, 1043   Cyrus the Younger, who died in 401 B.C. leading an army in revolt against his brother Artaxerxes II, King of Persia, was 'not only a lord of gardens, but a manual planter thereof' (Sir Thomas Browne, *The Garden of Cyrus* (1658), chap. i. At Sardis on 'Ionia's shore', the central part of the west coast of Asia Minor, Cyrus created the famous garden, or 'paradise', described by Xenophon, *Oeconomicus* IV.20–4, and by Browne.

p. 117, 1048   When this was first published (1744) Pitt's great years as Secretary of State and Prime Minister were still to come, but he was known as a fine orator and vigorous opponent of Walpole.

p. 117, 1050   'The Temple of Virtue in Stowe Gardens.' (T.) William Kent's design for a Temple of Ancient Virtue first appeared in Isaac Ware's *Designs of Inigo Jones and others* (1735). When the Temple was built shortly afterwards it housed statues only of ancient Greek heroes; while, as a form of concrete sarcasm, the contrasting Temple of Modern Virtue, built about the same time, was an empty, shapeless ruin. Possibly T. means the Shrine of British Worthies designed by James Gibbs about 1732 which, over the years, came to contain busts of Alfred, the Black Prince, Elizabeth, William III, Raleigh, Drake, Sir Thomas Gresham, Hampden, Bacon, Locke, Newton, Shakespeare, Milton, Pope, Inigo Jones, and Sir John Barnard (an opponent of Walpole). Cf. *Su.* 1442 end-note.

p. 118, 1054–60   These lines allude to some of the principles of that informal 'landscape gardening' developed in eighteenth-century England. The garden was to be a 'regulated wild' (1055) or 'Nature methodized' (cf. Pope, *Essay on Criticism*, p. 89—a text much quoted by gardeners). In thus regulating or methodizing 'common nature'—the actual landscape—the gardener sought 'the purest truth of Nature' (1058–9), that is Nature as she must have been at the Creation before man's fall degraded both the world and himself. Like other artists gardeners 'should imitate the Divine Maker and form to themselves, as well as they are able, a model of the superior beauties and endeavour to amend and correct common nature and to represent it as it was first created.' (Dryden's translation of Bellori in *A Parallel of Poetry and Painting* (1695), see *Essays of John Dryden*, ed. W. P. Ker (1926), ii.118.) The objects in a garden were intended to produce pleasing or inspiring associations in the mind of the beholder: 'objects should indeed be less calculated to strike the immediate eye, than the judgement or well-formed imagination, as in painting.' (William Shenstone, 'Unconnected thoughts on Gardening', *Collected Works* (1765), ii.112.) The classical temples in their 'regulated' but natural-seeming settings at Stowe were intended to evoke the landscape of Greece and Rome (though the actual models were all Roman), while the dedications of and objects in these temples gave reminders of classical heroes and virtues (cf. 1055–6).

p. 118, 1061–9   According to Lord Chesterfield, William Pitt had 'a most happy turn to poetry, but he seldom indulged and seldomer avowed it.' But T.'s reference in these lines may be to Pitt's already famous oratory (cf. 1065–9). T. had already drawn the 'tragic scene' (1062) three times with *Sophonisba* (1730),

Agamemnon (1738), and *Edward and Eleanora* (1739). Two more tragedies, *Tancred and Sigismunda* (1745) and *Coriolanus* (1749) were to come. 'Corruption' (1069) may well stand for Walpole whom Pitt helped to bring down in 1742. T.'s tragedies were political, mostly anti-Walpole, pieces; cf. *Cas. Ind.* I.xxxii. 6–9.

p. 118, 1070   The Elysian Fields, landscaped by William Kent about 1735, were the 'wildest' or least formal part of the garden at Stowe. Kent planted evergreens there—a comparatively new device in English gardens—to suggest the cypress groves of antiquity (cf. *Au.* 1055–6). In classical mythology Elysium was the place where heroes, patriots, and others favoured by the gods enjoyed after death a happy existence.

p. 118, 1072   Viscount Cobham, soldier and politician, left Walpole's ministry in 1733 in order to cultivate his garden and a crop of gifted dissidents who became known as 'Boy Patriots' or 'Cobham's Cubs'. Prominent among these were Pitt (cf. *Au.* 1048) and Lyttelton (cf. *Sp.* 906). On *Au.* 1072–4, cf. Virgil, *Georgics* II.276–87; Marvell, *Upon Appleton House*, xxxvi–xlvi; and Pope's compliment to another soldier turned gardener, the Earl of Peterborough, *Imitations of Horace*, Sat. II.i.129–32.

p. 118, 1075–81   England was not prosecuting the War of Austrian Succession with much vigour, and, indeed, had not declared war formally until Spring 1744. The preceding hostilities had produced hardly any English victories apart from Porto Bello (cf. *Su.* 1041 end-note) in 1739 and Dettingen in 1743.

p. 119, 1082–1102   Transferred, with alterations in 1730 from *Winter.* 1088–93 closely echo *P.L.* I.288–91. For 'deluge' (1098) and 'tide' (1101) cf. *Su.* 84 end-note.

p. 120, 1108–37   T.'s description of the aurora borealis (not what we should call 'meteors', 1109) was transferred, with alterations, in 1730 from *Summer*; cf. *Su.* 1701 end-note. The aurora appears as vari-coloured, flickering streamers of light radiating towards the northern horizon from a point between fifty and several hundred miles from the earth's surface ('high to the crown of heaven', 1111). Very fine examples were seen in northern Europe on 6 Mar. 1716 and 19 Oct. 1726 see *McKillop*, pp. 64–6), but the phenomenon was not 'new' (1137), since Aristotle, Seneca, and Pliny had all referred to it. For 1116–21 cf. *P.L.* II. 533–8, Shakespeare, *Julius Caesar* ll. ii. 19–20. T. goes on to draw his customary distinction between the reactions of the foolish herd and the enlightened few, cf. *Sp.* 210–17.

p. 120, 1150–64   Transferred, with alterations, in 1730 from *Summer*; cf. *Su.* 1681 end-note. Wild-fire (1152) or *ignis fatuus* is a phosphorescent light seen flitting over marshy ground, possibly due to spontaneous combustion of gas from decaying organic matter; cf. *P.L.* IX.634–42. The innoxious meteor (1162) is St. Elmo's Fire—the glow accompanying discharges of atmospheric electricity which usually appears as a tip of light on the extremities of objects (such as ships' spars or the heads of horses and men) during stormy weather; cf. Virgil, *Aeneid* II.680–6 ('innoxia'), Shakespeare, *Tempest* I.ii.196–201.

p. 121, 1172–1200   'The common way of killing the bees and saving the honey is to dig a hole, hard by, a little bigger than the bottom of the hive, into which stick one or two matches of brimstone five or six inches long, so that the top of them may be even with the surface top of the hole. The matches being fired, gently and dexterously lift off the hive, and set it over the hole, and immediately close up the hive at the bottom, that none of the smoke may get out, and in a few minutes the bees will be all dead.' (John Laurence, *A New System of Agriculture* (1727, p. 108.) Cf. Virgil, *Georgics* IV.228–30.) On the anthropomorphic periphrases cf. *Sp.* 132 end-note.

p. 122, 1235–8   Here begins a passage (1235–1373) modelled upon Virgil, *Georgics* II.458–542, which was probably the classical text most often imitated or translated in eighteenth-century England. However, where Virgil describes principally the joys of the frugal, hardy, pious husbandman (with a short digression on the poet's own happiness in rural retirement), T. devotes his account of the 'happy man' almost wholly to the hedonist-philosopher-poet. Such an adaptation of Virgil's lines was extremely common in the eighteenth century: 'There is, indeed, scarcely any writer who has not celebrated the happiness of rural privacy.' (Johnson, *Rambler* 135.) On such poetry of retirement see M-S. Røstvig, *The Happy Man: Studies in the Metamorphoses of a Classical Ideal* (2 vols., Oslo, 2nd. edn. 1958–62).

p. 123, 1278–86   This Virgilian theme became more urgent in eighteenth-century England as men grew concerned over the activities of West Indian planters and servants of the East India Company; cf. Burke, *Speech on the Impeachment of Warren Hastings* (1788) and the powerful lines in John Langhorne, *The Country Justice*, iii (1777), 76–83. T. displays a different attitude to trade in *Au.* 118–34.

p. 126, 1352–73   Adapted and expanded from Virgil, *Georgics* II.490–3, but T. makes this philosophic rapture his climax, as Virgil does not. For the rhapsodic manner cf. *Wi.* 106–17 end-note. For the 'chain of being' idea running through this passage cf. *Su.* 334 end-note. For the human mind and its place in the rising system (1361–2) cf. *Su.* 1788–1805 end-notes.

WINTER

p. 129, 1–16   Praised by the painter Constable (1836) 'as a beautiful instance of the poet identifying his own feelings with external nature', (C.R. Leslie, *Memoirs of Constable*, ed. J. Mayne (London, 1951), p. 328.) For 'smiled' cf. *Sp.* 84 end-note.

p. 130, 17–40   First added in 1730 to replace the prose dedication of *Winter* (1726); hence T. says he 'renews' his song after singing the other seasons (17–22). Spencer Compton (1673–1743), the Whig politician created Earl of Wilmington in 1730, was Speaker of the House of Commons when he received the dedication of the first edition of *Winter*. On Walpole's fall in 1742 he became Prime Minister —but in name only.

p. 130, 46–9   Cf. *Su.* 1620 footnote, *Au.* 722–7 end-note.

p. 131, 57–60   Cf. *Lucretius* VI.1090–1102.

p. 131, 63–5   After harvest the stubble was ploughed in and sheep were folded (hence 'untended') out in the field and fed with turnips ('wholesome root') through the winter, so that their dung would restore the land's fertility. Defoe observed this practice in his *Tour*, vol. i (1724), Letter i, 'Suffolk'. This was part of the so-called 'Norfolk system' of husbandry which was spreading slowly into suitable parts of Britain in the eighteenth century.

p. 131, 67   Cf. *Su.* 960 end-note.

p. 131, 72–80   Cf. Virgil, *Georgics* I.322–31. The 'Father' in Virgil is, of course, Jupiter, but T.'s conception is influenced by the O.T. Jehovah; cf. *Wi.* 197–201.

p. 132, 106–17   This passage may owe a suggestion to Milton's *Paradise Regained*, 'The Father . . . in whose hand all times and seasons roll' (III.186–7), but the tone and general cast of thought follow Theocles' famous outburst upon 'mighty Nature, wise substitute of Providence, impowered Creatress' in Shaftesbury's *The Moralists, a Philosophical Rhapsody* (1709). This praise of Nature's hand, rather than God's, takes T. very close to 'natural religion' or deism. Cf. *Sp.* 556–62, *Au.* 1352, *Hymn* 1–3.

p. 133, 118–52 These various signs of an impending storm are from Virgil, *Georgics* I.351–92, 427–9, 453. 'Pensive' (135) is possibly a mistranslation of *Georgics* I.390 'pensa', i.e. 'daily allotment or task' (referring to the amount of wool each girl had to card). The significance of 136–7 is that sudden, small gusts of draught which precede the storm cause the taper to gutter.

p. 134, 193 Cf. *Su.* 960 end-note.

p. 135, 244 After the sheaves were threshed, by flail, in the barn, the grain was winnowed, i.e. it was thrown up by shovels or sieves while a current of air passing between two opposite open doors (or generated by a large fan) blew away the chaff. At this time the barn doorways were besieged by fowl hungry for the grain.

p. 138, 348–58 Cf. *Sp.* 878–903 end-note.

p. 138, 359 'The Jail Committee, in the year 1729' (T.); i.e. the Parliamentary Committee under the chairmanship of James Oglethorpe to investigate allegations of torture in English gaols. See A. A. Ettinger, *James Oglethorpe* (London, 1937), where there are accounts of gaolers' cruelties referred to by T. (359–88). Most of the long passage 276–413 describing miseries and cruelties in the natural and the social worlds was first added in the 1730 edition.

p. 139, 405–6 For the belief that the lion instinctively reverences beauty cf. *F.Q.* I.III.v–vi.

p. 140, 414–423 First added in 1744, based on *An Account of the Glaciers or Ice Alps in Savoy* (1744) by William Windham and Peter Martel; see *McKillop*, pp. 142–3.

p. 140, 439 Socrates (469–399 B.C.), the great moral philosopher of Athens, turned aside from the physical speculations of earlier thinkers in order to study virtue, which he equated with knowledge. Falsely accused of blasphemy and of corrupting Athenian youth, he displayed fearless composure at his trial and while awaiting execution by poison. The oracle of Delphi called him 'wisest of mankind'.

p. 140, 446 Solon (639–558 B.C.) was credited by later Athenians with having established most of the city's democratic institutions. His 'tender laws' superseded the harsh ('Draconian') code instituted by Dracon.

p. 140, 453 Lycurgus, the legendary Spartan law-giver, promoted temperance and restrained luxury by many devices, including the prohibition of gold and silver. The laws attributed to him may be dated about 600 B.C.

p. 141, 457 Leonidas, King of Sparta, led 6000 Greeks who, in 480 B.C., held back a huge invading Persian army in the pass of Thermopylae until his position was turned, and he and many of his soldiers killed. He was regarded as a model of all the Spartan qualities valued by Lycurgus.

p. 141, 464 The strategy of the Athenian military leader Themistocles (d. 459 B.C.) brought victory over the Persians at Salamis in 480 B.C., but, having come into conflict with Cimon about 472 B.C., he was ostracized never to return.

p. 141, 466 Cimon (*c.* 512–449 B.C.), was accused of incest in youth, helped Aristides form the Delian League of Greek states against Persia, and became the most powerful Athenian leader after the ostracism of Themistocles and the death of Aristides, 468 B.C. He gained victories over the Persians by land and sea.

p. 141, 474 Timoleon (d. 336), the Corinthian, conspired about 365 B.C. to kill his own brother Timophanes who was trying to make himself tyrant. In 1730

Bubb Dodington (cf. *Su.* 29) tried to persuade T. to write an epic poem on Timoleon; cf. *Letters and Documents*, pp. 74–5.

p. 141, 476 Pelopidas (d. 364 B.C.) held a command under his friend the brilliant military tactitian Epaminondas (*c.* 420–362 B.C.) when the latter led the Thebans to the victory over Sparta at Leuctra (371 B.C.) which gave Thebes supremacy in Greece until Epaminondas' death.

p. 141, 481 The Athenian general and orator Phocion sought to prevent Athens from going to war with the Macedonia of Philip and Alexander the Great. In 318 B.C. he was sentenced to death by poison on a charge of treason.

p. 141, 488 Agis IV (*c.* 262–241 B.C.), King of Sparta, attempted to cure his kingdom's ills by a return to Lycurgus' constitution but was deposed and murdered.

p. 141, 491 Aratus of Sicyon in Achaea (271–213 B.C.), statesman and general, from 245 to 215 B.C. directed the Achaean League of Greek cities that had freed themselves from Macedonian rule.

p. 142, 494 Philopoemen (*c.* 250–183 B.C.) of Megalopolis in Arcadia, a highly successful general of the Achaean League who repeatedly defeated the Spartans, is often regarded as the last great man produced by Greece.

p. 142, 503 Numa, the legendary second king of Rome, is called a 'better founder' than Romulus the first king because his long reign was peaceful and enlightened. It was believed that he began the worship of Vesta, Roman goddess of the blazing hearth.

p. 142, 504 Servius was according to legend the sixth king of Rome. To his reign, in the sixth century B.C., were attributed certain forms of government that endured throughout the whole history of the Roman Republic.

p. 142, 507 The 'public father' was actually Lucius Junius Brutus the nephew of Tarquinius Superbus, last king of Rome. After the expulsion of the Tarquins and the end of the Roman monarchy in 510 B.C. he became one of the first two Consuls, and in his office, it was said, sentenced to death his two sons who had plotted to restore the Tarquins.

p. 142, 510 Camillus, the Roman dictator and general of the early fourth century B.C., was exiled but then recalled to lead the Romans to victory over the Gauls, the Volsci, and the Aequi.

p. 142, 511 Fabricius was three times Consul in the early third century B.C., and a type of the old Roman frugality and integrity. In 280 B.C. he was the Republic's ambassador to the Greek king Pyrrhus, and, though poor, resisted all Pyrrhus's attempts to bribe him.

p. 142, 513 Regulus was Consul in 267 and 256 B.C., and one of the commanders of Roman expeditions to Africa in the First Punic War. He was captured, and in 250 B.C. the Carthaginians sent him with an embassy to Rome to propose peace, making him swear to return if negotiations failed, but he advised the Romans to continue the war and returned to Carthage and a cruel death.

p. 142, 517 Though all of this generalized praise might well be offered to Scipio Africanus Major (cf. *Cas. Ind.* I.xvii.8), T. may refer here to Scipio Aemilianus Africanus Numantinus (184–129 B.C.) who wept over Carthage after he had destroyed it. A highly cultivated man, he was, in retirement, the centre of a brilliant literary and philosophical circle.

p. 142, 521 Tully is the name by which Marcus Tullius Cicero was often referred to by English writers down to the nineteenth century. Cicero's oratory helped to suppress Catiline's anarchist conspiracy, 63 B.C. After Julius Caesar's death Cicero opposed the tyrannical ambitions of Mark Antony who in 43 B.C. had him put to death.

p. 143, 424–540   Milton's *Il Penseroso* 77–119 furnished the hint for this setting and catalogue. In the first edition (1726) the catalogue included only Socrates, Solon, Lycurgus, Numa, Cimon, Aristides, Cato, Timoleon, Scipio, Epaminondas, Virgil, Homer, and Milton. In 1730 Pelopidas was added, and in 1744 the remaining names.

p. 143, 550–4   First added 1730; cf. *Su.* 1427. Pope's translation of Homer's *Iliad* was published 1715–20, and his *Odyssey* 1725–6. He befriended T. who was introduced to him in 1725 by Duncan Forbes (cf. *Au.* 944). The compliment in 554 recognizes Pope's successful self-cultivation as the virtuous recluse or Horatian happy man at Twickenham.

p. 143, 555   James Hammond (1710–42), M.P. and poet, was one of the Cobham-Lyttelton-Pitt circle of 'youthful patriots' (*Wi.* 565, cf. *Au.* 1042–81 and notes, *Sp.* 906 end-note), and died while on a visit to Stowe. His love elegies, published posthumously in 1743 were much admired (but not by Johnson, see *Lives of the Poets*, 'Hammond') T.'s tribute (555–71) was first added in the 1744 edition of *The Seasons*.

p. 144, 575–7   The first was the traditional interpretation of Gen. 1; cf. 2 Macc. 7:28, 'God made [heaven and earth] of things that were not.' The second—that the material universe was created by God not out of nothing but out of his own being—was inferred and developed from Plato's suggestion in *Timaeus* 29 that the Creator formed the material world as a copy of an eternal pattern. This notion was elaborated by the first-century philosopher Philo (*De Opificio Mundi* v–vii), and was much discussed by seventeenth-century English theologians. It has been argued, from *P.L.* VII.166–73 and from *De Doctrina Christiana* (not published till 1825), that Milton believed that God created the universe out of his own being (cf. Denis Saurat, *Milton: Man and Thinker*, rev. 1944).

p. 144, 579–82   Summarizes the intention of *The Seasons*.

p. 144, 583–7   T. could have found this notion in Shaftesbury's *Inquiry concerning Virtue* (1699), but the moral thought of the age was dominated by 'a firm persuasion of an omnipotent, omniscient, and most benign Universal Parent, disposing of all things in this system for the very best.' (Francis Hutcheson, *System of Moral Philosophy* (1755), i.215.) Cf. Pope, *Essay on Man* (1733–4), *passim*.

p. 144, 587–93   The influence of climate and other natural causes upon the national character and history of nations was a favourite topic for popular historians of the period; e.g. Sir William Temple, *Observations upon the United Provinces* of the Netherlands (1673), Goldsmith, *The Traveller* (1764). For 'double suns' (591) see *Su.* 645 footnote.

p. 145, 603–8   The old notion of the great chain of being (cf. *Su.* 334 end-note) was reinterpreted in the seventeenth and eighteenth centuries to include the idea of progress in the present and future states. So the future life may be seen as the infinite ascent of mind from stage to stage, and immortality as an endless extension of knowledge. For popular statements of this view see *Spectator* 111 and 237 by Addison, and 635 by Henry Grove. For modern accounts see A. O. Lovejoy, *The Great Chain of Being* (1936), chap. 9, and *McKillop*, pp. 21–5. T. wrote in a letter to William Cranstoun, 20 Oct. 1735: 'This, I think, we may be sure of: that a future state must be better than this; and so on through the never ceasing succession of future states; every one rising upon the last, an everlasting new display of infinite goodness.' (*Letters and Documents*, p. 100). Cf. *Sp.* 336–78 end-note, *Su.* 1796–1805 end-note, *Hymn* 108–16, *Liberty*, III (1735), 68–70.

p. 145, 609–16   Cf. Locke, *Essay concerning Human Understanding* II.xi.2. As usual, T.'s terms hover between personification and abstraction.

p. 146, 637–45   Cf. *Su.* 342–8.

p. 146, 572–655   Most of this passage was first added in 1730, but expanded and much revised in 1744. Lines 617–55 owe some hints to Milton's *L'Allegro* 100–38.

p. 146, 664   Philip Dormer Stanhope, fourth Earl of Chesterfield (1694–1773), the politician, wit and letter-writer. Like nearly every other politician, commended in *The Seasons*, he was a leading member of the Prince of Wales's circle of Whigs opposed to Walpole and George II. In 1744, after the extinction of Walpole's 'corrupted power' (*Wi.* 670), Chesterfield entered the government under Pelham (cf. *Su.* 1432). The fact that it is the Rural Muse who praises the highly polished, utterly urbane Lord Chesterfield indicates that there is no necessary connection between urban life and corruption. The whole passage 656–90 was first added in 1744.

p. 147, 694   See *Sp.* 563 end-note. It was thought that 'a windy season and serene sky' favoured the production of nitre, 'and that the east and north winds only bring with them the primogenial acid of the air which saturates the alkaline sulphureous parts of the earth and converts them into nitre . . . long frosts and snows, especially after a hot summer mellow the ground and render it exceeding fertile, because the earth calcined and rendered alkaline by the summer heats is by the frost and snow abundantly supplied with an acid and rendered nitrous.' (Anon., *The Rational Farmer* (1743), pp. 50–1.) Cf. *Au.* 4–5, *Wi.* 706–8; John Philips, *Cyder* (1708), II.184–8.

p. 147, 705–6   Cf. *Sp.* 111–13 end-note, but the phrase also hints at T.'s usual distinction between the herd and the enlightened few.

p. 148, 711   'The water which . . . snow yields when melted . . . is the purest.' (Anon., *The Rational Farmer* (1743), p. 105.)

p. 148, 716   Spirit of wine, or ethyl alcohol (illusive, cf. Lat. *illudere*, to trick; 'wine is a mocker', Prov. 20:1) was used in thermometers in T.'s day. Members of a scientific expedition in 1736–7 found that their spirit thermometers froze (Pierre Maupertuis, *The Figure of the Earth*, English trans. (1738), p. 85), but this must have been because the spirit of wine contained some water.

p. 148, 714–20   'Cold and freezing seem to proceed from some saline substance floating in the air; we see that all salts, but more eminently some, mixed with ice prodigiously increase the effects and force of cold. . . . Microscopical observations inform us that the figures of some salts. before they shoot into masses, are thin double-wedged. . . . The dimensions of freezed bodies are increased by the insinuations of these crystal wedges in their pores, and the particles of congealed water are kept at some distance from one another by the figure of these crystals which in freezing insinuate themselves in their pores.' (George Cheyne, *Philosophical Principles of Religion: Natural and Revealed*, 1715, pp. 61–3.) The microscope had revealed many variations in the shapes of snow crystals. See McKillop, p. 60.

p. 149, 780–1   Cf. *Su.* 1620 footnote.

p. 150, 695–793   In 1730 this passage on cold weather was expanded to 95 lines from the 22 lines of the first edition—chiefly by the addition of scientific information or speculation. In 1744 it was slightly expanded and revised.

p. 150, 809–14 Taken from Johannes Scheffer, *Lapponia* (1673, English trans. 1674), chap. xxix. Other parts of T.'s northern descriptions come from Scheffer; see *McKillop*, pp. 112–22.

p. 151, 816–26 Cf. Virgil, *Georgics* III.369–75.

p. 151, 840 'The wandering Scythian clans.' (T.) For the notion of the far north as the 'hive of nations' whose incursions into the declining Roman Empire reinvigorated an enfeebled Europe cf. Sir William Temple, 'Of Heroic Virtue' in *Miscellanea*, vol, ii (1692) and T., *Liberty*, III (1735), 510–38, IV (1736), 370–8.

p. 151, 843–50 Such idealization of the Lapps (cf. *Wi.* 877–86) is found in T.'s source—Olaf Rudbeck, *Lapland Illustrated*, appended to the 1704 edition of Scheffer's *Lapponia* (cf. *Wi.* 809–14 end-note).

p. 151, 851–6 T. may have gained his information about the all-useful reindeer from Olaus Magnus, *A Compendious History of the Goths, Swedes and Vandals* (English trans. 1658), XVII.xxi, which, like Rudbeck's book, idealizes the noble savages of the north.

p. 152, 859–64 The long winter night in the far north is illuminated by the aurora borealis (cf. *Au.* 1108–37) and starlight and moonlight through clear skies, reflected from the snow. T. found this information in Scheffer's *Lapponia*, (cf. *Wi.* 809–14 end-note) and Pierre Maupertuis, *The Figure of the Earth* (English trans. 1738), p. 78.

p. 152, 875–6 'M. de Maupertuis, in his book on the figure of the Earth, after having described the beautiful lake and mountain of Niemi in Lapland, says: "From this height we had occasion several times to see those vapours rise from the lake which the people of the country call *Haltios*, and which they deem to be the guardian spirits of the mountains. We had been frighted with stories of bears that haunted this place, but saw none. It seemed rather a place of resort for fairies and genii than bears."' 'The same author observes: "I was surprised to see upon the banks of this river (the Tenglio) roses of as lively a red as any that are in our gardens."' (T.)

p. 153, 894–901 Cf. the description of the Italian Alps, translated from Silius Italicus, *Punica*, iii, 477–92, in Addison, *Remarks on several parts of Italy* (rev. 1718), Letter xviii, 'Bolonia etc.'

p. 153, 904–12 Takes hints from Friedrich Martens, *Voyage into Spitzbergen and Greenland* (1694)—a work also used by Pope for his *Temple of Fame*.

p. 153, 925 'Sir Hugh Willoughby, sent by Queen Elizabeth to discover the north-east passage' (T.). Willoughby and his crew entered an inlet, subsequently known as Arzina (cf. *Wi.* 930), near the present border between Norway and Russia, intending to pass the winter of 1553–4 there, but they were ill-provisioned and all died. Their bodies were found some years afterwards, and Willoughby's journal was printed in Hakluyt's *Principal Navigations* and in many other collections. The description of the crew frozen in activity seems to be T.'s own, and is, of course, fictitious. Later attempts (cf. *Au.* 927–9) on the north-east passage were made by Pet and Jackson in 1580, by Barents in 1594–7 and by expeditions set in motion by Peter the Great and commanded by Vitus Baring in 1725–8 and 1740–1.

p. 154, 936–49 Cf. Virgil, *Georgics* III.349–83.

p. 154, 955   Peter the Great (1672–1725), Czar of Russia, travelled in 1697–8 through Western Europe to study government, commerce and industry, and even learned handicrafts in the shipbuilding yards of Holland and England (cf. *Wi.* 969). On his return home he reorganized his backward country's army, navy, civil government, education, social life, and culture. After he captured part of the Baltic coast he founded in 1703 a new capital city, St. Petersburg (cf. 973); he planned to join the Baltic and the Black Sea by canals (cf. 975–6). Though Peter did eventually defeat Charles XII, he did not awe the Ottomans (cf. 980–1), for though he attacked Turkey in 1711 he was forced to accept a humiliating peace and the loss of territory. The passage 950–87 was first added in the 1744 edition and was based on Friedrich Christian Weber, *The Present State of Russia* (English trans. 1722–3). On T.'s admiration for material progress cf. *Au.* 43–150.

p. 155, 794–987   T.'s first descriptive excursion into the frigid zone was added in 1730 and consisted of only 56 lines. It was greatly expanded to its present length in 1744.

p. 155, 1001–8   Cf. *P.L.* I.207–8, II.285–90.

p. 156, 1028–46   Cf. Job 14:1–15.

p. 156, 1049   Cf. *Sp.*111–13 end-note.

A HYMN

p. 159, 1–3   Cf. *Wi.* 106–7 end-note. On account of its supposed deism the *Hymn* was omitted from the edition of *The Seasons* which Lyttelton (cf. *Sp.* 906) prepared for publication after T.'s death. T.'s *Hymn* is modelled in a general way upon *P.L.* V.153–208 and Psalm 148 but restates and harmonizes many of the scientific, philosophical, and religious notions introduced earlier in the poem.

p. 159, 21–6   Contradicts the attitude of *Sp.* 317–20, since the *Hymn* corrects and extends the limited view of Nature found earlier in the poem. On 'kind art' (23) cf. *Su.* 185–96 end-note.

p. 160, 68   On light as liquid cf. *Su.* 84 end-note.

p. 161, 107   Newton's description of infinite space as 'the sensorium of the Godhead' was quoted by Addison, *Spectator* 565. In the *Hymn*, as in the whole of *The Seasons*, T. emphasizes God's immanence—never his transcendence.

p. 162, 112   Cf. *Sp.* 84 end-note. In the *Hymn* the subject óf 'smiles' is raised progressively from a natural object, the 'forests' (6), to 'creation' (81), to God's love (112).

p. 162, 114–17   Cf. *Wi.* 603–8 end-note, *Su.* 176–81 end-note.

The Castle of Indolence

CANTO 1

p. 165, i.3–4   The sentence pronounced upon Adam, cf. Gen. 3:19.

p. 166, ii–vi   Cf. the Hermitage and the House of Morpheus in *F.Q.* I.i.34, 41. For stanzas v and vi, where the beauties of the natural scene soothe the mind into a reverie in which dreams mingle with the appearances of external nature, cf. *Sp.* 458–68, *Au.* 1029–33.

p. 168, ix–xii Cf. *F.Q.* II.vi.15–17—Phaedria's song (which includes the allusion to Matt. 6:26–9)—and T.'s poetic 'Paraphrase of the latter part of the sixth chapter of St. Matthew' (*Miscellaneous Poems*, ed. J. Ralph). Stanza xi perverts the Lucretian philosophy of *Au.* 44–8 where Industry is 'the raiser of human kind, by Nature cast . . . out'. For 'cares that eat away' cf. Horace, *Odes* II.xi.18. Stanza xii alludes to the punishment of Sisyphus in Hades, as described by Homer, *Odyssey* XI.593–601.

p. 169, xiii Behind the Enchanter's appeal lies the authority of the conclusion to Virgil, *Georgics* II; cf. *Au.* 1287–1310.

p. 169, xiv.9 The inhabitants of the wealthy city of Sybaris, capital of Magna Graecia in southern Italy, were noted for luxury. 'The Sybarites were also the first to forbid noise-producing crafts from being established within the city, such as blacksmiths, carpenters and the like, their object being to have their sleep undisturbed in any way; it was not permitted even to keep a cock inside the city' (Athenaeus, *Deipnosophistae* XII.518).

p. 169, xv.8 On the social sense see *Sp.* 878–903 end-note.

p. 171, xix Cf. Eccles. 2:18–23, Psalm 39:6.

p. 171, xx Cf. Milton, *Lycidas* 77, *P.L.* VIII.1–3, I.781–6, *Su.* 1671–5.

p. 172, xxiv–xxv The porter owes hints to Pleasure's porter at the Bower of Bliss (*F.Q.* II.xii.46), and his page to Falstaff's page (2 *Henry IV*).

p. 173, xxviii 'Do what you will' was the rule of the Abbey of Theleme in Rabelais, *Gargantua and Pantagruel* (trans. Urquhart and Motteux, I.lvii); cf. *Cas. Ind.* I.xxxv.

p. 174, xxxi The revelation that the poet himself lives there makes the Castle in some sense both objective and subjective. Lines 1–5 echo Virgil, *Aeneid* VI.264–7.

p. 174, xxxii Cf. *Au.* 1061–5.

p. 175, xxxiv. 1–5 Modelled in a general way on the banqueting hall in *Comus*. Cf. the luxurious table condemned in *Au.* 1246–50.

p. 176, xxxviii.8–9 Claude Gelée (1600–82) was named Lorrain from his birthplace but spent most of his life in and near Rome where he painted gentle landscapes with grazing flocks, calm waters, luminous skies and blue distance which image a perfect harmony between man and nature, and convey the spirit of the Golden Age. Salvator Rosa (1615–73) was an Italian whose best-known paintings were landscapes containing precipices, mountains, torrents, wolves and brigands. Nicolas Poussin (1594–1665), like Claude, was a Frenchman who worked in Rome. He studied the antique more intensively and recreated it more perfectly than any other painter of his century; his greatest landscape paintings are nobly austere and almost geometrically ordered. For the influence of these three painters on eighteenth-century English poetry see Elizabeth W. Manwaring, *Italian Landscape in Eighteenth Century England* (1925), as corrected by Jean Hagstrum, *The Sister Arts* (1958).

p. 177, xl.9 'This is not imagination of the author, there being in fact such an instrument, called Aeolus's harp, which, when placed against a little rushing or current of air, produces the effect here described.' (T.) This instrument was said to have been invented by a Jesuit, Athanasius Kircher, about 1650, and rediscovered by a Scotsman, James Oswald, in the 1740s. Oswald made his Aeolian harp out of a lute, but examples of the instrument which survive today consist of twelve strings over a rectangular frame and sounding board. The harp, properly tuned, was placed in the open part of a sash-window and emitted a sound when a current of air passed over it. Cf. T.'s 'Ode on Aeolus's Harp' (1748, reprinted in *Robertson*, pp. 432–3). There are many references to the instrument in the poetry of the century following *Cas. Ind.* Robert Bloomfield the poet wrote an account of the harp of Aeolus in *Nature's Music* (1808), and a harp made by him is preserved in the museum at Bury St. Edmunds. The most-accessible modern account is Geoffrey Grigson, *The Harp of Aeolus* (1948). Aeolus in classical mythology was the god of the winds.

p. 177, xli.9 Cf. *P.L.* V.294–7 (with a hint from Milton, *L'Allegro* 134), and Pope, *Essay on Criticism*, 155. On the superiority of Nature to Art (a commonplace) cf. *Sp.* 468–79.

p. 177, xlii.7 'The Arabian Caliphs had poets among the officers of their court whose office it was to do what is here mentioned.' (T.)

p. 178, xliii.7 Cf. *Su.* 960 end-note.

p. 179, xlix.2 Cf. Merlin's globe, *F.Q.* III.ii.18–20.

p. 180, l–li Cf. *Wi.* 644–5. It was proverbial that the miser's son would be a spendthrift; cf. Cotta and his son in Pope's *Epistle to Bathurst* 179–218.

p. 183, lx.3 John Armstrong, M.D. (1709–79), physician and poet, author of *The Art of Preserving Health* (1744) and of stanzas lxxiv–lxxvii of *The Castle of Indolence*, Canto I. T. wrote of him in a letter of 1748: 'the Doctor . . . does not decrease in spleen; but there is a certain kind of spleen that is both humane and agreeable, like Jacques' in the play [*As You Like It*]. I sometimes have a touch of it.' (*Letters and Documents*, p. 198). On spleen, or melancholy, cf. *Au.* 1004–5, *Cas. Ind.* I.lxxv.7 end-notes.

p. 185, lxviii.1 'The following lines of this stanza were writ by a friend of the author.' (T.); the friend was Lyttelton (cf. *Sp.* 906 end-note) and the bard T.

p. 187, lxxiii Cf. *F.Q.* II.v.27, Acrasia's dungeon.

p. 187, lxxv.7 In the eighteenth century the terms 'spleen' and 'melancholy' embraced a whole range of hysterical disorders, and there was much medical writing on the subject. For a modern account see C. A. Moore, 'The English Malady' in *Backgrounds of English Literature*, 1700–1760 (1953), pp. 179–235. Cf. *Au.* 1004–5, *Cas. Ind.* I.lx end-notes.

p. 188, lxxiv–lxxvii Contributed by Armstrong, cf. *Cas. Ind.* I.lx.3.

CANTO II

p. 189, ii.5 Good poets had been likened to bees in Sir William Temple's essay *Of Poetry* (1692) and in the famous fable in Swift's *Battle of the Books* (1704). T.'s wasp-like tribe are the booksellers, i.e. publishers, of his day. In a letter to Aaron Hill, 11 May 1736, T. wrote: 'With regard to arts and learning, one may venture to say that they may yet stand their ground, were they but merely protected. In lieu of all patrons that have been, are, or will be in England I wish we had one good Act of Parliament for securing to authors the property of their own works . . . can it be that those who impress paper with what constitutes the best and everlasting riches of all civilized nations and of all ages should have less property in the paper so enriched than those who deal in the rags which make that paper ?' (*Letters and Documents*, p. 106). T. is referring to several test-cases in the 1730s which upheld the booksellers' common-law, perpetual copyright in works assigned to them by authors. (Two famous later judgements in which this right was upheld in 1769 and rejected in 1774 both involved T.'s *The Seasons*.)

p. 189, iii   See *Introduction*, p. xviii above.

p. 190, v.2   The name Selvaggio is coined from Spenser's adjective 'salvage' (wild, *F.Q.* I.vi.23.4) in the account of Satyrane's birth which provided suggestions for this episode in *Cas. Ind.*

p. 190, v.9   Cf. *F.Q.* VII.vii.29.8.

p. 191, xi.9   Cf. *Au.* 50.

p. 194, xv–xxi   The spread of all the arts of civilization, as the course of empire passes from Egypt, Greece, and Rome to Britain, is the theme of T.'s *Liberty* (1735–6); cf. also *Au.* 43–150, *Su.* 1758–81.

p. 195, xxiii   Cf. *Cas. Ind.* II.ii. Until the late 1730s T. depended heavily upon patrons, but later he regretted the fulsome flattery he had once bestowed on them. Smollett, in the Dedication of *Ferdinand Count Fathom* (1753) says that T., had he lived, would have retracted some of his encomiums on patrons. T.'s remarks in this stanza perhaps owe something to Pope's satires upon Bubb Dodington, sometimes called the modern Maecenas, and an early patron of T.; see *Su.* 29 end-note.

p. 196, xxviii   In 1746 T. had visited the Leasowes, William Shenstone's well-known 'ornamented farm' where there was an attempt to combine small-scale landscape gardening with productive agriculture; see *Letters and Documents*, pp. 185–6. On nature and art in landscape-gardening see *Au.* 1054–60 end-note.

p. 201, xli.7   Cf. the magic dust in Milton's *Comus* 164–5.

p. 202, xlvii   The theme of *The Seasons*.

p. 203, xlviii   For this notion—so important to T.—of a spiritual progress upwards through infinite states of being see *Wi.* 603–8 end-note. It is appropriate in the mouth of a Druid wight because the ancient Druids taught the Pythagorean doctrine of metempsychosis (Caesar, *Gallic War* VI.14); cf. *Sp.* 336–78 end-note.

p. 203, xlix.3   Cf. live ether, *Sp.* 563 end-note, and ethereal nitre, *Wi.* 694 end-note.

p. 206, lxii.3   Cf. Prov. 22:13.

p. 207, lxiii   See *Cas. Ind.* II.xlviii end-note and references.

p. 208, lxviii   Cf. the Cave of Despair, *F.Q.* I.ix.33–6.

p. 209, lxxii.8   Cf. Rev.7:17, 21:4, Milton, *Lycidas* 181.

p. 212, lxxxi   The dirtiness of the low-lying market-town of Brentford was well known, and may have been a stock joke in neighbouring, fashionable and far more salubrious Richmond where T. and his friends lived. Gay's *Epistle to Lord Burlington* (1715) alludes to the 'dirty streets' of 'Brentford's tedious town'.

Index